"I Can See You Naked"

Historical Footnote

In the ancient folklore
of presentation instruction,
it was widely held
that visualizing your audience naked
helped to reduce nervousness.

The concept lingers
to this very day.

"I Can See You Naked"

A New Revised Edition of the National Bestseller on Making Fearless Presentations

by Ron Hoff

Andrews and McMeel

A Universal Press Syndicate Company

Kansas City

Designed and illustrated by Barrie Maguire

Library of Congress Cataloging-in-Publication Data
Hoff, Ron.
    "I can see you naked". / by Ron Hoff. — New rev. ed.
        p.   cm.
    Includes bibliographical references and index.
    ISBN 0–8362–8000–8 : $16.95 — ISBN 0–8362–8008–3 : $9.95
    1. Public speaking I. Title.
PN4121.H456   1992
808.5'1—dc20   92–26641
                                                        CIP

Contents

CONTENTS

PART SIX

How to deal with questions.

Prologue

This may be the best piece of advice in this book:

When something strikes you as funny, don't let it get away. Hold on to it for dear life. It could be *gold*. My theory is this: everything that strikes you as funny is going to turn up on television some day.

I'll just give you this one example—because it relates directly to the book you're reading.

For as long as I can remember, I've always thought that the old idea of visualizing an audience *naked*, as a way to control nervousness, was a funny sort of notion. It just struck me funny.

I mean, it's not one of those ideas that flits in and out of your mind. It sticks. And it asks for some kind of response.

So, I made it the title of a book on presentations.

"I Can See You Naked."

Need I tell you what happened next?

The idea spread across the networks like a giggle through a classroom. I'm watching "Cheers" one night—one of the great TV comedies of the millenium—*and there it is!* The idea of visualizing an audience *au naturel* is part of the story. The audience is howling like crazy.

"Cheers" isn't the only one. "The Brady Bunch" had picked up on it. They had *great* fun with it. The idea floats across outer space, coming to rest on other TV transmitters. Soon, "Golden Girls" builds a scene around it—and the audience is in stitches.

Millions upon millions of people are howling their heads off about this quirky notion of speakers talking to naked audiences. It's hilarious. Dynamite. A TV writer's dream come true.

Then, amidst the laughter, a question hit me.

Had my book unleashed all of this hilarity?

Surely not. But how many speakers would now visualize their next audience in a state of dishabille? I shuddered to think of it.

If you're a presenter, a naked audience is not going to improve your concentration. Eye contact is going to be a real problem for you. And you're going to be very self-conscious about that $600 designer suit you're wearing.

This was all dutifully explained in *"I Can See You Naked"*—the first edition. But something told me it was time for new emphasis. Even with the relaxed morality that pervades our TV sets and movie screens, there remains a statement that must be resaid:

Never speak to a naked audience. It can be distracting.

There are all kinds of other psychological exercises that can be tapped to rid yourself of nervousness in the face of an awaiting audience. One woman even wrote to tell me that Chapter 13 which starts, "It's the night before your big presentation" enabled her to keep her *sanity.* Can you imagine? I considered changing the title of the book to reflect that thought, then decided that a promise of sanity was probably more than I could deliver—times being what they are.

As with the first edition, this new, expanded edition is dedicated to helping you be a better presenter. But it is also dedicated to candor, to saying things that—for one reason or another—never show up in other books on presentation.

Who else would tell you "to keep an eye out for the barracuda?" Chapter 51. Who else would tell you that "you may have been in the wrong place at the wrong time?" Chapter 17. Who else would employ the Mafia to give you a pointer or two on presentations? Chapter 31.

In short, this is a very different book on presentations. It's even different from the first edition of *"I Can See You Naked."* Which still strikes me as a funny notion, *great* for the sitcoms—but now there are other things to laugh about, look at, learn from, and *try* as you get ready to make your next presentation.

—RON HOFF
September, 1992

PART ONE

"What is a presentation? What am I getting myself into?"

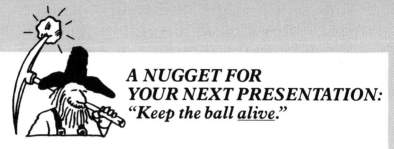

A NUGGET FOR YOUR NEXT PRESENTATION: *"Keep the ball alive."*

Presentation is, more and more, a *visual* medium. The audience thinks visually—and it will help you, the presenter, to think in terms of pictures. If a mental image helps you to hold a thought or concept in your brain, *use it!* So it's a little weird or goofy. You're more likely to remember it. Besides, it's just for you. Here's a visual idea, a nugget that puts the whole subject of presentation into a picture. It's a bit odd, but it makes a point that could be useful in your next presentation.

NUGGET: Think of your next presentation as a big, buoyant medicine ball which you must keep "alive." It's your responsibility to keep that ball up in the air, guiding it deftly, tapping it ever higher, perhaps hitting it smartly with your head. Occasionally you'll boost the ball toward someone in your audience. That ball will move around a lot, people will get involved with it, but it will always come back to you—because you're the one who keeps it "alive." Besides, it's your ball.

1

What is a presentation? It *sounds* like something you do in costume.

You have been asked to make a presentation.

Congratulations!

Somebody thinks you know something that is worth hearing or seeing—maybe both.

You have, in fact, entered a charmed circle. The majority of people are never asked. They never hear those flattering, felicitous words, *"We'd like you to make a presentation to us."*

You accept. The date of the presentation seems quite remote—and you suspect it may never arrive at all.

The precise hour and place assume minor importance when the date is so far away—and you jot the particulars into your "plan ahead" calendar.

The whole crazy notion remains in some far recess of your brain until several days prior to the actual presentation date.

Then comes the unsettling question, *"What have I let myself in for?"*

In struggling to deal with this issue, some people have even been known to admit, "I'm not sure I know what a presentation *is*. It sort of sounds like something that should be done in costume."

Let's nail it down, here and now.

At one end of the spectrum, there is what is loosely called a speech. The very word sends chills up the spine. When people say, "You're not going to make a speech, are you?"—they really and truly *hope that you will not.*

Speeches are presentations that *explode* subjects. Cast an eye at the sketches on the opposite page and you'll get the idea. Speeches have a way of getting fatter and fatter as they are being given. (How often have you said to yourself, "What *is* that guy talking about?") As speeches expand, they rumble and ramble, and generally create a lot of smoke. (Ever noticed how much coughing a really *bad* speech can generate?)

Most speeches have very little impact because they don't ask you to *do* anything. I asked an ex-boss of mine what he wanted to accomplish in an upcoming speech. He said, "Oh, I just want to open their minds up." Fine. Great. Admirable. But most people are not sitting around waiting to have their minds opened up. They are waiting for you to drive home a specific point or idea *that they can really use.*

"... a torpedo is always better than a cannon."

A free-wheeling cannon, often called a "speech," creates lots of smoke! Explodes a subject. It takes a subject of some interest and expands it. It is essentially an inside/out presentation.

A torpedo that speeds precisely to its mark. Starts narrowly and gets sharper. It is essentially an outside/in presentation.

Which brings us to the type of presentation you're most likely to be involved in. It fires quickly from a solid base of preselected information that is already important to the audience. It analyzes that information and sharpens it, bringing it ever closer to the audience's real needs. Near the end, the presentation is speeding swiftly along to a single point that "homes in" *precisely* on its bid for action.

An effective presentation (the kind that you will make) will be a torpedo, not a cannon.

Two to remember

In any presentation that you will make, two things are happening simultaneously:

5

1. *The presenter is making a commitment* to the audience. The presenter is working to prove something that will win the support of the audience—that will generate *action*.

2. *The audience is making a judgment* on the commitment. "Does this thing make any sense?" "Are those facts *accurate?*" "Do I really trust this person?"

By the final moment of the presentation, *if* the presenter has fulfilled his or her mission, the audience will unfold its arms and say, "By golly, I see what you mean. I agree. I'll give it a shot."

Here's what you'll want to stick in your mind . . . it's the best definition you'll find of the presentation that you'll be making:

A presentation is a commitment by the presenter to help the audience do something. Simultaneously, throughout the presentation, the audience is evaluating the presenter's ability to deliver—to make good on the commitment.

Then, of course, the audience renders its verdict. Just like in a courtroom. (See panel titled, "Find yourself in this list of presenters—all are presenting today.")

Commitment/judgment

"I will," says the presenter, "I promise." "Let's see if you're up to it," says the audience.

Can a presentation be that simple?

Actually, the presenter gets a "perk"—a little something special—to make it even simpler.

Presenter's "perk":

The presenter can see how the presentation is doing, every step of the way, by merely looking at the audience. Body language, we call it.

And you'll know how to read it—as well as *facial* language—before you're halfway through this book.

"Find yourself in this list of presenters—all are presenting today."

- An attorney stands before a jury to summarize the reasons that her client, accused of larceny, should be allowed to return "to his rightful place in society." She is making a presentation.
- The treasurer of a midsized research firm stands before his executive committee to report that expenses are running far behind budget and the committee should make immediate cutbacks. He is making a presentation.
- The group manager of a major oil company appears before the company's board of directors to recommend that a new refinery be acquired in South America. She is making a presentation.
- The president of a commercial realty firm tells a potential client why her firm should get the assignment to locate the needed floor space instead of her three competitors who are cooling their heels outside the door. She is making a competitive presentation.
- A marketing student stands on a small platform in front of his Corporate Strategies class and dissects a case history. Summarizing, he tells what the bankrupt subject *should have done*. He is making a presentation.
- A writer pulls a thick screenplay out of her bag and proceeds to "sell the concept"—in twenty minutes or less—to a group of Hollywood executives who may, or may not, spend ten million dollars to get it produced and distributed. She is making a presentation. "Pitching," it's called in Hollywood.
- A woman rises to her feet to review a novel she has just read. Her book club settles back to listen. At the end, she will recommend the book or not. She is making a presentation.
- An instructor at a small midwestern college reads a poem by T. S. Eliot to her class and explains how to build images into original fiction. She is making a presentation.
- A representative of a major publishing company gets up before a group of schoolteachers to prove why her company's educational program will supply the teachers' needs more effectively than the other publishers competing for the contract. She is making a competitive presentation.
- A banker stands before a group of pharmaceutical executives and tries to win their corporate account, realizing full well that six other banks are attempting to do the same thing. She is making a competitive presentation.
- Two candidates for high office stand on a stage and try to win the votes of the people in the auditorium. The candidates are really making competitive presentations to the audience.

Presentations that defy definition.

Before we leave Chapter One, let's not ignore some presentations that don't quite fit the mold—but you encounter them almost every day of your life. And once you recognize them for what they are—presentations that sort of sneak up on you, presentations that tend to defy definition—you will not only enjoy them, you'll detect techniques that *you* can use or adapt.

- *The presentation of the menu.*
  Some restaurants offer *spectacular* presentations of their daily entrees. Waiters and waitresses recite menus with absolute mastery of the language as well as the nuances of the presentation of each dish. Adjectives are chosen as carefully as the condiments. Props and audio/visuals may be used. Perhaps we see a selection of fish, immaculately presented on a silver platter—like jewels from the sea.
- *The presentation of the team.*
  Watch professional athletic teams as they are introduced. Such energy! Such charisma! Such style! Even during warm-ups, the Los Angeles Lakers of the middle 1980s (Kareem, "Magic," "Silk") presented themselves so confidently that you sensed they would never lose. They seldom did.
- *The presentation of the captain of the plane.*
  A voice-only presentation (usually), but what a voice! So comforting. So deep (usually) and wonderfully wise. Have you ever wondered why it isn't a woman? I have.
- *The presentation of places.*
  Try this. Next time you are flying to a major city, notice how it presents itself to you just before you land. I have never been able to find Los Angeles. It's there, but it just doesn't present itself very well. Other cities soar up at you, dazzle you, with their famous landmarks. Golf courses also present themselves with dozens of different personalities. The presentation of a single golf hole (like the seventh at Pebble Beach) can be a work of art. Theaters present themselves differently. As do the plays inside the theaters.
- *The presentation of owners and entrepreneurs.*
  Walk down a street and into a store. *Any* store. Inside, what kind of presentation is being made? Does the owner smile and call you by name? Or, does the person behind the counter take your money without looking up—without saying a word? "Thank you" never hurt a presentation of any kind—*ever.*

Every day, you'll run into *dozens* of presentations that may not *seem* like presentations, but they are. Ever take a taxi? Get a haircut? Barbers and cabbies are *presenting* all the time. And, more often than not, the presenter is taking his or her measure of *you*. Which means *you* are making a presentation, too!

2

"I need you.
You need me."

No, that is not the whispered sentiment of a star-crossed lover. Nor is it part of a hurried conversation on the baseball field between pitcher and catcher.

It is the core of a relationship that should exist between presenter and audience.

It is important to any understanding of the dynamics of presentation because it suggests a partnership rather than a performance, a linkage rather than a confrontation, coming closer rather than pulling apart.

What we're talking about here is the heart of our headline: *needs*. No presentation should occur without them. Since they are so fundamental to the success of your next presentation, they deserve some thoughtful examination (and some graphics to stick in your mind):

Every presentation begins in this way. The audience *needs* something—usually *help*. (Ask a seasoned salesman what he wants to get out of a presentation and invariably he will say, "Just give me *one* idea, that's all I ask, something I can use tomorrow.")

By coming to your presentation, by simply showing up, your audience is expressing a need for help, counsel, wisdom, inspiration—maybe even something that can change its life. Not its collective life—its personal, individual lives.

If truth be told, the audience arrives on the scene with the ardent hope that the presenter knows something that it does not.

Maybe the presenter has a secret, and is willing to share it with the audience. If not, the presenter may have a fresh way of looking at things—one that the audience can apply—profitably. Perhaps tomorrow.

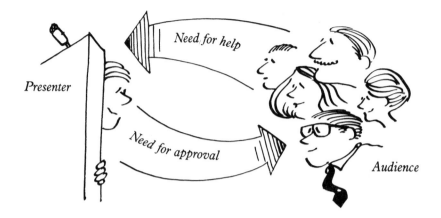

The presenter has needs, too, of course. *Many.* But nothing quite equals the presenter's need for *approval.* Only the audience can give it, but it can be rendered in many forms—from a simple vote (a raising of hands), to a signature on a document (such as a long-term contract), to an outburst of applause.

Without some indication of approval, response, endorsement, confirmation—*something!*—the presenter is lost at sea, adrift, seeking a signal.

This can be tough on the ego. (*No* response is, in many ways, worse than outright rejection.) But it can also leave the presenter without authorization to *do anything.*

How many meetings have you left with the uneasy feeling that nobody had an inkling of what to do next?

This may not be the fault of the audience alone. Maybe the first link in our circuit was never made. Maybe the audience was there, registering a need, but the presenter did what thousands of presenters do: *talked about himself, or herself.* The audience withdrew, sensing that its need was being ignored. Here's what happens:

Nothing happens. The area between audience and presenter remains a void. *No needs are met.* No help is offered. No approval is given. Everybody goes home. Another useless meeting. The audience says, "Boy, was that a dreary meeting." The presenter says, "That audience was dead." The *fulfillment* of needs is essential.

■

Let's assume we've got our circuit going. The circulation in our circle of needs is flowing smoothly. There are no gaps, no hitches.

Gradually, a gratifying sense of *rapport* begins to fill the room. The distance between audience and presenter seems less.

The prognosis for this presentation looks very good indeed.

There are few things in life that can match the exhilaration of a meeting where everything is going well.

But, before the euphoria carries us blissfully away, is there nothing else? No other overriding need?

There is. However, it applies to *brilliant* presentations only. So, if you are simply striving for brilliance rather than insisting on it—consider the following "need" as an intriguing possibility and nothing more. If brilliance is *necessary* to you, listen up.

■

In every *brilliant* presentation, there is what Spalding Gray—the noted writer, actor, and monologist—calls "the perfect moment." He refers to it in his presentation of "Swimming to Cambodia"—a monologue which enjoyed great success at Lincoln Center in New York and, later, as a film. It's worth thinking about.

"The perfect moment" is a burst of incandescence that ignites the entire presentation and gives it an everlasting impression on the audience's memory.

"Swimming to Cambodia" demonstrated its own "perfect moment"—as performed by Mr. Gray—when he described his experience of swimming in the towering surf of the Indian Ocean.

Joe Froschl, an advertising agency executive in New York City, has his own language for this moment of enlightenment. He calls it "a flash of insight that gives us a reason to believe."

Fred Lemont, an experienced marketing consultant and exceptional presenter, calls it a dramatic point in a presentation "which everybody can rally 'round."

"A perfect moment" can be crafted into your presentation and rehearsed to perfection—or it may occur suddenly as an idea erupts in a shower of sparks.

"A perfect moment":

A young business executive named Richard Foody stands before us. He wears a dark blue suit and white shirt. He is nervous. He fluffs some words. He is going to tell us about skiing, but he is starting his presentation in the same way that he might approach a steep, downhill slope. *Very, very* carefully. He is telling us, rather matter-of-factly, that you need certain things before you can start to ski. Gloves. He slips them on. A ski cap. He pulls one over his ears. A number (skiing is like everything else— you have to have a number!).

He hangs the cardboard number around his neck (his coat has been discarded; his tie, loosened). Suddenly, he looks very different. A strangeness has set in—call it "a perfect moment," or at least the start of one. He crouches down, his eyes glistening, and describes the breathless anticipation of "pushing off." His body sways as he speeds down the slope. He's really into it—into his "moment"—carrying us with him. Then, astonishingly, *he falls down.* His feet fly out from under him, and he's down—in a heap. Right in front of us! He looks around, struggles to his feet, chuckles self-consciously. He starts talking to us again, like a stream of consciousness, words coming faster and much easier than before. He realizes he has almost completed his fearsome run down the slope—*and he's home, free!* Well, almost free. What's a little spill when you're out to conquer a mountain—and, most important, your own fears of it? He looks totally different now—confident, elated, in control. He rips off his number and holds it high over his head. There is a kind of radiant jubilation about him. "Just grab your number," he shouts, *"and go."*

Later, it dawned on me that he wasn't just talking about skiing, he was talking about "taking a chance"—doing something different—making a commitment to life. And, shortly thereafter, he moved on to a much bigger job with a different company.

"Perfect moments" may sound a bit weird, but they are very easy to identify. They tend to engulf audiences in a sudden awareness that something unusual has happened. They communicate on a higher level of involvement. And they often conclude in a feeling of emotional closeness between presenter and audience—as if they had shared some kind of transcendent experience.

The vital reminder

It's pleasant to think about the "perfect moments" of your life. It's fun to think about capturing one for your next presentation. But it's *vital* to remember what presentation is all about: *It's about meeting needs.* It's about completing the circle that revolves around rapport. It's the honest realization and resulting reward of "I need you. You need me."

3

Escaping the script.
Discovering the memory map.

In the beginning, there was the script.

It was the exact text of the presentation, double- or triple-spaced by a manual typewriter on $8\frac{1}{2}'' \times 11''$ sheets of white paper.

It was generally stapled together by the typist so the speaker wouldn't lose the pages, or get them in the wrong order, on the way to the meeting.

Then, at the meeting, the speaker would pull the staples out of the script while standing behind the lectern.

(There were times when the speaker couldn't get the staples out—and he or she would flip the pages over the top of the lectern. Every minute or so, another page would appear. It would dangle, along with the other flipped pages, on the audience side of the lectern. Often, members of the audience would *count* the pages as they flew over the top, guessing how many remained to be read. This made the time go faster.)

Notes on $3'' \times 5''$ cards were a big step forward. They freed the speaker from the lectern. The cards could also be shuffled in moments of anxiety—but "notes" instead of a "script" conveyed a far more self-assured impression to the audience. (Scripts almost immediately beg the question, "I wonder if the speaker really wrote this thing.")

In addition to words on paper, speakers have been known to put little notes on their cuffs, their fingernails, and their palms. (Anthony Quinn, the actor, revealed that he often writes reminders on the tips of his fingers in order to emphasize certain qualities in his onstage performance. "More warmth," for example.)

These jottings work with varying degrees of success—usually depending on the speaker's belief in their usefulness. This suggests one of the eternal laws of presentation technique: "If it works, *do it.*"

Television came along and introduced us to teleprompters, giant cue cards, and the like. Some of the nation's more heralded speakers have been known to position a script in front of them and turn a page every now and then while actually reading, word for word, from an off-camera teleprompter. This touch of craftiness led the audience to believe that the speaker knew his on-camera script *so well* that only a rare downward glance or page turn was necessary.

Television also brought us the *storyboard*—a sort of audio/visual device that enabled advertisers to get the gist of a commercial before it was produced. The finished commercial usually had all kinds of

---

Mandela—without notes

When Nelson Mandela made his "Victory Tour" of the United States following his twenty-seven-year imprisonment in South Africa, he and President George Bush stood side by side and exchanged statements on the White House lawn.

President Bush spoke in his usual ceremonial style, talking almost casually from a prepared script. The seventy-one-year-old Mandela, in his somber, navy blue suit, spoke almost formally—never looking down, never referring to a note or script of any kind. His English was impeccable. His sentences were clear and remarkably candid.

George Bush seemed almost awestruck by Mandela's directness and ability to say exactly what he meant without written words to guide him. As the two men walked away, the parabolic microphones picked up George Bush saying, "Good statement. No notes. It's wonderful."

It is always impressive to see someone talk precisely without a script of any kind. But it cannot happen unless the speaker *sees* the message forming in his or her mind. And, in most cases, the message is a *picture* in the mind's eye which prompts the words to flow.

---

directorial touches to polish up the production values, but advertisers got an *impression* of the selling idea by studying the dozen or so sketches on the "board."

■

Enter Ben Goodspeed, business analyst, author, and presenter. While I was interviewing him in his office, he showed me something that resembled a storyboard—but it was much *looser,* required no special format, and seemed beautifully simple.

It was a hand-drawn *road map* of a presentation that Ben was going to give in Minneapolis on the following Tuesday (this happened over ten years ago).

Ben's squiggly drawing had a kind of childlike charm to it. There were lines going every which way, and a smattering of words. I wasn't quite sure I totally understood the message (more about that in a minute), but it looked like a great leap forward for presenters who had previously used scripts and notes.

He suggested that I keep it and study it. ("I've got it all in my mind," he said.)

It was a one-page visualization of a presentation . . . and its objective was simple and precise: to aid the memory of the presenter. It was a presentation memory map. And any presenter who has ever been stalked by the fear of forgetting should try one.

Let's ease into this idea, because it requires a whole new way of preparing your mind to remember something.

Ask yourself, "If my presentation were going to be laid out like a Monopoly board, or a Candy Land® board, or almost *any* kind of game board, what would it look like?"

This does something quite miraculous. It gets you thinking in terms of *graphic* relationships instead of *word* relationships. It also forces you to work on a *single* surface where you can see the whole thing at one time.

The Candy Land game board, if studied as a way to remember your next presentation, can be a lively revelation.

Please note that each locality has a vivid *picture* and *illustrated* personality to remember it by.

Gloppy, a lovable brown lump, lives in the Molasses Swamp. Lord Licorice, dressed appropriately in black, lives in the Licorice Castle.

You get the idea. There's at least one picture per neighborhood. The course to be followed is colorfully clear. And the words are few and vivid.

The entire board is a delightful piece of almost-instant communication, presented in the way that most people remember things, *pictorially.*

Now, let me show you a raw example of a presentation memory map. It was sketched by the speaker for a presentation to the Young President's Organization in New York City. If you don't quite understand the *subject* of the speech, don't worry about it (nobody can really get inside somebody else's brain). Just consider the *concept* of the map and what you might do with it.

This idea of visualizing your next presentation can help you in two very specific ways:

■ In the process of creating the visuals for your memory map, you are drawing pictures in your brain that will last much, much longer than words. With those pictures indelibly in your head, you're going to find that your presentation comes to mind almost effortlessly.

■ You can use your memory map as a teleprompter. Take it with you to your presentation and put it any place that you can see it. You'll find that you can "read it" from ten feet or more—and that glancing at it, from time to time, will show you *instantaneously* where you are. You'll also discover that you're less nervous when your memory map is at hand.

There aren't any rules to follow in trying this exercise, but here are some "suggestions" you might want to consider:

1. Best way to *start* is to jot down the basic points you want to cover. A few words per point.
2. Visualize those points with your own graphics. The roughest sketches, the skinniest stick figures will be fine—just as long as they represent pictures in your mind.
3. Have a pathway, a route. Want to use green arrows? Traffic symbols? Big, blocky numbers? Or maybe the route is so obvious that you don't need any of those things. Whatever works for you, *do it.*
4. Keep everything on one surface. That doesn't mean you're prevented from attaching something to that surface—maybe a snapshot, a clipping, whatever. But your memory map

Part Map, Part Picture, Part Game
It's an easy way to visualize your next presentation.

This "Presentation on Perceptions" starts in the lower left (with the big eyeball)—swings up through the billboard (with the point of view)—moves quickly through the supporting exhibits (beginning with Gerald Ford's perception as being clumsy)—returns to the point of view—presents the idea (The Perception Process)—and closes in the lower right with "The Next Step . . ."

This is how the flow goes.

Don't try to understand this one. Try your own!

should remain a single, self-contained piece of communication.

5. Don't fuss with it. Fill the page. Think of Candy Land—or your favorite board game. Use colors and free-flowing shapes. *Let go.*

Once you've seen your presentation in this way, you'll feel differently about it. It's more creative. It's more dynamic. And—best of all—it's uniquely yours. (Nobody else will even be able to figure it out!)

4

Have you got what it takes to be a superb presenter? A twenty-eight-point checklist.

☐ Do you ever wonder what the other person is thinking about while *you're* talking? Do you instinctively put yourself in the other person's situation?

☐ Do you really get a kick out of helping other people solve *their* problems?

☐ Do you use the word "you" more than "I"?

☐ Have you ever watched a debate on TV (or elsewhere) and thought, "That's something I'd like to try"?

☐ While watching TV panel shows, do you sometimes answer the questions before the experts do?

☐ Do you have a good memory?

☐ Do you enjoy "board games" like Monopoly? Do you think you could create one?

☐ Are you sensitive to the sensitivities of other people? (See Chapter 44 for examples.)

☐ When you get into an animated conversation, do you sometimes find yourself taking a *differing* point of view just because you enjoy the argument?

☐ Can you cut through a rambling, foggy conversation—dig out the main point—and *say it* so that everybody understands and *agrees?*

☐ Do you have a high energy level? Do other people seem to be talking slowly to you?

☐ Have you ever listened to your own voice—just to see what you sound like?

☐ Have you ever watched yourself on film or videotape—just to see how you handle yourself, how you move, how you might be perceived?

☐ Is there a bit of cheerleader in you? Do you usually lead the applause?

☐ Do you like to tell people what you've learned? Would you make a good teacher?

☐ Do you think graphically? As you talk, do you see pictures forming in your mind?

☐ If you were to look out the nearest window right now, could you describe what you see in some detail?

☐ Does the prospect of actually trying the exercise in the preceding question appeal to you?

☐ Are you a good editor? Can you digest lots of material into simple, clear language?

☐ Do you like the feeling of being "in control"?

☐ Can you handle pressure without blowing your top? Can you deal with provocative questions without flaring up?

☐ Do you like to show people the work you've done and explain how you did it?

☐ Do you like to demonstrate what you're talking about? Do you tend to "act out" what you're describing?

☐ Are you an optimist? Do you bounce back in a hurry?

☐ Were you in the senior play in high school?

☐ Do you look people in the eye when you *talk* to them?

☐ Do you look people in the eye when *they're* talking to you?

☐ Do people turn to you when it's time for the meeting to be summed up?

If you answered "yes" to at least half of these questions, you're in good shape to become a superb presenter. If you scored less than that, all is not lost. At least you're honest, and *that*—as has been dramatically demonstrated—is clearly the most important requisite of all. We'll also give you an extra point for "tenaciousness" if you'll just hang in there.

This is a "dive in" page.
Subject: fuddy duddy fundamentals

Know how people read this book? They jump around. Precious few "self-help" books are read straight through. Alas. You have no idea how hard that is for an author to admit. Let's face it. Audiences of *all* kinds read/listen/watch *only what interests them.*

People like to "dive in" on books like this one. So, this is a "dive in" page. It looks at some presentation "fundamentals" which have probably served their purpose (and their time). Granted, that's sensitive ground, but we'll give it to you in "short pops"—and if you want more on anything in particular, we'll head you in the right direction.

1. *"Don't be nervous."* Telling presenters not to be nervous is like telling them to stop breathing. Everybody's nervous. *Everybody.* Which is good. A certain amount of nervousness gives your presentation an edge. Otherwise, you'd be flat as Kansas. (See Part Three, Chapter 9.)

2. *"Use a podium."* Why? It restricts all movement and makes you look like a monster. (See Chapter 15.)

3. *"State your objective."* Hey, no offense—but we don't *care* what your objective is. What we care about (we, being your audience) is *our* objective. The "Me Generation" may be history, but people are still interested in what you can do for *them*, not what you can do for *you.*

4. *"Speak slowly."* Slow speakers can drive you nuts. It's like watching cement harden. News anchors on the networks speak between 165 and 195 words per minute (I've clocked

them). Most presenters speak considerably slower than that—about 120 wpm.

5. *"Tell a joke to get started."* In most meetings, if you start with a joke just because you think it's funny, you're a candidate for immediate tune-out. A relevant, true story is so much better than a concocted joke that there is no comparison. (See Chapter 21 on humor.)

6. *"Turn the lights low to show your slides."* That's like saying, "Nighty, night . . ."

7. *"Cover all bases."* "We try to cover everything and the audience remembers nothing." That may be the most prevalent self-criticism that I hear from presenters who have had bum luck in competitive presentations.

8. *"Make it flow."* Old-fashioned presentations used to flow along like maple syrup—with smooth, immaculate bridges and transitions. Now, TV has changed all that. Break it up. Jolt people. Surprise people. (See Chapter 14.)

9. *"Summarize at the end."* No—summarize, summarize, summarize. *You should be summarizing all the way through.* We call it "Planting flags" in this book. Keep making it easy for people to remember. (See Chapter 14.)

10. *"Keep control at all times."* Don't try to be Captain Queeg. You're likely to have a mutiny on your hands. Let an audience wrangle if it wants to. They'll feel better afterward, and you will come across as somebody who has enough confidence to give the audience some intellectual freedom.

The worst enemy of presentation is rigidity. The world has changed. Television is here. Holistics is here. Information delivery has gone through its biggest transformation in history. No wonder the old fundamentals of presentation are being debunked. Onward, friend, we've hardly started.

PART TWO

The first ninety seconds: They're absolutely crucial.

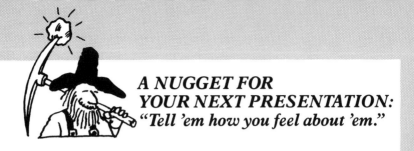

A NUGGET FOR YOUR NEXT PRESENTATION:
"Tell 'em how you feel about 'em."

The first ninety seconds of any presentation are crucial. Maybe the audience has never seen you before. The eye is taking snapshots of you, impressions are being registered.

As college professor Ralph Podrian puts it, "Your audience will scan every personal detail about you for clues to character and temperament." Think back. How many times have you heard someone in an audience say, "I knew in the first couple of minutes it wasn't going to be any good." Or, conversely, "The minute she started, the very *first* minute, I just knew it was going to be *sensational.*"

> **NUGGET: Never hesitate to let your audience know that you're *delighted* that they're there. Tell 'em, right off the bat. "I've been looking forward to this moment for a long time. . . ." What does that say? It says you're prepared. You're confident. You're eager to get into it. *You're enthused about sharing this particular subject with this particular group of people.* The only possible hitch: You'd better mean it!**

5

Stand or sit?
What's a presenter to do?

Y̲ou stand up.

You sit down.

Sounds so easy. Ask almost anybody, and he or she would say those are the two basic positions for making a presentation.

Up. Down. *Simple.*

But if it's so simple, why do we have so many presenters doing all those strange "in between" things?

■ There's the guy who wraps himself around the podium like a vine around a tree. Neither sitting nor standing, he's sort of communing with the furniture.

■ Then, there's the woman who just leans back against a table and talks. No, she's really *resting* on the table, arms extended—a body in repose. Graceful, yet mannered.

■ Of course, there are those presenters who lean against walls and rub their backs against the rough surface texture. I had a civics teacher who did that all the time. Arms folded, always scratching his back. It seemed to help him talk.

■ There are also those terribly earnest people who put one foot on a chair and lean forward on the upraised knee. The "Knute Rockne" position.

Let's face it: *Presenters don't like to stand up unsupported.*

They'd rather sit. In a recent meeting, a young market analyst was asked to make his presentation.

"Oh, should I stand?" he asked hesitantly (already the audience was forming an impression of something less than decisiveness).

"Yes, why don't you?" the chairman said.

The young man smiled a wan smile, rose to his feet, and immediately grabbed hold of the back of his chair. Ah . . . *blessed support!* And there he stood, clutching onto that chair as if it might march off to some other meeting.

So, why don't we just sit down and make our presentations?

A lot of people do. If you're presenting to one other person, you may want to sit down and make your presentation. One-on-one, eyeball-to-eyeball. And if the mood is casual and conversational, sitting down is often best.

Or, if it's an "open discussion," with five or six participants, you could look pretty silly jumping up and down every time you wanted to say something.

All other times, however, you stand. Unsupported.

I can see you now, recoiling in horror. Hold on.

Before you rush madly to the next chapter, consider a few phrases. *"Standing ovation."* Did you ever hear of a "sitting ovation?" *"There's a real stand-up kind of guy."* Did you ever hear of a sitdown kind of guy—or gal?

"Stand up for what's right." Nobody ever said anything about "sitting down" for your principles. Did you ever see an attorney *sitting down* to deliver a closing argument?

"Stand up and be counted." The other posture just wouldn't make much sense.

People stand up for what they believe in—the home team charges onto the field, the maestro takes a bow, the mayor waves to his supporters. Bravo! Hooray! Good show! *Everybody stands.*

Even Dan Rather started standing recently. (He said your voice sounds better when you're standing.) Nobody watching at home really knew he was standing. I understand he's sitting now. Funny thing about newscasters, they seem to be standing even when they're sitting. Head up, eyes sharp, spine erect, they've perfected *a stand-up kind of sitting!*

You want to stand up when you're in a group of people because it gives you authority—automatically, instantly. It signals the rest of the group to shut up and listen. It's a nonverbal command for attention.

But here's the main reason for standing.

You can be your own best audio/visual aid when you are standing up.

You can move. You can travel all over the room so that people will have to keep their eyes glued on you. When you're sitting, their eyes are more likely to close.

You can make eye contact equally with everybody in the meeting. Moving from person to person, you can achieve an up-close intimacy you could never sustain sitting in one place.

You can attend to props without saying things like, "will somebody please punch up the video?" You just step forward and punch it up yourself.

You can send signals more clearly. A colleague of mine said recently, "I like presenters who stand up. It means they aren't going to speak as long. And when they sit down, I know it's over."

You can communicate more memorably. When you're moving around, people are taking mental snapshots of you all the time. Each snapshot reveals something about you. When you're sitting down, you're sedentary. You may be communicating verbally, but you're not nearly as interesting. You're giving up more than half of your ability to be remembered.

You become the best audio/visual aid you'll ever have. You're a motion picture. You're a narrator (you can converse, if you want to). You're a pointer. You're a "live" dramatization of the message you want to send. You can be instantly reactive (like a computer).

Or, think of it this way: You don't have the *problems* of other audio/visual aids. You don't have to have the room darkened in order to be seen. You don't burn out. You don't jam up. You don't break. You're not one-dimensional. You're cheap (well, cheaper than most A/V). You won't fall off the wall, and you don't need a technician to operate you.

How to stand on your own.

For anybody who's ever had that "I've got to find something to lean against" feeling, here's a small ritual that is absolutely guaranteed to work:

1. Before you get up to present, pick out *the exact spot* where you're going to stand. Just as professional basketball stars have precisely identified the points on the court from which they will invariably score, you've got *your spot* where you'll feel most comfortable.
2. Keep both feet *flat on the floor before* you get up to present. This helps the circulation. It also helps you to rise smartly to a standing position without unwinding your legs.
3. Move briskly to "your spot." Let them read your body language. You're prepared, eager to get going. This isn't going to be one of those takes-forever-to-get-going speeches.
4. Look at your audience, acknowledge their interest in you— but keep things perking.

NOTE: **Some speakers will stand up and peer into every eye in the audience. This usually reduces the group to abject silence. Oh, oh. Something ominous is going to happen. What is this—hypnosis or what? Speakers who try to mesmerize people often suffer from hyperactive egos. Pretentious speakers are a bore.**

5. *Move* at the earliest opportunity—to an audio/visual aid or toward a friendly face in your audience. Both are worthy objectives to get your presentation off on the right foot.

Here's something else to think about: if you're sitting down, the other person can always stand up. For possible repercussions, see the panel below.

How to avoid being stood up

Want to know the worst feeling in the world?

You sit down across from the person you're presenting to. It's just the two of you. You're comfortable.

Your presentation is going nicely. You're making points. *Suddenly, the other person stands up.*

Even though the other person hasn't said a word, you've been dismissed. You're outta there. You leave mumbling, "*That's* never gonna happen to me again."

TRY THIS: **Make a presentation that will give you a legitimate reason to stand when you start. Almost every office, these days, has a flip chart on the wall—or a presentation board—or a chalkboard. Ask permission to use it and put something on it that will get things going. Whatever you've planned. A provocative question. An intriguing formula. A surprising statistic. You're standing, and the floor is yours. What's more, you've got a much better chance of keeping it until you're finished.**

6

How to "warm up"
an audience without a
Catskills comic or a
Big Ten cheerleader.

There is much to be said for "warming up" an audience.

This simply means to soften the strangeness, defuse the defenses, and slice through the natural reluctance to expose feelings and emotions openly.

Without a "warm-up," an audience can be a very cold pool on a gray day.

It's an art to unfrost an audience. It's like an emotional massage, coaxing the face to smile, the senses to respond, the arterial system to open up. Any stand-up comic or Big Ten cheerleader can do it in minutes.

Of course, if you don't happen to have a stable of joke-writers in your entourage—or a squad of cheerleaders—the "warming up" process is going to become your task.

This prompts yet another question.

Who warms *you* up?

The answer sounds impossible, but it's really fairly easy.

You've got to warm yourself up while you're warming up your audience. Before you dismiss that advice as clearly preposterous, keep in mind one small truism which will carry you through many a tough spot in a presentation: *The audience reflects the attitude and manner of the presenter.* Thus, while *you're* getting warmed up, *your audience* won't be more than a few steps behind.

There are two things *you* can do *alone* (that is, *without* cheerleaders or Catskills comics to warm you and your audience) and you can do both of them in those crucial first ninety seconds.

1. *Start by focusing on a friend—one who is committed to your support.* (Spouses, blood relatives, and paid shills don't count.) It must be a legitimate member of the audience who is not a member of your handpicked team. (It just doesn't help very much if you look at your mother and she smiles back at you. Some small modicum of objectivity is necessary.)

If you look over your audience and find that you don't have a single, solitary, legitimate supporter in the whole place, you might as well pick up your easels and chalkboards and head for home. You haven't done your audience analysis, *or* you're talking to the most hostile audience on the face of the earth.

Once you've established contact with your one, true, legitimate friend—*lock in.* Let the eye contact register. Let that person know, by your manner, that he or she is damn important. From that moment on, you and that person have an understanding that is going to develop into a relationship.

> **IMPORTANT:** **Most presenters think that they're just standing up there, in front of the audience, *building a case*. Actually that's half of it. They should be *building a relationship* with every person in the room. (See Chapter 50—A guide to relationships.)**

Once you've made a friend in your audience, you can move on, to another face, lock in, and read the reaction. A steady, open exchange—maybe even a smile or a nod—and you've got another friend.

Your audience is "warming up"—you're doing it by yourself and only seven seconds have gone by.

It's a little like calling the roll—only doing it by eye contact. "Yes, you're here. Thanks for coming." "Yes, you're with me. Good for you." "Are you with me? I'll be back to see how you're doing later on."

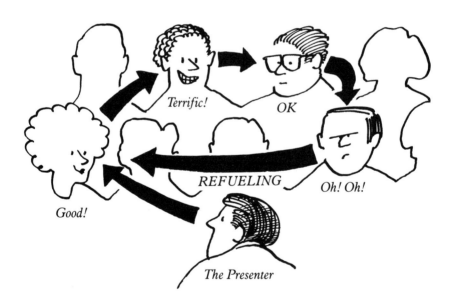

"Warming up an audience" is like calling the roll via eye contact. You can tell who's with you. If you hit a cold fish, don't hesitate to return for refueling.

You've reached a question mark. Face averted. No eye contact. Arms folded. Leaning back and away.

The "warming up" has cooled off. Never mind. You simply go back for a little "refueling." You need reinforcement. Everybody does—especially during those first ninety seconds. So, back you go to a friend, a *known* supporter, and you solidify that connection—confirming it—and all the while you're gathering strength to continue your quest for more friends. You've got plenty of time. Oodles of it. Only twenty seconds have elapsed and you've got more than a minute to make more friends before your first ninety seconds are gone.

So, refueled and recharged by refreshing a few friendships, you're changing the atmosphere from frosty to warm, from static to reactive. You can almost feel the climate change.

But, while all of this crucial chemistry is taking place, what are you saying? Is it chatter or solid gold? *What are you saying up there?* Listen.

2. *You're saying something that you really enjoy—that is easy for you to relate—that is relevant.* Maybe it's one line. Or, it could be a favorite quote from a favorite writer. Or, a bit of news that is positive. It doesn't have to be a leg-slapper of a joke, or a feature story for Tom Brokaw. It's *for you*, and the relationship you want to build with your audience. It should not have any hard-to-pronounce words or hard-to-digest theories. It should roll right out of your mouth—without the slightest suggestion of pretentiousness.

Maybe a couple of snapshots will help:

Snapshot: A slender woman in her late twenties gets up to make a presentation to a business group in Cincinnati. She stands there, establishes eye contact, smiles, and says in a soft voice, "Who would like to play hookey with me this afternoon?" You can *feel* the audience defrost. People in the audience smile at each other, smile at the presenter, and lean forward. The ice is broken. She *has* them. The warming-up period took all of ten seconds. The chill is off the room, and the presenter is moving gracefully into her presentation. Her subject is perfect for her lead-in: We should use our leisure time more imaginatively, not following the same frazzled routine.

Snapshot: An intense young researcher doesn't look so tense this morning. He's smiling. He gathers his audience and says, "Got an invitation for you. Let's have some tea . . . and celebrate."

The audience is fully awake now. It has been asked to participate in *good news*. Only six seconds have elapsed.

Here comes the tea, right on cue. Everything is perfect. The tea service looks like a spread out of *House Beautiful.* "The tea that you're about to taste," says the research director, savoring the word *taste,* "is our newest instant tea—and it's just been tested in the marketplace. It looks like we've got a winner. Congratulations."

Twenty-one seconds have elapsed. The atmosphere in the room is glowing.

So, as the tea is served, the research director moves into the topline results of the test. The audience is sipping from the cups of victory, and the numbers *tinkle* with good cheer. Whatever the young research director recommends, chances for approval are now as hot as the tea. *Good news,* coupled with an invitation to *participate* in it, can "warm up" an audience almost instantly.

■

You've seen presenters like this research director, and the woman in Cincinnati. They look into your eyes, say a few words in very simple language, and the atmosphere changes. This is not somebody reading a speech-writer's script or rambling through a few obligatory remarks. There is no pretense.

This is a relationship in the making—friendships forming, real feelings being transmitted. And, always, eyes are making contact.

"Warming up" an audience can be done well within your first ninety seconds. Just start making friends, and talking in a way that comes easily and naturally for you. You'll be warmed up in no time. And audiences are never far behind.

7

Some little questions
that can make a big difference
in the first ninety seconds.

Sometimes, during those crucial first ninety seconds, you can get things moving your way by asking your audience to help you. Casually. Almost offhandedly.

If you're presenting in a small meeting room—perhaps in a not-so-new hotel conference room—where the audio/visual equipment is a bit antiquated and you never really know what's going to happen next ("Pardon me," the waiter asks, "but is this the meeting that ordered the plum danish and decaf?"), an audience really *can* serve as a kind of volunteer support system.

It's a little tricky, though, so it's best to know what you can ask your audience to do with some reasonable expectation of success and, on the other hand, what can cause confusion, consternation, and delay.

1. *When you ask your audience to get involved with the lighting, you're courting disaster.* "Could somebody please hit the light switch back there. I've got a few transparencies to show up here." Suddenly the room is plunged into inky darkness and the speaker can't find his notes, his slides, the projector, the audience, anything. "No, no—can you bring up the dimmers?" It turns out there are no dimmers. "What about the sidelights, the wall lights?" The well-meaning guy sitting back by the light panel starts throwing switches with reckless abandon. Lights flash on and off in blinding combinations. The chandeliers blink. Spotlights appear from out of nowhere. It's like a Light Show at Atlantic City. The overall effect is not without dazzlement, but it can be rudely disruptive.

The answer is for *you* to have all the lights set exactly where you want them for the showing of your slides. There is a midpoint of illumination where you can see your audience, they can see you, and the slides are clear and bright on the screen. This is a point which the poor devil sitting back by the light panel is unlikely to discover—perhaps in his lifetime.

Unexpected Darkness—A True Story: The most unnerving experience of my speaking career involved the lights in a cavernous auditorium in Dallas, Texas. I had started my presentation on a vast platform that seemed more like a mesa high above the audience. There were only a few hundred hearty souls in an arena that must have seated ten thousand. But I could see them and they could see me—the lighting was just fine. The presentation began. After about three minutes, every light in the auditorium began to dim. It was eerie, like a very slow power failure. As we all descended into darkness, a spotlight of ferocious intensity suddenly attached itself to me. I looked for my audience and saw only blackness beyond the blinding whiteness of the spotlight. Was anybody there? I couldn't see a single solitary person. It was like being alone in an aircraft hangar. But I labored on, good soldier and all that. When the normal lights returned, there were the people—just as I had left them—but I had the strangest feeling about them. *I felt that I hadn't talked to them at all.*

There's a moral to this story: don't let unexpected darkness disconnect you from your audience. If that ever happens to you, throw discretion to the wind and *save* your audience. Just say, "Please bring the lights back up." That's what I should have done.

2. *When you ask questions that relate to the comfort and convenience of your audience, you'd better have the answers.* When you start out by asking your audience, "Is it too cold for you in here?" or "How's the ventilation?"—you're showing your concern. *Good.* Audiences like that. They're people, after all, and they like the idea that you're watching out for them—responsible, in a way, for their welfare. They're already appreciative. But you'd better have a pretty good idea of where to find the building engineer or the superintendent should you receive a rousing chorus of complaints.

I've heard presenters ask, "Is that music in the next room too loud for you?" without having the foggiest idea of what to do about it. (Ask the hotel manager or meeting manager to intercede—you stay out of it. An argument with the presenter in the next room is something you don't really need.)

Show concern, yes, but don't bring up problems that you don't know how to remedy. It's strange, but drawing attention to an unfixable problem will only make it more distracting.

3. *Ask your audience about things that are directly within your control. Demonstrate your concern.* Here's a suggestion for the first ninety seconds of your presentation that's a far better icebreaker than telling a joke—and it will use up much less time:

■ "Can everybody see this chart from where you're sitting? How about the back of the room? . . . What if I move this easel forward a few feet? Is that better?"

Important Note: Of course you checked out the meeting room long before the audience arrived. You've made your decisions on where you want your props and audio/visual gear. What you're doing now is making some slight adjustments to, ostensibly, accommodate your audience. However, you're also accomplishing some other things that can be every bit as important:

—You're showing that you're not paralyzed by your own rigid planning. You're flexible. Nothing is set in stone.

—You're involving them in a nice way. You've hardly started and already *they're* participating, making a meaningful contribution to *your* presentation. That's gratifying for them, and genuinely help-ful to you.

The key point: demonstrate your concern authoritatively, not tentatively. You're not worried or fretful about the lights, the mike, the props. You don't want to give that impression. You're starting up a dialogue. You're getting a relationship underway. And just maybe you're also alleviating a bit of your own nervousness.

All that, within the first ninety seconds!

8

"Who's going to be Stanley Kubrick?"

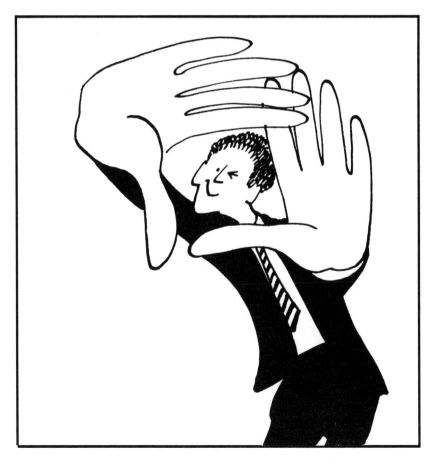

Every presentation needs a Stanley Kubrick. A *director*, that is. Man or woman (Elaine May would have worked just as well in our headline).

What we're saying here is that every presentation needs *somebody* (no codirectors, please) to steer things during rehearsals, to keep things on an even keel during the presentation, to be responsible for the entire effort.

Stanley Kubricks are especially important in *team* presentations. That is, where there's more than one presenter and everybody has the same goal—usually to get something approved. Like a budget, or a strategy, or a schedule, or an acquisition.

When *no one* is officially in charge, *everybody* can be foggy at best and stormy at worst. Rehearsals can be ignored. Time restraints can be flouted. And the various sections of the presentation can become little unconnected islands of opinion. Before you know it, the presentation doesn't really understand what it's about. *It needs a Stanley Kubrick.*

Of course, responsibility also brings accountability—so a Stanley Kubrick whose presentation doesn't get approved probably isn't going to be Stanley Kubrick for very long. Fair's fair.

Could you qualify for the director's chair? Would you make a successful Stanley Kubrick? Sit down right there and scan the requirements:

Job Profile:　　Presentation Director

- Must be authoritative, capable of telling a senior executive or high-ranking officer that his or her part of the presentation must be drastically cut or changed. An unusual level of job security is helpful.
- Must understand that successful presentations answer the *needs* of the audience and are not promotional pulpits for the presenters.
- Must be able to resolve differences of opinion, especially during rehearsals, without causing ruffled feathers.
- Must know how to "cast" a presentation so that the presenters fill their most effective roles. Strengths must be compounded; weaknesses, minimized. It's a little like organizing a repertory company in the theater.
- Must have an up-to-date knowledge of audio/visual aids.
- Must know exactly what the audience is looking for. Should be able to see the world from inside "their boxes" (see Chapter 39).

- Must be willing to insist on rehearsals even when the presenters think they're perfect.
- Must be skilled at compassionate criticism (see Chapter 60).
- Must have considerable motivational ability. Needs to be tough *and* inspiring.
- Must have the guts to call an "audible" when something unexpected happens during the presentation. Doesn't panic under fire.
- Must have the patience to drill his team on the question/answer process (see Chapters 52, 53, 54, 55). Must have the depth of knowledge to handle the unanticipated questions.
- Must be willing to bend the corporate culture, eager to experiment, open to new ways of presenting people, products, and processes. Must be willing to say, "I know we've never done it this way before, but . . ."
- Must have a "grand vision" of the presentation that enables him or her to evaluate all of the "pieces" in terms of a single, desired impression.
- Must be an eternal optimist, able to withstand heavy bombardment and carry on.

How did you do?

If you didn't measure up to *all* of those "musts," you can still be a director—of a little different definition.

You see, every single presenter needs help, support, guidance—a kind of *personal* Stanley Kubrick. A manager, time-keeper, A/V expert, critic, and supporter—all helpfully packaged in one person.

This could be you—for a spouse, business associate, brother-in-law, neighbor, or *anybody* preparing a presentation alone. Then, when *you're* working on a presentation and need your own personal Stanley Kubrick, the roles can be reversed—and *you'll* have a solid source of support.

Presentations need Stanley Kubricks—*and* Elaine Mays. They're invaluable. They can make a decisive difference. But please, only one to a presentation.

PART THREE

Nervousness.
How to tame the fear
that's in us all.

A NUGGET FOR YOUR NEXT PRESENTATION: *"Knees knocking? Don't tell us."*

The hotel ballroom was filled to overflowing. It had been a good year. The employees were bubbling—full of anticipation. Visions of Christmas bonuses filled the air. The chairman of the corporation stood up and quickly introduced the treasurer—who, everybody knew, was to be the bearer of grand financial tidings. The treasurer moved unsteadily downstage. He positioned himself behind the lectern, which was simply a canted shelf on a metal pole, and held on to it for dear life. His first words:

> "I'm so nervous this morning. I hope you can't see how badly my knees are shaking."

The reaction was immediate and eminently predictable. Everybody's gaze shifted to his knees and stayed there for the rest of the presentation.

NUGGET: If you're nervous, don't announce it. Once you do, your audience feels obligated to worry about you. Presenters who cause worry don't inspire great confidence.

9

How to get the best out of nervousness— and control the rest.

Show me a person who says, "I never feel the slightest bit nervous when I get up to present," and I will show you a person who is not to be trusted.

That person, no matter how reputable, is *lying*.

Here's the truth of it: some of the world's most famous presenters have freely admitted to nervousness and stage fright—Sir Lawrence Olivier, Helen Hayes, Maureen Stapleton, Luciano Pavarotti, Willard Scott—and many more. You are not alone.

If you're *alive,* your nervous system is going to be going full throttle, or close to it, when you get up to present yourself.

Being nervous is being alive—so how can it be all bad?

It's not.

Contrary to popular belief, nervousness is *good* for you and your presentation—that is, up to a certain point which I have dubbed the Crossover Point.

So, let's explore the *good* side of nervousness.

Positive nervousness activates the adrenaline supply. It makes the eyes shine. It puts an edge on what you're presenting. It generates a respectful attention within your audience (after all, nervousness proves that you think your audience is worth being nervous about). It creates an atmosphere that has a bit of drama in it.

Those are all decent virtues—not to be minimized by hardliners who view nervousness as some kind of paralyzing ogre.

But now we're approaching the Crossover Point. To see it more clearly, settle into this church pew with me on a recent Sunday morning in New York City.

Quiet please, the service is under way. It's a full house and things are moving along smoothly. The scripture has been read. The offering has been collected. The ushers move down the aisles, their collection plates heaped with wads of cash and little white envelopes.

As the ushers gather at the front of the church, a woman in her mid-fifties climbs the stairs to the altar.

She looks solemn, heavily laden—though she is carrying only a small piece of rumpled paper. She stations herself behind the altar, looking first right and then left as if she were sizing up a dangerous intersection. There is no joy in her manner. Her spirits show no sign of heavenly levitation.

Silence. Then, her voice—small and constricted—tumbles out upon the congregation. She is nervous, obviously, but the words emerge—forming sacred platitudes—and the audience is attentive, even smiling a bit, nodding in appreciation of the woman's valor.

Suddenly, there's a problem. The words aren't coming out right. There are awkward gaps. Meanings fall apart.

Like a car running out of gasoline, the woman's voice is chugging to a standstill. Her throat has become so constricted by nervousness that she is running out of breath.

The congregation shifts uneasily; the minister looks up from his meditation.

We have arrived at the Crossover Point. The audience no longer regards the presenter's nervousness as an endearing life sign but, instead, sees it as a darkening cloud. The nervousness of the presenter has become so worrisome to the audience that it has, in fact, made *the audience nervous.*

Back to the woman at the altar.

She stops. Is she finished? Apparently. The minister moves toward her, reaching for her elbow, whispering a few consoling words in her ear. Steering her gently, he escorts her down the steps and back to her seat in the congregation.

The lady is pale, shaken, but she doesn't realize what she has done for us. She has taken us to the Crossover Point *and* shown us what can happen when nervousness creeps over the line, causing such anguish for the presenter that it spreads to the audience.

Here are some astonishingly simple things the church member could have done, and *you* can do before your next presentation: Louis Nizer, the famed trial lawyer, has nailed the culprit quite emphatically. He says, "A speaker's nervousness or distress is the most communicable disease in the world."

The Reverend Jesse Jackson makes the same point, a tad less dramatically, "I've learned that nervous speakers make people nervous."

First, don't fight it. You don't get anywhere by waging war against nervousness. It'll wear you down. You *accept* it as a positive influence. At the very least, it prevents you from being flat. Then, like Sugar Ray Leonard, you "finesse" your way along—with a lot of technique and no small amount of self-assurance. Keep it positive and joyful. You can *ease* your way through it a lot more effectively than by hammering and pounding.

Second, take a brisk walk. While everybody else is loading up on Danish and crumb cake, take a five-minute walk. That should get you around the block. If you haven't got five minutes, walk around the hallways outside of your meeting room. Walking *before* presenting gets your whole body loosened up (it is *guaranteed* to prevent knees from shaking during crucial presentations). Walking burns off excess nervousness (it is also good for hypertension). It gets you moving forward physically and mentally. It projects you into your presentation in a nonviolent, nonstressed way. You walk in with a glow.

Third, don't sit there with your legs crossed. One of them is liable to go to sleep. It happens frequently. Presenters often get up to speak and find that they sort of lunge forward, one leg functioning and the other floundering. If you're the next presenter, put both feet on the floor and lean forward. Wiggle your toes. It's okay. No one will know what you're doing and you'll have solid proof that both feet are fully awake and ready to go.

Fourth, while you're sitting there waiting to present, let your arms dangle at your sides. Make believe that your fingers and arms are supported by the carpet. If you can't feel the carpet, just let your arms hang there—detached. Feel the tension draining out of them and onto the carpet. Remember: you're not *fighting* anything. You're just letting it drift away.

Fifth, while your arms are dangling there, twirl your wrists, so that your fingers shake loosely. Athletes do this all the time, usually while waiting on the sidelines, just before entering a game. You're shaking the stress out of them—not violently, *gently*. Coaxing them to ease off, not badgering them. You'll find that all of these sly, little exercises increase the circulation—the blood supply—and anything that improves circulation reduces stress.

Sixth, pretend that you're wearing an overcoat and you can feel it resting on your shoulders. Shoulders "hunch up" when you're cold or nervous. And when your shoulders are tight, the rest of your body feels tense. The gentle pressure of an imagined overcoat will relax your shoulders and encourage the rest of you to do the same.

Seventh, waggle your jaw back and forth three or four times. If you hear your bones grinding, you're probably tense—and the exercise will help you open your mouth. This, to a presenter, is akin to helping a professional quarterback throw the football. Nothing is worse than presenters who suffer from the "tight jaw syndrome." They appear, from time to time, on the "MacNeil/Lehrer NewsHour."

Eighth, try that trusty old standby—deep breathing. All you have to remember is this: your breath goes in, your stomach goes out. Inhale, stomach out. (You should feel it against your belt, if you've got one on.) Exhale, stomach in. Do it for *two* minutes. It *ventilates* the body. Before you try this exercise, it helps to have a well-ventilated room.

Create Your Own
Anti-Nervousness Routine

(Here's one that works. Feel free to use it
—*before every presentation.*)

1. *Take a five-minute walk.* Exercise relaxes. Gets your blood going.

2. *Check yourself out.* Everything intact? Do you look as good as you can reasonably look?

3. *Deep breathing exercises.* Do the same number every time . . . no more, no less.

4. *Ask yourself, "What's my objective today?"* Should be one simple sentence . . . always related to the audience's self-interest.

5. *Say something to somebody.* Do your vocal chords work? Great! Can you smile? Terrific! There's less and less for you to worry about.

6. *Take care of superstition.* Glance at your good luck charm. It should be something that makes you feel good—like a St. Patrick's Day card that always brings you luck.

This is vital: Always do the same routine. Exactly the same. That's the secret.

Ninth, say "Let go." It's a suggestion to yourself, not an order. Tell your brain, your muscles, your nerves, your arterial system *to ease off and let go.* "Let go" will do more to diffuse negative nervousness than any other combination of words in the English language. And nobody can make them work for you as well as you can.

Tenth, don't be self-conscious about having a warm-up routine— such as the one on the preceding page or any combination of suggestions from page 53 on. Athletes warm up. Opera singers vocalize. Dancers cavort about. Presenters, on the other hand, seem to do a lot of standing around before they perform. *Why is that?* Could it be that speakers don't think of themselves as *doing anything* (how much practice does it take to stand behind a podium?), and therefore feel a little silly doing warm-up exercises? Actually, presentation is enormously demanding on the vocal chords, the nervous system, bodily coordination, and the circulatory system. If those things aren't working, if they're not warmed up and ready to support you, you can be tense, awkward, dreadfully uncomfortable, and thick in the brain. The exercises we've described in this chapter aren't going to make people think you've lost your marbles—chances are, they won't even notice. And if they do, so what? Everybody exercises these days. It's a sign of self-pride and professionalism. Besides, I've never heard a single program chairman say, "Oh my, don't invite *that* speaker. He does funny little exercises before he begins." Have your own warm-up routine. You'll speak better, feel better, and get more applause.

Maybe the woman who lost her voice in New York City will get wind of this book and try some warm-up exercises before she blesses her next offering. If she does, I hope I'm part of her audience. Her voice will fill the chapel and all of those present, heavenly and otherwise, will be mightily pleased.

10

Sometimes,
the best offense is to
let your guard down.

See if this sounds familiar to you. . . .

You're in a conference room of one of the world's great multinational marketing companies. An executive in his early thirties has been asked to identify his most serious weakness as a presenter (he handles some very tough accounts).

"It happens, invariably, when I let my guard down. Suddenly, one of those killer questions comes zinging at me. You know the kind. They hit you on your blind side and cut you off at the knees. When I'm defenseless, I'm vulnerable. I can't afford to risk it. When I get up there in front of a client, I *have to be* on guard. It's a plain and simple case of self-defense."

Suddenly, I had this vision of hundreds of presenters, men and women, standing on stages or platforms with their guards up—fighters in boxing gloves, gunslingers with pistols cocked, gladiators with spears sharpened. They were all *covered, shielded,* protecting themselves.

From what?

From their audiences, you ninny—all those people out there with their killer questions and their bolo knives aimed at the knees (or higher).

"Presenters on Guard" I titled this strange vision before it faded into the very same people with arms folded over chests, fingers slightly clenched, jaw muscles tightening up, neck veins starting to show, bodies back-pedaling—away from the questioner, to the refuge of a table, a podium, *anything.* And, always, the eyes, narrowed—that old "fight or flee" look.

Good grief, what a ghastly portrait, what a terrible, terrifying perception we've allowed to form—maybe even *encouraged.* The audience, attacking. The presenter, tensed, ready to scramble.

From behind his trusty armaments, the presenter says, "I can take anything you can dish out."

"Well, try a little of *this,* " the audience replies, lunging forward with a deadly Kung Fu chop.

It's a Grade B movie, a zany cover for a comic book. Far worse, it's a self-destructing perception for anybody who'd like to win an audience without beating it to death.

I would submit to you that very few presentations end with the audience saying, "Well, that presenter really beat our brains out. He thrashed us good and proper."

A presentation is not a boxing match. It is not a mighty contest to be won by the person who keeps "his dukes up," his battle station barricaded.

Here's a revolutionary idea:

The presenter's best chance to win is by offering his or her knowledge, talent, ideas, wisdom *openly*—in a heart-felt desire to *help* rather than a self-protecting *fear* of being outgunned or sold down the river.

The whole thing is disarmingly simple:

- Open up rather than hunker down.
- Share what you know rather than guarding what you don't.
- Respect your resistance.

Is it too wild an idea to envision yourself standing there with no thought of covering up or ducking away?

Snapshot: Your arms hang loosely at your sides. Your veins are open. Your mind is clear. You're opened up, not clenched up. You're *flowing*, moving effortlessly *into* it, enjoying the tide, not fighting it.

Idea: Let's say you start behind a lectern or podium, acknowledge your introduction, then move out from behind the barrier and closer to your audience. You speak as you move. You have sent a signal. *You feel more comfortable, closer to them.* The relationship has started in an *open* atmosphere.

Idea: You have a script. You glance at it, then put it down and move toward your audience. You may return to your starting point—you may not—but a signal has been sent. *You have moved from a protected position into a more spontaneous one.* You have said, in effect, "Let's just discuss this thing. *Openly,* with nothing between us."

Idea (for wearers of glasses only): You've talked for a few minutes on a formal level. Now, you want to lower that level, to shift into a more personal, "off-the-cuff" manner. You simply reach up and remove your glasses. No big deal. No showy theatrics. Maybe you just hold them there, in one hand. What's happened? You've changed the mood. Such a little thing to do. But, with an almost incidental kind of gesture, you've removed a barrier, lowered your guard. And the audience senses it without being smitten by it.

"Opening up" can be helped along with a few, simple barrier-breaking ideas. But it's mainly a matter of *attitude*—how you feel about yourself and about your audience that day.

If you're confident, feeling good, it's going to be easy. You'll regard every comment, every question, every answer as a way to help your audience. *Everything* in your presentation will be designed to win *without attacking*. To win their votes by offering them the benefit of your brains, energy, or whatever you've got to give. An *unguarded* commitment.

As I say, it's a wild notion.

P.S.: Later, I watched the executive who said that "letting his guard down" was his most troubling weakness. His presentation was carefully controlled, consciously conservative, and utterly bland. He succeeded in not offending anybody. He never let his guard down. Not once. And I still wonder what he is really all about.

11

"Hands never seem to be much of a problem until . . ."

Hands often speak louder than words.

Hands resting on hips during a question/answer session can say, "I don't really like that question. In fact, it's *stupid*. But I'll answer it anyway."

One hand nervously twirling a mustache or lock of hair can say, "Give me a minute, will you? I'll have to think about that one."

Hands in pockets often suggest an admission that the speaker doesn't know what to do with them. NOTE: A celebrated Chicago attorney, C. Barry Montgomery, had thirty-five suits custom tailored with no pants pockets. He didn't want to be tempted.

Hands jangling coins in pockets suggest a kind of Captain Queeg disorder. It can be distracting to an audience, but the jangling speaker seldom hears a thing.

Hands clasped together just above the waistline suggest a rather delicate form of annoyance. Caspar Weinberger, appearing before the Oxford Union—a debating society—held his hands in this way. It didn't do much for his image as Secretary of Defense.

Speakers love to twiddle with their hands. They twiddle with electric cords winding them into coils which are then unwound.

Some things seem to need *shaking*. Chalk is one. For some reason, chalk is invariably *shaken*—like dice.

What's to be done about all this twirling, jangling, twiddling, and shaking?

First, you've got to be aware of what you're doing.

Next presentation you give, tell a friend to do nothing but watch your hands and give you a full report. Or, give the presentation in front of a videotape camera—then see your hands as others see them.

Once you know what you're doing, you'll know what to *stop* doing.

Here's a trick that works.

Stand in front of a full-length mirror with a large book in each hand. Then, *talk*. At times, you'll raise one hand or the other in a gesture even though the books are heavy. Those are the *real* gestures. *Save* them. Eliminate all others. Those are *nervous* gestures.

You'll also discover that the books will tell you *exactly* how your hands should be positioned—bent slightly at the biggest knuckle—comfortably close to your body. Not moving except when there's an important point to be made.

Then, when you get up to speak—visualize yourself in the mirror with the books. Concentrate on it. You'll find that your hands stay where they belong—and you won't twirl, twiddle, or shake again.

12

The world's smallest secret
—for presenters who like
to stay in touch.

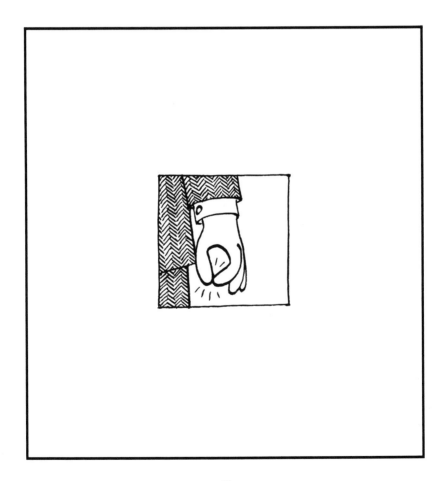

Insight: Presenters like to stay in touch with themselves. Watch them. There are those who will clasp one hand in the other and use them, both hands, like a fig leaf. They will even *walk around* with their hands in this strangely protective position.

Then, there are those who clasp their hands higher up—in a sort of angelic position. Jack Benny used to do this. It finally became one of his trademarks.

I have even seen presenters clasp their hands behind their necks— in a sort of supreme, self-conscious nonchalance.

The Pope can often be seen "looking through the chapel." To do this, you merely put your two hands together, tips of fingers touching each other, and form a "church" or "chapel." Then, you peer through.

And who could forget Johnny Carson, arms folded—hands clasping upper arms . . . in touch with himself.

Presenters seem to gain confidence, or safety, by getting into contact with themselves—generally by doing something with their hands.

The only trouble is, most of these hand mannerisms draw attention to themselves, thereby distracting from more important things such as eyes.

If you are a person who likes to keep in touch, who just feels better by having some tactile reassurance that you are alive, I have the world's smallest secret for you. It is so small, and so secret, that nobody in your audience will know you're doing it.

I don't want to make too much of this because it may sound outrageous to you. On the other hand (so to speak), it could be a lifesaver.

Here's the secret:

Let your hands hang comfortably at your sides (as you're supposed to do), and then touch thumb and forefinger on each hand. Like in the drawing on the previous page.

It has the same effect as hands touching each other (you know you're there), only you don't appear to be self-conscious or nervous. You look perfect. *Marvelous.* You're in touch with yourself—feeling the warmth of your own body heat—but you're the only body who knows it!

13

The night before:
How to get psychologically prepared.

It's the night before your presentation.

You're presenting to a group of approximately twenty-five people from your regional trade association and everything's all set.

The hotel is booked. Ballroom B, 10:00 A.M., tomorrow.

You've checked everything out (it's an old hotel, but comfortable). The audio/visual equipment works. The lighting seems okay. You've strolled around the ballroom a few times and tried the steps leading to the speaker's platform. (This is important. The steps are usually creaky, and the platform tends to sound like an old attic floor.)

You've worked hard on your presentation. You've analyzed your audience. And you're sitting there, by yourself, at just a little after 7:00 P.M.—the night before. You've got about six waking hours until your presentation. *What are you going to do?*

■ You put your nervous system on "fluid drive." From now on, you're just going to *glide.* Any crashing calamities or "crises"—unless life-risking—will be quietly put aside until after ten o'clock tomorrow. Your mind is reserved for your presentation and your private thoughts about it.

■ Have a quiet dinner, with a quiet person. Nice, but quiet. Don't talk business if you can possibly avoid it. If you're alone, *glide.*

■ If you have made a cassette tape of your presentation, play it by yourself. Just let the words and the thoughts sink in. You're not listening to be critical. You're listening to absorb, to remember.

■ If you haven't made an audiotape of your presentation, take the time to do it. Just "talk it" into the tape. It doesn't have to be perfect. But once you've got that cassette deck in your hand, you'll feel better. You'll know that the presentation *exists,* that it's *tangible,* that there's *substance* to it.

■ Let's hear it now, *and time it.* If the tape runs too long, don't say, "Well, I'll just talk faster tomorrow." It won't work. Edit one self-contained section. You can determine *exactly* how many minutes you're cutting by timing that precise section of the tape. Don't fool around with other sections of your presentation, or trim a word here and a phrase there. Keep the editing clean, simple, surgical. *One chunk.* Excise it, snip it out, and know *for sure* that you'll stop on time.

■ Practice positive self-imagery. As you hear your voice, letting the words sink into your consciousness, see yourself up on the platform in that room. The verbal and the nonverbal begin to blend together, reinforcing each other. Also, you're minimizing the possibility of surprise. You hear what you sound like. You visualize what you look like. And you're already familiar with the environment—so what's to worry about? Relax. *Glide.*

■ The night before is the time for settling into your presentation. It is not the time for massive, unsettling changes.

NOTE: Competitive presentations are infamous for dress rehearsals that are rewritten and restructured into the wee small hours of the morning. Strategies are changed. Presenters are cut. Tempers explode. Audio/visuals are scrapped, costs go crazy. In virtually all cases, the "night before" scrambles are self-defeating. If you are ever caught in one of these madcap affairs, there's a chapter in this book that might pull you out. It's Chapter 51—"The Deadly Game."

■ Go to bed at a reasonable hour—and make a few reasonable resolutions:

1. That you'll give one last listen to your cassette deck while you're getting dressed in the morning.
2. That you'll take a brisk walk before 10:00 A.M.
3. That you'll bound up those creaky steps, take command of that waiting platform, and really *help* that audience.

It's 11:00 P.M. The night before. Lights out. Sleep well. You're going to be terrific.

PART FOUR

"I'm so boring
I even bore myself!"
How to get
out of the gray.

A NUGGET FOR
YOUR NEXT PRESENTATION:
"Use your camcorder as a notebook."

In preparing a presentation, it *was* the common custom to "check out the library." Then, conduct a few interviews, notebook in hand. You ended up with a lot of words on paper. Result: a verbal presentation, frequently boring.

NUGGET: Use your camcorder as a notebook. Cover the subject with a video camera, just as a TV reporter would do. Then, show your tape in your presentation *to bring your subject to life*! It's a lot more exciting to *see* your subject in action than to listen to words, words, words. P.S.: The cameras are getting smaller and smaller (would you believe one-and-a-half pounds!).

14

What TV has taught us,
but most presenters ignore.

There's a new game in town, and—in its own electronic mode—it has changed not only the way we watch the three major TV networks, it has changed the way we watch everthing else, *including "live" presentations of all kinds.*

Zipping, Zapping, and Grazing

This new national pastime is called "zapping around." At least, that's what I call it—because none of the other electronic "buzz words" quite capture the gist of it.

Allow me just a few seconds to set this thing up:

■ *"Zipping"* is what happens when VCR users push the fast forward button and "zip" through any previously recorded material they would prefer to skip. "Zipping" gives you a squealy, squawky scramble of sound and picture.

■ *"Zapping"* is what happens when you lower the boom on a particularly odious commercial—or an overdose of "trash TV"—or whatever form of enlightenment is driving you crazy.

■ *"Grazing"* is leisurely "zapping." Since 75 percent of all TV homes now have a remote control for the TV or VCR, there's quite a lot of "grazing" going on.

The newest national pastime is none of the above. It is in fact, quite innocuous in comparison (unless you happen to be a sponsor).

"Zapping Around." A compulsion.

"Zapping around" is something quite different. It gets in your brain. It activates your nervous system. There's a *compulsion* to it that your occasional zapper or grazer simply doesn't feel and probably never will.

"Zapping around" (sometimes called "channel surfing") means flicking your way, backward or forward, through a rapid succession of images. The routine requires that you perceive instantly, evaluate quickly, and *zap* every five seconds *or less.* If you dally more than five seconds between zaps, you can consider yourself grounded. The objective: *anything* that captures your attention.

A few suggestions:

—*"Zapping around" is more stimulating when played alone.* It takes a bit of the edge off when you have to ask your companion, "Do you mind if I change the channel?"

— *"Zapping around" can provide significant stress relief.* There's something therapeutic about having the power to play Steven Spielberg on dozens of different channels.

So, if the room is reasonably dark and the rest of the family has trundled off to bed, you're in good shape to do a little experimental "zapping around."

You're into it now . . .

You're off to a fast start, moving through channels like a breeze through bedsheets, and you're about to make a discovery which may change presentations forever.

> **You tap into a spokesperson standing behind a hotel lectern. Velvet curtains provide a somber backdrop. Has somebody died? The speaker looks for a cue. The script makes little, rustling noises. What do you do?**

Silly question. *Zap!* You're "zapping around"—moving on. That pathetic speaker is history!

Ten seconds later, after a few old movies and a videotext of coming community events, you happen upon a female speaker sitting behind a table. It's a Congressional hearing of some kind. People seem to be listening (or *are* they?). The woman is reading in a flat voice because her chin is resting squarely against her chest. She looks up, adjusts her glasses, moistens her finger, and flips the page of her manuscript. You, of course, do the humane thing. You *zap* her. She wasn't suffering. *You* were.

Get the message?

What we are beginning to see here is something that every presenter should recognize:

> **The presentations we are most likely to zap—usually within the first five seconds—apply the very same presentation techniques that we use in meetings every day. If corporate managers ever saw their own meetings on TV, they would zap them into oblivion in the flick of an eyelash!**

Keep zapping around. Now, after an interlude of soccer games, get-rich schemes, another rerun of "Miami Vice," and a chorus from the Beach Boys—we are in the middle of a group of people sitting around a conference table.

They talk but they don't move. They discuss but they don't decide. They are decent, but terribly dull! There are no graphics— just words, filling the air with a kind of verbal fog.

What have we here?

We have a mixed group of experts on economic policy, but it could be any meeting of any experts in any organization. Who knows? It might even fit the profile of one of your meetings.

How would your presentation play on television?
(Would you watch it or zap it in the first five seconds?)

The biggest zapper of them all!

Zap the meeting with your remote, then take a little breather from all of your "zapping around" to ponder this point:

The human brain is the biggest zapper of them all. It can do to a "live" business presentation exactly what your remote control can do to a tedious piece of TV programming. Only the brain simply disconnects and starts to daydream.

TV has taught our brains to disengage and think about something else—sex, grocery shopping, bowling, whatever. After all, our brains have been on TV "overload" for years. The A. C. Nielsen people say that the average adult now spends twenty-four hours a week in front of the set (the average child spends thirty hours). Other researchers peg the adult viewing time at over seven hours *per day!*

Now, the flabbergaster:

Is it possible that our TV-saturated brains are zapping all or part of the thirty-three million presentations that occur in the U.S. every business day?

Because if it's true—if we're disconnecting out of meetings during the day for the same reasons that we're zapping dull programming at night—then American organizations are wasting untold *billions* of dollars.

Seventy percent of all executive time is now spent in meetings. According to the people who attend those meetings, 49 percent of that time is an utter waste. Almost half!

What happens in those meetings? For the most part, *presentations*—presentations of the type that you just clobbered as you went "zapping around."

Remember when President Reagan said that he often attended eighty meetings a day during the Iran-Contra affair—and, considering *that*, how could he really be expected to remember *anything*?

It's a fair question. Who could blame him for zapping thirty to forty of those meetings? *Anybody* would glaze over.

Is there a "quick fix" for this pernicious problem?

No. Not an *instant* remedy—but there are some hopeful signposts. And, not surprisingly, those signals are images on the face of the tube.

Watch any nightly news show on any network. Let's look in on ABC's "World News Tonight."

Short Stories

The anchor tells us that the economy has just taken another hit. The president is concerned. The unemployed are up in arms. Their benefits must be extended. But the president says no. It's a political seesaw, a national issue that reaches right into the pocketbook.

How much time does this developing story occupy on the ABC evening news? Ten minutes? Seven minutes? Five? None of the above. Exactly two minutes and five seconds.

A ferocious storm crashes into the east coast. Sixty-foot waves wash over expensive beach houses. Even the president's vacation home is gutted. The damage is immense. The storm is bigger than Hurricane Bob—and it's not over yet.

This story is covered in two minutes, twelve seconds. NBC does it even shorter.

Very seldom, according to Robert Goldberg and Gerald Jay Goldberg in their book *Anchors*, does *any* network news story exceed three minutes. The entire day, around the world, is covered in twenty-two minutes (allowing time for commercials—and they, too, are getting shorter).

Or, consider "L.A. Law" on NBC. It is really an *assortment* of stories. On a recent show, the audience was exposed to each story for no longer than three minutes at a time. Most of the segments were *two* minutes! The show moved the viewer from story to story at a remarkable rate of speed—almost like the audience was "zapping around." There's no doubt about it: "L.A. Law" has been produced to "sync up" with the ravenous attention span of its audience.

Everything moves faster. Our brains adapt faster, absorb faster, reach conclusions faster. Recently, a trade book called *Smart Moves* by Sam Deep and Lyle Sussman announced that people talk, on average, at a rate of 120 words per minute. The brain can absorb the meaning of words when spoken at 480 wpm. We've got a lot of unused capacity up there!

Add to all of this heady evidence a recent statistic from *Business Week*, and the future of presentations seems clear.

According to *Business Week*, the typical U.S. executive has an on-the-job attention span of six minutes.

Every six minutes, something happens to disrupt his/her attention. An important client is on the phone. The stock market is acting strange, and decisions must be made—*instantly*. A dangerous competitor is doing mean and nasty things. A son is calling desperately from college. Somebody just floated a take-over rumor. And so it goes. Every six minutes a bell goes off in the executive brain.

Peter Jennings	Tom Brokaw	Dan Rather
Anchor,	Anchor,	Anchor,
"World News Tonight"	"NBC Nightly News"	"CBS Evening News"

NOTE: Guess how much time the three network anchors—Jennings, Brokaw, and Rather—spent on camera during their nightly newscasts. *Five-and-a-half to six minutes each!*

A presentation that is planned with that specific knowledge is bound to be more successful than one that tries to confine the brain for long periods of time. TV has taught us that, over and over. When left to our own devices, we prefer shorter "takes," shorter scenes.

Actually, it's not difficult to build "live" presentations in shorter, more compact segments. Segments that are "in sync" with the quicker, visually stimulated way our brains work these days.

A few tips may be in order:

1. *Think of your presentation in scenes.* Each scene has one important point to make. So, to start, simply list the points you want your audience to remember. Now, build your scenes—of about six minutes or less per scene—around the points on your list. Remember you've got plenty of time—much longer than any of the three TV networks give to 90 percent of the stories they cover.

2. *Plant a "flag" in every scene.* A "flag" nails down exactly what you want your audience to take away. It is *deliberately* interruptive. Here are a few examples:

- "*Let me make a point here* . . . here's what this means in terms of cutting *your* operating costs this year."
- "*Let me nail this point down for you* . . . we must increase our store traffic by at least 15 percent."

"Flags" wake people up. They jolt the pacing of drifty meetings.

They summarize and shorten. They make people reach for their pencils. (See Chapter 48 for more on this technique.)

3. *Use different audio/visual techniques to segment your presentation.* Use computer-generated slides for six minutes. Make your point, plant a "flag" or two, then turn up the lights and move to your electronic blackboard—and your next scene. Let the media help you segment the subject by changing the environment. TV transports people from city to city, nation to nation. The *least* a presenter can do is bring new audio/visual into play, and give us the *impression* that we're not locked into one spot.

4. *If you have a presentation team, change presenters every six minutes.* There's very little that can't be explained in six minutes or less. According to Tom Theobold, chairman and CEO of Continental Illinois Corporation, "Most meetings really *start* about halfway through." That's where the meeting moves from the people doing the presenting toward the people in the audience. Drop this little bombshell into your next presentation rehearsal: "What do you suppose would happen if we start this thing about halfway through?" One result: the meeting would end on time.

5. *The whole room is your theater!* Choreograph your presentation. Let your first presenter make his or her opening remarks from the front of the room, then let another speaker take over at a presentation board at the side of the room. Then, roll your film or your videotape and have a member of your team talking to the audience from the videotape! Then, go into your audience for questions. Watch Arsenio Hall some night.

6. *Give each six-minute segment its own headline*—ten words or less. Set it in type and blow it up big. Post it where everybody can see it. Example: "Our Strategy for Marketing in Germany." State your case, then post another board with another subject. Put the second board on a ledge or easel next to the first. Headlines provide breaks (just as they do in newspapers) and help the audience keep everything straight. They also provide an index of where you've been.

7. *Colors can help you (and your audience) identify your segments.* If the strategy segment is presented on blue boards, let the sales promotion be on orange boards. Let the pay-out be on green. Color-code your scenes. Then, when all of the boards are displayed around the room, the brain will recall your segments in seconds, nonverbally. NOTE: Recently, a Mafia Commission trial in New York City used colored velcro strips to identify crime families, how they were organized, who was dead, who was alive, and who was in prison. It was all done by colors—posted on the walls of the courtroom. And it was mesmerizing.

"Let's nail this down."

In the 1990s, when change is so easy—as easy as tapping a remote access button—the worst thing that can happen to *any* speaker is for the audience to think, "This is *dull*. Nothing's happening. I'm movin' on."

That speaker is history!

That presentation is going to get zapped—electronically or mentally (it's all the same). Our brains are always "zapping around."

Presentations don't have to be meat for the mental zapper. They don't have to last as long as a sleepless night. They don't have to be all of the things that made David Greising, business columnist of the *Chicago Sun-Times*, tell me, "I'm just not very interested in presentations. They are so bloody dull."

Here's the "flag": *The point is so simple, so clear—mark it down somewhere. It's time for our presentations to catch up with our brains.*

15

"Podiums are poison.
Lecterns are lethal."

Lecterns have one reason for being: They hold up the speaker's script. Sometimes they also hold up the speaker.

Lecterns have all kinds of bad side effects. They put a barrier between you and your audience when you should be doing everything in your power to clear all obstacles away.

Sometimes, lecterns have "ads" on them. These "ads" may provide the name of the hotel where the meeting is being held (just in case the audience has lost all sense of time and place). Sometimes, lecterns have the name of the sponsoring organization on them. Whatever message the lectern is trying to convey, it is probably not the same as yours. Also, many lecterns come right up to the speaker's Adam's apple. With your head bobbing about on the name of the hotel or sponsoring organization, the effect can be very distracting— if not very disturbing.

Lecterns have another bad habit. They often have tiny tubular lights tucked away under their brows. If you have many hollows in your face, the upward bounce of light can make you look like Frankenstein, Dracula—or worse. Once, when I was presenting behind a rather tall lectern at Ogilvy & Mather, Inc.—a distinguished advertising agency headquartered in New York City—David Ogilvy, the founder, interrupted me from the back of the room. "Ron," he said, "behind that lectern, you look for all the world like a defrocked Baptist minister."

Of course you can turn off the lectern light. That produces another bad side effect. *You disappear.* Like a vampire at dawn. Also, if you're counting on the lectern to cast a little light on your script, you probably won't be able to read it in the dark.

That may be a blessing, but not unless your mind is prepared to perform *spontaneously.* If you aren't ready to forge ahead completely on your own, the first signs of panic may begin to creep in. You've seen it happen. The speaker grabs hold of both sides of the lectern, knuckles white, as if it were a lifeboat, slowly taking water.

The best presenters may stand behind the lectern or podium for a few seconds, then—as if freed from it by some cosmic force—move out into a pool of light, probably closer to the audience. This well-thought-out piece of business has some salubrious effects. It says you are more confident of your material than previous speakers who have remained rooted behind the podium. It also suggests a desire to cast aside all foolishness and get down to the nub of it.

Eye contact is much easier to maintain when you aren't locked in place by a dimly lit manuscript, and the whole presentation takes on a different attitude. It becomes more conversational, more personal, less stuffy. Three-by-five-inch cards can be pulled out if you need a few key words to keep you on track. Almost anything is better than standing behind an ad for the local hotel *and reading!*

Now, if you're thinking, "Billy Graham uses a podium," I would only add what Herman Kahn, the brilliant futurist, used to say: "Yes, that's so. But he's got the Bible. Nobody argues with a man carrying the Bible."

Sometimes, a podium is an ad. Sometimes it is placed where it gives the audience ideas—not necessarily good for you.

16

"There's nothing more boring than something that never moves."

I am sitting on the soft grass of Lincoln Park in Chicago watching Alexander Hamilton.

He is standing maybe 200 yards from me, looking north toward Diversey—a singularly uninspiring convergence of roads, bewildering traffic signals, and impatient cars.

Mr. Hamilton is done up rather smartly. He appears to be slathered with gold leaf, and he shimmers in the afternoon sun.

He's impressive all right, but he doesn't move. He's as stationary as most of the cars that queue up on Diversey.

Even though he's dazzling in gold leaf, it must be said that Alexander Hamilton gets pretty dull after you've watched him for a minute or two.

Ever noticed what happens when you're watching something that *never* moves? Your eyes glaze. Ever watched somebody on television who just sits there, or stands there, talking endlessly? Your mind drifts off.

What if Alexander Hamilton, all golden and glittery in the afternoon sun, suddenly turned and motioned for me to take a walk with him through Lincoln Park?

First, I'd suspect I had become an unwitting participant in a TV commercial (probably for a bank). But I wouldn't waste much time thinking about it. I'd want to hear what he had to say. What does he think about Chicago? Any ideas on the traffic flow? And how did he get into that mess with Aaron Burr? Once he moved, *he'd have my undivided attention* (he'd also have a ten-dollar bill from my wallet—and my best ballpoint for his autograph).

But Hamilton, alas, doesn't move. Neither do most presenters—but they don't have as good an excuse as he does.

They stand up in their finery and remain as stationary as statues. They speak, but they don't move.

When a speaker doesn't move, that's really making it difficult for any well-meaning audience to pay wholehearted attention. Static speakers produce listless audiences.

Sitting still, immaculately robed and soberly groomed, may work for Judge Joseph A. Wapner on TV's immensely popular "The People's Court," but I've noticed that even the judge gets up and rushes out "to chambers" from time to time.

The case for *moving* during your presentation can be stated in the most elementary terms.

■ *It proves you're alive.* You are not plugged into the floor. You're not a computer. You are still with us. You, in fact, have an admirable supply of energy. *You're moving.*

■ *It forces your audience to keep their eyes open.* When you move, your audience is obligated to follow the action. Since physiologists tell us that 80 percent of all human motivation is optically stimulated, you'd be silly not to give our eyes a little workout.

■ *When you move, you're reducing your own stress.* Your vital juices are flowing. Psychiatrists tell us that exercise is the best way to control stress. So, you're helping yourself.

■ Also, when you're physically moving from one point to another, you have a legitimate excuse to pause and collect your thoughts. A moment or two not only helps you to get back on track, it gives your audience a momentary "recess." A little silence can be a wonderful thing.

With many of the wireless electronic controls now available, you can forsake the podium and circulate among your audience—lavishing as much attention on the back of the room as you give to the people up front.

This not only keeps everybody involved, it gives you an opportunity to generate a bit of "dynamic tension" throughout the room.

When an authoritative presenter moves into "pockets" of people, tension is created and audiences are likely to stay alert. ("Oh, oh. Is she coming over here? I'd better get with it.")

Staying in touch with an audience, moving among them, interacting, gives everybody a feeling of participation. It keeps the attention level up. *It keeps things moving.*

Those are benefits that don't come easily if you're rooted in one spot, behind a lectern, speaking to people who may be daydreaming in the noonday sun.

You've got a terrific advantage over presenters who are sculpted, taped, filmed, or otherwise reproduced. *You're alive.* So, maybe you think of yourself a little differently. Maybe you see yourself, not as Alexander Hamilton, but as the best traffic cop in your city.

Here's a picture for your self-imagery file:

You, as a presenter, aren't just a stately spokesperson up there, you're a leader—helping people, showing them what to do, where to go, how to get there.

As a presenter, your body begins to move like a traffic cop—pointing to a graph on a videotape slide, showing the intricate workings of a new product, working out an equation on a greenboard, marking up a production schedule, recommending when to "stop" and when to "start."

Presenters who see themselves as traffic cops find themselves moving actively through statements like these:

- "This is the cut-off point. Right here."
- "Look how these two plans compare. Follow me on this, point by point."
- "There are five steps in this resolution. I'm going to show you each one separately."
- "Think of this as a road map, and we've got six months to make the trip."

These comments bring your entire body into play. You use your A/V equipment, you use your audience, and you use your "open aisles" and "walking space" as elements which can motivate and facilitate motion. And you do it without cords and cable that can trip you up, or fluttering scripts that can get in your way.

17

How do you create excitement if you're not Madonna, Prince, or Zig Ziglar?

*E*xciting is one of the most popular words in the English language. It has long since gone beyond being a "buzzword" and is now
close to being one of those words which means almost anything.
 If you're in the communications business (which is where I
come from), "exciting" is a word that attends every meeting:

> "Hey, this is the most *exciting* concept I've seen
> in ages."

> "Is this *exciting*—or what?"

> "I just love what you've done with this . . .
> really, really, *exciting.*"

Having heard this word used to describe everything from rap
music to floor polish, you begin to get a pretty fair notion of what it
really means. Here's what I suspect it means:

> *"This is pretty good."*

So, as we apply "exciting" to presentations and presenters, we
need to proceed cautiously.
 One thing we *cannot* do is get "exciting" mixed up with "intense." "Exciting" is *ex*ternal, as the word suggests. Celebratory.
Outgoing. "Intense" is *in*ternal, highly charged—like energy being
poured into a funnel.
 Both words, as described here, are desirable in the vast majority
of presentations. However, if given their druthers, most presenters
would take a truly *exciting* presentation over an *intense* one any day.
 An exciting presentation is more commercial. It will sell better
at the box office. The Nielsen ratings will jump faster, higher. And
the sales force will certainly like it better.
 "Exciting presentations" have been so thoroughly studied, analyzed, and applauded that I didn't think there were any questions
left:
 Wrong. There's *one*. And I wasn't ready for it.
 "How do you get excited?"
 The questioner was dead serious.
 "I know presentations are supposed to be exciting and all that,"
he said, "but what if I just don't happen to *feel excited* that day? What
if the subject I'm presenting doesn't really excite me?"
 My questioner was the CEO of an automotive marketing agency

in Irvine, California. It was a CEO-type of question. Out of the blue, yet so simple. The *obvious* question.

I gave him my tried-and-true response to all CEO questions.

"That's a terrific question. Let me think about it for a few minutes."

CEOs will usually go along with this overt play for time, but they never forget the question.

A couple of things struck me—both pretty obvious, but worth noting:

■ Unless you are Madonna or Prince or some other high-voltage performer, the audience is not going to get excited in anticipation of your presentation. That may not be fair. But that's just the way it is. Until you get up to speak, they're going to sit on their hands and wait for lightning to strike. Steve Martin doesn't have this problem. *You do.* That's the bad news.

■ Even the best presenters in the world aren't exciting *all the time.* That's why we've got "sound bites" and "sight bites" and all the rest. Even if you could sustain a constant level of tingling excitement, your audience would grow faint of heart and swoon (which hasn't happened since Frank Sinatra played the Paramount). So, you don't have to be exciting *all the time.* That's the good news.

But—even if you're going to be exciting only *part* of the time—it's hopelessly hard to do if you're going to "get up there" and read somebody else's script. You're going to be as exciting as water dripping.

Same thing applies to the presentation of someone else's idea. In coaching advertising and marketing professionals over the years, I've heard this lament many times:

"It's practically impossible to get excited when you're presenting someone else's brainstorm. You just don't feel the same when it's not your work."

Okay. That sets us up for our first "generator" for making excitement (even if you don't feel particularly excited).

Generator #1. You must be more than the messenger. Unless the message contains "a piece of you," it's very hard to generate an exciting presentation. You must *discover something* that can improve, enlarge, or enlighten the core idea. It doesn't have to be a mesmerizing discovery. It can be a minor discovery, but it's enough to give you a fully justified feeling that you are *a part of* what's being presented. Maybe you've created some dazzling graphics on your desktop computer.

Maybe you've given the presentation a *title* that captures the concept *brilliantly.* Maybe you've discovered a different way of expressing the basic proposition. Just a few words perhaps, but a significant contribution nonetheless. With "a piece of you" in the presentation, you'll be amazed at what happens to your excitement level. It will take off like a Harrier jet—straight up.

Generator #2. *You should have a stake in the outcome.* Of course, you already have a stake in it: your reputation. You want the audience to think well of you. That's a given. But if you can envision the possibility of a *special* reward at the end of your presentation, your juices are bound to flow more actively. Maybe it's a chunk of new business after a long dry spell. Maybe it's a nice commission. Maybe you'll be bumped up to a new place in the pecking order. Maybe, it's the feeling that you are involved in an issue that could be crucial to your city—or your country. The bigger the stake, the more likely that your excitement will percolate—and it will happen naturally, without a lot of internalized cheerleading by you.

Generator #3. *You must believe it, all of it, without reservation.* It must come right out of your own experience. Some of the most exciting speakers in America speak directly from the gut—or so it seems.

A case in point: Zig Ziglar. Zig, as he is called, is a superanimated author, sales consultant, and motivational speaker. Before Zig bounds into view, audiences are warned they're going to be *"Ziglarized"*—which, loosely translated, means they are going to be on the receiving end of so much raw energy and excitement that the walls may crumble. "I was born in L.A.," he proclaims in his booming baritone. "That's lower Alabama." And so it goes. He is *so* excited that nothing he does seems like too much. His excitement is Vesuvian.

Sales people *love* Zig. "You were born to win," he cries. Audiences soak it up. But what they're *really* soaking up is the unbridled conviction that Ziglar presents to them. "I was stone broke and in debt at the age of forty-five." Now Zig sells cassette albums, books, "combo packages," and seminar sessions in packed ballrooms. For forty-five bucks, Zig will light your fire for a couple of hours. His message is simple: "Never give up."

To a salesperson whose life is full of rejection, Zig is the messiah of resilience. His history proves it. But his delivery, incandescently convincing, makes it exciting.

Generator #4. *You must be willing to shoot the moon.* That means to risk losing control—ever so slightly—in the desire to generate a storm of excitement. Not many business presenters are willing to "go over the top." That's for rock stars and evangelists. Well, maybe. But you don't see many corporate speakers who make us yearn for *less* excitement. Most are about as exciting as an empty mailbox. See "Be a bit of Springsteen" on page 286.

Generator #5. *You must have no questions, no qualms about your total command of the knowledge required.* If there are any gaps in your knowledge, your excitement will fall right through—leaving you, as they say, with egg on your face. It's hard to be exciting with egg on your face.

Generator #6. *You must connect your knowledge to their needs.* That's when the excitement meter begins to dance up the scale. The audience realizes that what you have been saying will work *for them.* Now, *that's* exciting. *That's* explosive. The second any audience reaches that realization, *you* become pretty darn exciting yourself. At that point, you can hold them for hours. John Bradshaw, the bearded author, lecturer, and social scientist, is as expert at making that connection as any presenter you're likely to see. He talks on and on (usually about "dysfunctional families") and the audiences can't seem to get enough. I was in one of his audiences at the University of Illinois, and the excitement never wavered. Bradshaw makes *connections.* And connections make presenters exciting.

John Bradshaw keeps making connections with the childhood memories of his audience. You can actually feel the connections, like little mental jolts. This sustains the excitement level—of his delivery, and his audience's response.

Generator #7. *It doesn't hurt to have some friends in the audience—excitable friends.* As all presenters have learned, it's very hard to warm up a *cold* house. If *you*, the presenter, are running a little low on excitement—that cold house is going *remain* frozen in time, like a fish in a meat locker. A few friends, already sharing your feelings, will tend to thaw a chilled audience. More importantly, they'll warm you up, too!

Generator #8. *Leave a little something behind—the more exciting, the better.* It should be something that most people would be reluctant to throw away. And it should relate, somehow or other, to your message. Sales promotion catalogs are loaded with nifty little leave-behinds, from biofeedback cards that tell you—in glowing color—how *stressed* you are, to jelly beans (with your name imprinted on every bean), to the pictured "foot in your door" which has real, live shoestrings and the rich, resonant sound of china.

COURTESY: ADMARC ADVERTISING/DALLAS

Coming down to earth

Because "exciting" is so frivolously used, let me add one additional point to bring it gently down to earth.

It's not a generator of excitement. It's more like a requirement of candor. *Absolute* candor.

You've got to be in the right place at the right time.

If you're the last speaker of the day, and everybody has been sitting in the meeting room for eight hours—and there's cigar smoke hanging in layers somewhere near the ceiling—and eyes have glazed over long ago—it's going to be hard for you to generate a strong current of excitement.

Recently, I gave a presentation to a sizable group of marketing people in a musty old church in Portland, Oregon. It reeked of sermons somberly spoken.

So, I got up on the platform with my audio/visual fireworks and my devilish techniques for enticing new business. I tried to be exciting. Three hundred and fifty people looked up at me like I was an alien from some distant planet. I spoke for three hours. Finally, darkness settled over me like a cloud.

Later, my sponsor said he detected an atmosphere of "dissonance" during my presentation. I thanked him for such a charitable description.

I was in the wrong place at the wrong time.

Don't plan on a lot of excitement if you're presenting in a place where the air is heavy with "dissonance."

Excitement doesn't explode in every presentation. Sometimes, it can't. Wrong place. Wrong time.

But those times are rare. Most of the time the eight "generators" in this chapter will work. Try them. If you come across as "too exciting"—you can always cut back to seven.

18

They call it "chemistry."

Chemistry is one of those words that always makes me a little suspicious.

Let me give you a quote from a recent issue of ADWEEK, a trade publication in the communications field:

> "It's appropriate that the current review for the $40-million account is boiling down to chemistry. Either agency could handle the business. It's simply a question of the right chemistry."

What does that mean exactly? "Chemistry" has always struck me as a courteous cover-up, an excuse for something, maybe something too ghastly to say in plain language.

Oh, I've heard the delicate definitions: "It's the emotional climate that forms between the presenter and the audience, the degree of rapport."

Well, that's fine. But I remained leery of that word—suspicious that it was some misty euphemism—until I went to Cincinnati and met a man sitting in a hotel ballroom about ten rows back.

He'd been sitting there all day, listening quietly to the workshop I was conducting, and I suddenly realized he had been there for almost five hours without participating—*without, in fact, saying a word.*

So, I invited him to make a presentation to the rest of us—about thirty-five business professionals—confident that we could give him some "compassionate criticism."

"Just speak to us about anything that's important to you, see if you can make it important to us, and give us the first step to take so that we may share your enthusiasm," I told him.

He moved agreeably to the front of the room, settled himself in the center of the platform, and began.

I shall never forget it.

Though the rest of his body hardly moved, his head was like a radar sweep in a dangerous battle zone. It turned as methodically as a rotating summer fan, never stopping, moving in a perfect 180-degree sweep from side to side. His eyes were locked into a level just above the heads of his audience.

His voice carried over us like an announcement in the Atlanta airport transit system. (It had a nice, businesslike quality to it, but you suspect that it might be a computer.)

This fellow wasn't difficult to look at—or listen to. He was quite presentable. He seemed to be about forty, a little on the portly side, slightly balding, dressed conservatively in a dark gray suit and white shirt with a striped tie.

He was talking about the brain, and the voice seemed strangely detached from this small audience in Cincinnati. It's not right brain and left brain, he said, there are no hemispheres. "The brain is a patchwork quilt," he said, "with little patches for sex, memory, conscience, and all of life's major emotions."

The content of his presentation seemed fairly interesting (though it could have been coming from another planet). His head never stopped rotating—his voice never wavered—and his eyes stared steadfastly forward, moving quietly above the crowd. He seemed "programmed," a distant cousin of Max Headroom.

He summed up his presentation ("I don't agree with anything I have heard in this room about the brain") and returned to his seat. There was a courteous riffling of applause.

After allowing a moment or two for the presenter to get himself assembled, I asked the audience for comments.

Silence. No one uttered a sound.

I made a second call for comments—reminding the group that all remarks would be gratefully accepted *as compassionate criticism.*

Still, nothing. The room began to rustle uncomfortably.

Then, from somewhere midway back in the room, there came this voice—male, nervous, tentative—but clear, cutting right through the silence.

"I'm just not sure I'd want to see him again tomorrow."

That was all. Nobody laughed. Nobody gasped. Nobody did anything. But, suddenly, I knew what "chemistry" meant.

Chemistry means, "Do you really want to see that person again tomorrow?"

The second I heard that young man's brave contribution of compassionate criticism, I remembered a phone ringing on my desk several years ago, and a voice on the other end saying, "You know that third presenter in your presentation this morning?" "Yes, sure," I said, recognizing the voice of a new business prospect. "Well," said the voice, "we'd just rather not see that person again." And *that* sounded a lot like "chemistry" to me.

After all of this "lab work" in the mystical realm of "chemistry"—I felt that we owed our speaker, the man who told us about the brain, some honest comments. Here they are, as noted that day:

■ Seek out individuals in your audience to engage with your eyes. Collect friends as you move from person to person. Once you make contact and detect signs of agreement, *smile* and move on.

■ Head movement should be dictated by the individuals in your audience. You move in response to them, *on a personal basis*, not a mechanical rotating system. The presenter is *attracted* into the audience, not overseeing them.

■ There are some presenters who, without ever knowing it, prompt their audiences to think, *"Oh, come off of it."* This usually means the presenter is talking way above the audience—on a kind of elevated intellectual plain. An idea: when you're presenting, look at one person in your audience and say to yourself, "What's *really* going on in her mind?" If you detect distance, or resistance, she is probably thinking, "Oh, come off of it." Ease off. Soften your language. Try not to be so dogmatic. Ask your audience a question. Show that you're sensitive to *their* reaction. You *respect* them.

■ *Let your body demonstrate your enthusiasm for your subject and your interest in your audience.* Move. Draw us a picture of *our* brains if you're talking about brains. What are *our* brains doing as they listen to you? Show us how your "patchwork" theory works. Bring your subject closer to us. Give us a memory test or some other exercise we can do to prove your point. We don't really know what to do about your views—provocative though they may be.

■ *Give another presentation as soon as possible*—within a week. Get used to engaging audiences and drawing them into your subjects. Try offering your knowledge as an inspirational, participatory, exciting presentation rather than an intellectual disagreement.

It's entirely possible that "chemistry" is the most sensitive— and least talked about—subject in presentation. It may also be one of the most important.

What is this thing called "presence" (and how can you get some)?

■ Presenters with "presence" usually walk briskly, with a sense of purpose. They carry themselves well. Their attitude is outward, aware of their surroundings—not inward. When they speak, they are concerned about *you*, not themselves.

■ Nothing is tentative. They don't fuss with things. They don't hem and haw. They demonstrate the importance of their mission by being decisive and well-prepared.

■ They have a bit of manufactured magic about them. Barbara Bush has been dubbed "The Silver Fox" and, all of a sudden, she has "presence." Speakers with "presence" have their own personal magnetism—but the magic may have been spun to a high gloss by the media.

■ They move *into* an audience. Can you imagine Arsenio Hall starting his show in any other way than striding into the camera?

■ They project an attitude of *positiveness* about their own abilities that may border on arrogance, but the audience never worries about them. "Presence" guarantees that *the speaker can handle anything.*

■ They *look* good. They've gotten "a little dressed up"—reflecting their own sense of self-worth, but also complimenting the audience (see Chapter 33).

■ "Presence" is something that the audience *feels* about the presenter, often before the presenter even appears. In a sense, the audience creates an aura of expectation that the presenter simply fills.

19

"Great props don't have to be proper."

It was 10:30 on a slate-gray winter morning in Oshkosh, Wisconsin.

At the Oshkosh Hilton, an unusual presentation was taking place.

Janet Rothe, slightly nervous but definitely excited, was telling her colleagues about the benefits of using *dogs* in advertising.

This was not a pandering presentation to dog lovers. What's more, she had done her homework. This was serious business, and Janet wasn't joking.

She reeled off the names of major advertisers who have used dogs in national campaigns: RCA, Hewlett-Packard, J. C. Penney, Citicorp, the *Wall Street Journal*, and an almost endless number of beer companies.

Delving deeper into her research, she announced that more dogs are told "I love you" during their lives, on average, than human beings are told the same three words throughout their lifetimes.

The implication was clear: *dogs are more lovable than people.*

Now, hold on! Let's not get carried away here. Next thing you know, dogs will be cuddlier than babies. Janet Rothe sensed it was time for the demo. She walked over to the conference room door and turned the latch.

In the fluttering flip-flop of a tail wag, two dogs came bounding in. One was an elegant dalmation and the other was a somber but well-fed basset hound. Both were enchanted with the opportunity to attend a real, live business meeting. The dalmation worked one side of the room; the basset hound handled the other.

They nuzzled old friends, introduced themselves to strangers— never stopped moving. A couple of troupers.

Dogs often make joyous little yipping noises when pleased by the turn of events—and, in this case, members of the audience communicated in kind. It was strange. People and dogs exchanging totally incomprehensible noises.

It was at that moment—of delirious, incomprehensible joy— that I realized how perfectly dogs have mastered the techniques of presentation (see panel). They are absolute masters. And they make it look so easy.

A moment or two later, Janet Rothe asked the dogs to leave, and they did (the dogs, as you have guessed, belonged to Janet). She knew better than to compete for attention with a dalmation *or* a basset hound.

But Janet had made her point: dogs bring an aura of genuine joy to almost any situation, be it a TV commercial or a marketing meeting. As psychologists have long claimed, dogs have a therapeutic effect upon people.

Beyond this undeniable truth, Janet's presentation set forth a fool-proof principle you should use in your next presentation:

Never fail to work with "the product"—be it yours or theirs—when you make a presentation. The best idea: bring it to life—literally.

A presenter becomes more interesting when using a prop. The prop may be *your* product. Example: the dogs of Oshkosh, property of Janet Rothe. Or, the prop may be a product that means

The Dogs of Oshkosh—how could you miss with a couple of "props" like these? "Hopi" (left) and "Leo" (in the straw hat) are lively lessons in the art of presentation.

a great deal to the audience—it may, in fact, *be theirs*. Let's watch another presentation where the products work as props—but in a totally different way than the dogs of Oshkosh.

Products as props, in Chicago.

He had red hair. There was no question about it. He looked like an athlete, ruddy and robust. He might have been twenty-one, with all of the energy that a young red-headed man has at the age of twenty-one. His energy level edged him up close to nervousness, but he spoke out loud and clear:

"I'm from the *Chicago Sun-Times*. And I want you to be the marketing department of the *Chicago Tribune*. I'm here to sell you some space."

It took a moment for the audacity of this announcement to sink in. Was he serious? Yes, he seemed to be. He looked like he meant business.

The audience was there to judge his presentation. Twelve media marketing professionals. They were leaning forward now, intrigued.

NOTE: In case you haven't touched down in Chicago recently, the *Sun-Times* and the *Tribune* are the archest of rivals. They fight and scratch for every inch of advertising that comes along.

And this brash young man, named Todd Probasco, was going to sell an ad in the *Sun-Times* to the marketing manager of the *Tribune*. It was a mind-boggler.

The presentation began.

"All my life I've been a baseball player," the young man said.

"I must have played on every sandlot in Chicago. Every position, too. I even thought I'd play pro ball one day.

"Then," he said, "I realized I was twenty and it was time to get a job. I came to the *Sun-Times*. I left the sandlots and got a ticket in the bleachers. I became a lifelong Cubs fan."

Leaving his audience to appreciate the fact that the Cubs are owned by the *Tribune*, the young man took off his suit coat and pulled a Cubs jersey over his shirt and tie.

He then covered his red hair with a Cubs cap. He tugged it down, just like the players do, giving the bill a jaunty twist.

The audience realized what had happened. The presenter had become the prototypical, absolutely *perfect* Cubs fan. He had become the *market*. Even the marketing manager at the *Tribune* would have to give him points for that one.

"Now, I'd like to show you my product," he said.

He reached over to a nearby table and picked up a special edition of the *Sun-Times*. "This is called the *Final Markets Plus*," Todd said. "It comes out every day, after five, to catch the scores of the afternoon ball games and the closing prices of the stock exchanges.

"It's tailor-made for us upwardly mobile Cubs fans."

Now, he was leafing us through the first few pages of the paper. Sure enough. It was just as he described. Baseball scores. Finals. Market prices. Finals. Irresistible. So were the cap and jersey.

He filled in the media numbers as he took off his cap. He eased out of his jersey. More numbers. After all, this was a *business* call.

He placed the special edition of the paper back on the table, next to the cap.

"I'm going out to the game tomorrow," he said. "I've got a season ticket in the bleachers. But if you want to call me . . ." He handed everybody a card. "I get all messages right away."

"Thank you," he said, "for the Cubs, and for listening to me. The Cubs have given me a lot of good things. I just figured that this was something good I could do for you."

He sat down. Only the products remained. The baseball cap and the newspaper. They looked pretty good together. And the audience roared its approval. The young man with the red hair beamed. It's hard to resist a Cubs fan.

"Picking up a few tricks from the dogs of Oshkosh"

Maybe your next presentation *should* go to the dogs. When two dogs made their entrance at a business meeting I was attending recently, I jotted down a few things about their presentation technique:

1. Dogs always seem so glad to see you. (I've excused pit bulls from this analysis.)
2. There is no artifice or pretense about their greeting. They just come right up to you and make friends. They communicate friendly little noises—but never give you a long line of guff.
3. They show the same affectionate attention to everybody. They're demonstrative without being pushy.
4. Their message is simple: *We like you. We like being here. We'll help you in any way we can.*
5. They have no hidden agendas.
6. Their body language is telegraphic.
7. They don't do most of the things that dull presenters do: they don't carry scripts, don't monotone endlessly about themselves, don't lean on podiums, don't tell bad jokes or endless stories (not even endless shaggy dog stories).
8. Dogs have a great sense of knowing when they're no longer the center of attraction. They just go over and lie down. They don't go overtime.
9. They know who they are. Most of them have endearing personalities.
10. They're good friends. They don't come in, put on a show, and hurry out to a waiting limo or taxicab. They'll stay with you as long as you need them.

Dogs may know more about presentations than all of the speech coaches in the world. Next time you see a dog—in a business meeting or anywhere—go over and present yourself. Dogs are great listeners.

20

Participation: powerful, but explosive.

Participate. Make a mark. An X. A ✓. Anything will do *as long as you participate.*

It's easy. Consider these three scenarios and indicate (got your pencil?) which *one* would be most likely to remain in your memory.

The scene is common to all three storylines: *You are in the back seat of a cab riding down a state highway toward Tulsa, Oklahoma.*

■ *Scenario No. 1.* Your cab driver is an amiable sort, chattering away about tornadoes, telling tornado tales that date all the way back to stagecoach days. He's quite a talker. But eventually you arrive at your hotel, pay the driver, and he leaves.

■ *Scenario No. 2.* Same cab. Same driver. Same road. The cabbie is chattering away, only this time he hands you a magazine which shows a tornado spinning across the Oklahoma plains. You study it dutifully and hand it back. The ride proceeds, driver still gabbing until you climb out of the cab at the hotel.

■ *Scenario No. 3.* Your cab driver is chattering away when suddenly a funnel-shaped tornado appears dead ahead. Your cab driver screams, "Hit the floor!" and dives behind the dashboard. You and your cab are lifted off the road and hurled through the air. You land (still inside your cab) fifty feet away. There is a crunching noise, like that of a compactor in a junkyard. The cab driver isn't chattering, but he's alive. He reaches into the back seat and pulls a suitcase off your head. "Damn twisters," he says.

Wasn't too tough, was it?

For most people, *Scenario No. 1* would be quickly forgotten. Reason: the exchange was verbal, passive (and most cab drivers are crummy presenters).

Scenario No. 2 brings a new element to our story—a dramatic picture. The passenger looked at it, albeit briefly, and passed it back to the cabbie. A visual now reinforces the words. By adding a visual (a photo, a drawing, a graph, an exhibit of some kind), you more than double your chances of recall.

Scenario No. 3 is going to be remembered by driver and passenger almost *exactly* as it happened—and, chances are, they will never forget it. *People remember what they participate in.*

It's one thing to be *told*, informed. You're passive. You can take it or leave it. Words are easy to turn off. We retain less than 10 percent of the information we receive (a recent article in *Newsweek* estimates that it's *even less*—1 percent).

It's another thing to be *shown* what you've been told. You're still passive. But the more retentive nonverbal side of your brain has now been engaged. Your chances of remembering what you've been *told and shown* have now approached one out of four. *Much* better—you now have a picture to help you remember the words.

Live presentations have the capacity to confront you with words, pictures, *and active participation.* The possibility of participation *jolts* an audience into attentiveness.

In terms of recording an event or experience in the mind, nothing comes close to active participation. It triggers the senses. It creates a dynamic tension that flashes an immediate signal to everybody in the room—*"You are expected to be ready. You will be asked to contribute. You are going to be acted upon."*

Blood pressures inflate. Pulse rates accelerate. Often, participation brings with it a kind of reverberating *shock* value. Get ready for a tremor:

—A vice president is telling a meeting of managers that precious time and money are being wasted because of the outdated elevator service in a hotel where the company's trainees are being housed. He has calculated the average "wait time" per floor. He has also figured the "trip time" from each floor to the lobby. He has really done his homework, this fellow (his name is David Liemer, an associate creative director in New York). The audience is sitting there, calmly.

He asks them to stand up. He's serious. "Yes, please stand up— I want to show you something." His audience stands. The presenter tells the group that they will now wait for the elevator to arrive at the fifteenth floor. The audience *stands* there, obediently, as the presenter continues. But the atmosphere has changed: The problem has become *real.* The audience is beginning to *feel* it.

More statistics from David Liemer—translating "wait time" into costs. When the "wait time" is finally over (and the elevator has theoretically arrived), the presenter announces the beginning of "trip time." Now, a touch of participatory theater. David has made an audio tape of the actual "elevator music"—that is, the music "piped in" to lessen stress and strain. He plays the tape. It is *awful.* It is scratchy, tinny, awful. Worse, it repeats endlessly—the same tiresome piece of music. There are only a few concluding points to be made now, and the presenter shouts them over the relentless music. "Lobby floor," he hollers, "everybody can sit down." The whole thing has taken less than five minutes, but the audience has a new appreciation of the elevator problem. They have experienced it, participated in it. They can feel it in their legs and hear it resounding in their ears.

NOTE: A few days after the presentation, the elevator system was renovated and the music was put to rest.

Other participatory presentations reside in my mind, one in particular:

—Michael Colacchio, a New Yorker who taught a Chicago audience to speak Italian. He was remarkable. Not once did he utter a word of English. He simply *pantomimed* phrases—acting them out—adding the appropriate Italian words, linking them to the action. The audience participated throughout.

"Bartender, give me a drink" was pure pantomime—no English, not a word. Then, as the audience understood the action, the presenter began to make the connection. Speaking nothing but Italian, Colacchio added the words to define the action. *"Barista, mi porte una bevanda."* It became a kind of dramatized chant.

Soon, Colacchio was rushing about the room, pointing to his audience, identifying individuals (by first name, *in Italian*), encouraging participation. The decibel level was soaring as the audience repeated the words. *"Barista, mi porte . . ."* It was pandemonium. Everybody was speaking Italian! Well, *some* Italian. Enough to have a drink in Rome.

Audience participation is the fastest form of teaching—and the most titillating. It may be *the most* titillating at the Harvard Business School. I was there, for a two-week stint, when Professor Martin V. Marshall entered the amphitheater on the first day of the course, gazed around at the forty "students" in his marketing class, and said, *"Well, where do you want to start this thing?"*

The group was astounded. Professor Marshall moved into them. "I mean, how do you feel about it? See anything here that piques your interest?"

The class had been put on notice. The message was clear: "Be ready. You will be asked to contribute."

This is the most familiar and broadly used form of participation. The presenter *acts upon* the audience. The audience, or someone in it, *reacts*.

■ The congressional committee attacks, probing for answers. "Didn't you realize that you were violating the Boland Amendment?" The witness and his counsel react.

■ "Does everyone agree with that recommendation?" the chairman asks the board. "I'm not so sure," someone replies—and the issue is joined.

■ The presenter needn't be a challenger. "Can you help us out

on this, Margaret? What does your experience tell you?" The doctor
eases the staff toward discovery.

An exploratory interplay begins, and soon the atmosphere is
enriched with differing views. There is a cerebral tingle in participation, sharpened by the realization that inevitably, *someone will be next.*

Participation elevates the energy level of the audience (as has
been noted before, there's much to be said for an audience that stays
awake), but it does something equally important for a good presenter.

> **Audience participation is a *superb* tool for audience
> analysis. It keeps feeding information about the audi-
> ence to the presenter *during the presentation.* The fresh
> flow of data enables the presenter to personalize the
> message and make it more useful.**

This is powerful stuff, stimulating participation and shaping
your presentation accordingly. But, with all of the rewards of participation, there are also a few hazards, and some basic principles that
can be crucial.

Here's a short but beefy list that may help you avoid the hazards
and apply the basics:

■ *Check the dynamics in the room* before you ask your audience
to actively involve themselves in your presentation. Maybe they're
competitors and don't want to reveal anything. Maybe they're tired.
Maybe they're spoiling for a fight (the day-long session has been
nothing but bad news—and you're the last presenter). Stand in the
back of the room and take a reading of your audience. Listen to them.
Check the body language. If the mood is subdued, or the vibes are
ominous, don't push your audience to participate.

■ *Make the participation easy for everybody.* Audiences don't
want to be threatened. If they're worried about their ability to do
what you're suggesting, they probably won't do it. They won't even
try. They're not bad sports or anything. They just don't want to look
inadequate in front of their friends.

■ *Many forms of participation are subtle but effective.* They can
even be therapeutic. An example: "Let's take a stretch. Feel free to
yawn if you want to."

You'll find more subtle but effective forms of participation *in
church* than almost anyplace else.

> "Let's join together for the singing of hymn number
> 309. Please rise."

"If you don't have a hymnal, maybe your neighbor will share with you."

"Shall we stand for this morning's responsive reading?"

"Can I ask the deacons to please come forward?"

Then, as you file out, there's the pastor at the door ready to shake your hand. If you want to see participation being practiced in many gentle but telling ways, go to church.

■ *Involuntary participation can be disastrous.* If you're going to crush an egg in one hand to symbolize the fragility of some organizational structures, make sure it doesn't explode, splattering your audience. (An egg-splotched shirt or blouse can be very distracting.)

If you're going to pound your fist on the conference table for emphasis, make sure the coffee cups don't fly.

Participation shouldn't be an accident.

■ *If you're asking an audience to participate, you'd better be able to lead the drill.* If you're going to guide the group in a memory improvement session, better remember the names of the people in the class. Most forms of audience participation require at least a smattering of talent by the presenter.

■ *There should be a bit of the cheerleader in you.* Audiences are remarkably agreeable, open to suggestion. But it really helps if you're genuinely enthused, a true believer. If your audience senses that you're lukewarm about the whole thing, you really can't expect them to enter into it with much conviction. Audiences reflect the attitudes of presenters, particularly presenters who seek participation.

■ *Don't make one person responsible for the entire audience's participation.* Let me explain. There's always an element of doubt in audience participation. The old friend in the audience, the one person you *knew* would participate, suddenly clams up. "Why *me?*" he says. You back off. You don't rely on one person. Too chancy. "Charley here will carry the melody while the rest of us tap out the beat on the tabletop." What if Charley can't carry a tune in a bucket? Have at least *two* people who can bail you out.

■ *If somebody surprises you and refuses to participate, or tries and can't, just move right along.* No big deal. It may be tempting to say, "Come on, Charley, you can do it if you try"—but participation works best without pressure. With pressure, it can become intimidation. That turns Charley into a martyr and you into a tyrant.

■ *Participation should be fun.* Games make great participatory devices. Short, simple games. Example: *Perceptions:* "Let's play perceptions. Let's identify some major corporations in terms of the *Past*, the *Present*, or the *Future*. Tell me, where would you place each of these major corporations without really thinking about them? We're talking about *perceptions* here."

Games should move that fast. The audience is involved, participating, being entertained, without really thinking about it.

■

Nine times out of ten, audiences remember what they participate in. That makes participation a presentation powerhouse. But like most powerhouses, it can blow up if not handled with infinite care and respect.

21

Humor:
It's low tech on a high wire.

"I'm the president of the United States, and I am not going to eat any more broccoli."—President George Bush

Now, is that funny?

Yes, it is—*sort of* funny. But it's not a joke. This is a joke:

■ A couple of tourists were driving around Boston, trying to find the Harvard Business School. They realized they were lost, so they stopped a young student on the street and asked: "What's the best way to get to Harvard?"

The student thought for a moment, and finally said, "Study, man, that's the only way—study, study, study."

That joke is so old that it has been used by speakers throughout the country by merely adapting it to the local geography.

What's in? What's out

Now, those two minor offerings suggest something about the evolution of humor over the years—especially about humor in presentations which are likely to involve *you*.

Truth is in. *Concocted jokes* are out.

This is good news for you, as a presenter. It means that your audience is going to be a lot more interested in true, relevant, funny things than the old "traveling salesman" jokes which used to arouse more interest than they delivered.

There's a performer named Rick Reynolds who has made a career out of telling stories about himself—and all of them, according to him, are true. "Only the Truth is Funny" is the name of his show. His title is probably *not* true (I can remember a lot of Laurel and Hardy movies which were pure imagination and they were *hysterical*), but Mr. Reynolds has a point.

There's something about the *truth* that makes the humor bite a bit deeper. It becomes more meaningful, more memorable when it's true.

There's only one problem.

When you're in the middle of a situation which *could* be funny, it's often hard to recognize the potential for humor in it. It's just too close. The reality is simply too real. Here's a way to recognize humor in everyday life—*your* life:

If you ever say to yourself, "I just don't believe this. This really can't be happening to me," chances are you are in the midst of what could be a very funny story.

Let me give you a personal example. It is absolutely true.

Back in the early '80s, I wrote an article about then-President Reagan. The article appeared in the *New York Times.*

On the day following the appearance of the article, I flew to Dallas to call upon a client. Awaiting me was a pink "please call" slip from Ronald Reagan. There was a number on it. I called. To my astonishment, I got the White House. I said I was returning the president's call. (What *else* was I to say?) After a series of clicks and checks about my social security number—I was informed that the president was in a meeting. Fair enough. I didn't expect to pull him out of a cabinet session.

I returned to business. I had had my brush with history.

Several hours later, I was presenting some ads to an audience of six or seven people in a good-sized conference room.

Suddenly, the secretary of the general manager opened the door and announced in tones of resonating clarity, "Mr. Hoff, the president of the United States is on the phone."

Well, I was up to my ears in potato chip ads.

Potato chips! That's when I thought, "This really can't be happening to me." No way. Not in the middle of my *potato chips* presentation! But it was. And it struck me funny.

So, I stacked the ads, nodded to the group (as if this sort of thing happened all the time), turned to the secretary, and said, "I'll take the call."

I had a nervous three-minute conversation with the president (which he has forgotten long ago, and I never will), and—to this day—I cannot eat a potato chip without smiling.

That's a true story—and it always relates well to people who have to handle all kinds of situations when making presentations. It also makes an interesting point about humor:

The most laughable things invariably happen when an ordinary individual finds himself or herself in an extraordinary situation.

Humor, of course, is tricky. Jay Leno calls it "a high wire act . . . you go out and you talk, and it works or it doesn't."

He also calls it "low tech"—meaning only the human brain must light up.

Leno is an exemplar of many characteristics of the art of humor. His attitude toward life is essentially whimsical. ("They buried the oldest man in Japan today. He was 109—and he was *semi*-retired!") ("In 2014, we'll put astronauts on Mars—where there's no plant life—no water—no air."—*puzzled look*—"I don't get it. Why don't they just come to *L.A.*?")

He sees things differently, in a way that makes other people think, "That's right. Why didn't I see that?" Then, they laugh because he has voiced *creatively* what they have known all along, basically.

Leno also appears to be genuinely interested in people. It's an absolute requirement of comedy. If you're not inquisitive, you're not going to discover much humor in anything.

Humor includes an element of surprise, too. There's always a twist that catches you just a bit off-guard. Mort Sahl, one of the great stand-up comedians—and essentially a *political* satirist—used to say of certain candidates, "If he ran unopposed, he'd be defeated." What a surprising way to say, *he's a loser!*

Humor is surely the hardest of all subjects to fit into a "how to" book. Humor resists rules like jazz resists sheet music. But maybe there are a few observations worth noting:

Worth Noting

■ Don't try to write jokes. Even the most experienced scriptwriters in the world admit that it is excruciatingly difficult.

■ Stick with the truth.

■ Make fun of yourself, not your audience. NOTE: Even in Hollywood, where almost anything goes, one of the hottest comedy directors in town—Jim Abrahams—has a golden rule which he's followed in everything from *Airplane* to *Hot Shots*. It is this: *don't laugh at others when you can laugh at yourself.*

■ Don't build a presentation around a bunch of jokes you've collected. You are not a stand-up comedian. Fit relevant bits and pieces of humor *into* your message. The message is primary. The

humor enhances the message.

■ Be wary of the off-color, the four-letter words, the shocking, and the scandalous. Andrew Dice Clay does it—and George Carlin—and quite a few others—but they also alienate a lot of people.

■ Don't wait for laughs. If you get 'em, fine. If you don't, keep right on going. There's nothing more pathetic than a presenter pausing for laughter that never comes.

■ Do some testing. Try your funny bits on your spouse, or your kids, or your co-workers (kids are probably the best). If you bomb with your test audiences, you—at least—won't be surprised when you don't bring the house down during the real thing.

■ Don't laugh at your own jokes. The audience laughs—you rejoice, *inwardly.*

■ Beware of satire. Mort Sahl, Mark Russell, and a few others do it well. But most audiences can't really distinguish satire from reality. It's a little like the commercials that appear on "Saturday Night Live." It's hard to tell the commercials that are satirizing the ads from the commercials that *are* the ads.

■ People are more likely to laugh when they're seated close together. If they're scattered about, with empty seats in between, you're going to get less response to *everything.* Make sure they get together before you start.

Free the endorphins!

If you don't have humor in your presentation style, try it. *Go for it.* According to Dr. Robert B. Zajonc at the University of Michigan, smiling has great therapeutic value. It cools the blood in the region of the brain known as the hypothalamus, promoting the release of endorphins, the hormones which can suppress pain and make us feel good.

Just think—all of that good stuff *from smiling.*

Almost all audiences like to smile, to laugh. They're just sitting there waiting for an excuse to laugh out loud. And up you come. Tell 'em something that happened to you that they can identify with—and launch your presentation with a burst of laughter. Everybody will feel better. Including you.

22

"I'm speaking to what I see in your eyes."

—Mike Vance

Have you ever tried to have a conversation with a cab driver while you're in the back seat and he (or she) is weaving through heavy traffic?

It's very difficult, but it makes a dramatic point about eye contact.

It is virtually impossible to talk to the rear of a person's head. A floundering conversation has little hope of survival without some degree of eye contact. A cabbie talking to a rearview mirror is a miserable presentation technique.

Cab drivers have taught us something else about eye contact. Without it, it's impossible to tell if anybody is *listening*.

In a very real sense, listening isn't done with the ears, it's done with *the eyes*. ("Want to know if a person is listening to your words of wisdom? *Look at his eyes.*")

And as the eyes "listen," they *respond*—sending back more signals than you could stuff into a mainframe computer. Perhaps that is why Mike Vance—a superb professional speaker—says, "I'm speaking to what I see in your eyes."

This means, "I'm talking directly to the most sensitive and responsive channel of communication in the human system—and I'm editing as I go." That takes lots of experience but it is a skill that great presenters strive to achieve.

Why all this attention to the eyes?

The answer may sound melodramatic (but it's true): the *eyes* communicate a living presence that is indescribably powerful, and no camera in the world can transmit it with the same impact of a live presentation. (You may be looking at Dan Rather. But is he looking at *you?* Are you *sure?*) Live eyes are "the windows of the soul." Doctors peer into them to gauge your health. Lovers stare into them to share their deepest feelings. Hypnotists use them to cast us under a spell. And enemies try to *outstare* each other in order to express their hatred. Eyes are awesome.

The whole subject of eye contact and presentation may boil down to this small sliver of truth:

If you're *not* going to use eye contact in your presentation, you might as well Federal Express your message to the meeting.

Eye contact, if you are *not* employing it effectively, can do more to enhance your presentation skills than any other single improve-

117

ment you can make. Vocal cords may carry your message, but *eyes* hold your audience.

Since eye contact is so necessary to holding attention, let's spend a few moments answering the questions that seem to crop up most often:

1. *How do you do eye contact? What's the secret?* The secret is not "equal time." It's not a matter of "*three* seconds per person" or "*five* seconds per person" or any preordained length of equal time.

Eye contact is a matter of punctuation. It's the registration of an idea, a phrase, maybe even a single word, during a continuous linking-up of the eyes.

If you're getting a negative response, eyes averted, head turned away, maybe you want to concentrate on this person for a few more thoughts, or phrases, or words—perhaps *something* will strike home. (It is *not* an insult if a person is hesitant to look you in the eye. People don't relinquish their eyes easily—especially to strangers.)

If the eye contact is strong and solid, and the facial language is favorable, you move on—staying with each person as long as your instincts (and your eyes) tell you. You linger long enough to sense an acknowledgment by the person you're talking to. A bond, a linkage, is created in those few seconds and you both know that a highly personal exchange has occurred—and that, implicit in the dialogue, is the message that "you'll be back." The eyes say it all, talking back and forth, an exchange unique to "live" presentation.

Eye contact is doled out by words and thoughts, and measured by body language. But, somewhere near the unfathomable core of it, there is a bonding that is deeply alive and unique to the eyes.

Idea: To feel the depth and power of the eyes, and sneak in a little eye contact training, try this exercise tonight. Find a friend (or lover) and stare into her (his) eyes for *two* uninterrupted minutes. Rules: no laughing, no talking, no touching.

The two-minute continuous current: Can you do it?

2. What prevents eye contact? What are some of the most prevalent mistakes?

■ If you're standing in a pool of light, reading notes or a script, and the audience is bathed in blackness, you're not going to *see* any eyes—let alone make contact. Louis Nizer, the great trial lawyer, is adamant on this point. In his book, *Reflections Without Mirrors*, he says, "The firm rule is: a speech should be delivered without a single note, the speaker looking at his audience in the eye and timing his delivery to match its immediate comprehension." So, Mr. Vance and Mr. Nizer are saying the same thing here, only Mr. Nizer will not tolerate "a single note."

■ If you're just too far away from your audience to see them easily—if you're isolated—eye contact is going to be difficult.

■ "Cocktail Party Eyes" is the presenter's worst affliction. It is derived from all the cocktail parties you've ever attended. There are a variety of "Cocktail Party Eyes," many of which are shared by presenters when speaking to audiences. Here are a few different examples:

"Cocktail Party Eyes"

"Oh, oh . . . where's she going? Is she leaving with that guy?"	*"Frankly, I don't come here often. These aren't my kind of people."*	*"Where am I? Is this Toledo?"*	*"Is he going to the bar again?"*

Presenters with "Cocktail Party Eyes" never look directly at their audiences. They look around them, over them, even *through* them. There's a lot of self-consciousness in the presenter with "Cocktail Party Eyes"—but there's very *little* eye contact.

3. "How do I maintain eye contact when I'm really trying to concentrate on my presentation?" Speaking and eye contact aren't two separate actions. With a little experience, you find that one becomes a part of the other. That's really what Mike Vance was saying when he said "I'm speaking to what I see in your eyes." It requires confidence in your knowledge and a reasonable degree of self-esteem. You've got to believe in your ability to help others. As in all aspects of presentation, *preparation* is key. If you're not quite sure of your material, your eye contact will be tentative. Have complete command of your material, and your confidence will come right through your eyes.

■

One other little point that could be important: Think twice before you hand out papers for your audience to study—or give them other inducements to break eye contact. They may get so engrossed in the papers that they never come back to you. And, no matter what they say, people can't read and listen to you at the same time. Eye contact is so valuable. Be wary about giving it away.

23

Spend a day
with your voice.

A voice-over is seldom seen, rarely identified, but can become familiar to millions of Americans.

John Connell is one of those familiar voices. He is hired by advertisers or their agencies to deliver the narration in a TV or radio commercial.

Like many voice-overs, John was formerly an actor on Broadway, worked in television (he was "Young Doctor Malone"), and started doing commercials on the side. Through it all, his voice has mellowed and deepened, but it has never lost its youthful enthusiasm.

"It all comes out in the voice," John says. "Joy, nervousness, anticipation, authority, boredom. The voice gives the audience its first real clue about you. Yet the voice is often neglected."

Many presenters have never even heard their own voices. At least not as their audiences have heard them. Usually, when the voice is recorded for the first time, the response is incredulous, "Is that *me*? Do I really sound like *that*?"

Idea: spend a day or two with your own voice, and see if you're somebody you would like to listen to.

Simply get yourself a micro-cassette recorder (around sixty dollars at most department stores) and carry it around with you. Talk into it when you're in your car, walking through the park, sitting in your office, or waiting for an elevator. (Nobody will think you're crazy. *Everybody's* wired for *something* these days.)

Tell the recorder how you feel, where you're going, how the weather is. Tell it a joke, if you know one. Describe a movie, a book, a scene you saw on the street. Just talk—about anything that strikes you.

That night, push the "play" button and listen to yourself. Are you somebody you'd like to listen to? How would you describe your voice? Full or thin? Confident or shaky? Personal or distant? Fast or slow?

Describe your voice to your recorder after you have listened to yourself. Then, make at least three resolutions based upon your analysis. Examples: Pick up the pacing if you sound tentative (use more verbs). Eliminate those "you knows" if you have a lot of verbalized pauses. Speak up if you sound like a wimp. (This works particularly well in New York City.)

Then, next day, try your own advice. And listen to yourself again that night. *You're getting better acquainted with your voice.* You'll hear things you never heard before. You may notice that you laugh when you're surprised or self-conscious. You may find that your voice deepens when you become relaxed. You may detect that you pause before certain words. You may realize that the words are beginning to come more easily as you let your thoughts flow into your audio cassette. You may discover that you *like* to talk and that your voice doesn't sound so bad after all.

Most important, as you become better acquainted with your voice, you'll find that your "real talk" starts to reflect the improvements that you've suggested to your tape.

Spend some time with your voice. Other people do. By listening to yourself, and working on it, you may realize that it not only sounds better to *you*, it carries more weight with *them*.

24

"Rapture of the deep" can steal defeat from the jaws of victory.

There's nothing like a responsive audience to get the adrenaline going.

Sometimes a speaker can get so intoxicated by the laughs, smiles, chortles, and applause of even a small audience that all sense of time and purpose evaporates in a rising tide of euphoria.

Deep-sea divers encounter the same malaise. It is called "rapture of the deep" and sometimes it ends their diving days.

For a presenter, the rapture of acclaim may continue long after the audience has expressed itself and is ready to move on. The presenter's adrenaline invariably surges more strongly than the general response of the audience, so it's only natural that the presenter takes longer to normalize or "come out of it."

Hubert Humphrey, the late senator and vice president, was often accused of brilliance that could be beaten into boredom by verbosity. His comments, while smart and insightful, often became interminable. Nothing seemed to stop him, and moderators of talk shows could be heard—behind the senator's insistent, nonstop voice—trying to break in, change the subject, or call for a commercial.

> This problem is not without its humorous aspects, but it can be serious—particularly in "live" gatherings where nobody really wants to tell the invited speaker to "shut up and sit down." Also, in a business presentation, the speaker experiencing "rapture of the deep" may very likely be the most senior officer in the room. It's awkward to tell the chief that he (or she) exceeded the agreed-to time allotment fifteen minutes ago and everybody is getting slightly punchy.

What to do?

If you're on your own, and you don't have someone in the audience to save you from yourself, there are always watches and clocks with beepers, buzzers, and other forms of alarm. Some electronic podiums also have timers. These have merit, and your audience will admire your efforts at self-discipline—providing you stop shortly after the signal flashes, rings, pings, or whatever it does.

There is no humiliation in using mechanical or electronic reminders of the amount of time that has elapsed. After all, presidential debates have buzzers, politicians who serve on televised panels of inquiry have red lights, and theaters frequently seem to be infested with people whose digital watches sound off at moments of high drama.

You may also want to rehearse your presentation to a shorter time period than you have actually been allowed. If you have been given sixty minutes, for example, rehearse your presentation—under stringent timing—to quit at fifty minutes. That way, if you get swept into the heady currents of ego gratification—you'll still have ten minutes left to pull yourself out of it.

The best way, however, to deal with "rapture of the deep" is to have your own "Stanley Kubrick." That is, a director/critic/timekeeper.

If your "Stanley Kubrick" is imaginative, as all good directors are, he (or she) will come up with a signal to draw your attention to the situation without disrupting you or your audience.

A word of caution:

Don't let your timekeeper make the signal too *sudden* or too *subtle.* Keep in mind that the presenter is deeply into the subject, and feeling a certain intensity bordering on giddiness. If there is a sudden signal—a hand shoots up in the audience, for instance—the presenter is likely to be startled by it, unlikely to remember its prearranged meaning (I have seen presenters react to this kind of signal by calling on the timekeeper, thinking there was a question to be answered). A sudden signal may *shock* the presenter into silence. A subtle one may have lost its well-intended meaning in lingering euphoria.

Here's what your "Stanley Kubrick" can do:

Sit near the back of the room. When the presenter has exceeded the allotted time, "Stanley" stands up and moves to the rear, behind the audience. No big deal. Chances are, the audience doesn't even notice. People stand up all the time.

Maybe you, the presenter, get the signal right away, maybe not. But you'll *begin* to surface. You'll *begin* to be aware of what's happening.

There's "Stanley," after all, standing by himself—*right in your line of sight.* Nothing intimidating about him—but there he is, giving you an expression that says, "Good job. Time to close up."

A sensitive director/critic/timekeeper will allow you to continue bubbling to the surface for a few more minutes.

When it is clear that you should *stop,* that the audience is sagging, your own "Stanley"—still standing, but out of the audience's direct view—will give you the classic signal for "time!" It is pure, nonverbal language.

It may be the quickest, clearest language in the world. It is telegraphic, unmistakable—and it is *hospitable,* not cross and impatient like most broadcast signals. You know the ones.

A finger drawn menacingly across the throat, probably severing the vocal chords. This is unsettling, for the presenter.

Forefinger twirling impatiently in the air, indicating "Hurry up, you're running long." Again, that's rattlesome.

There are other signals, but the discreetness and congeniality of the classic "T" make it the best way to tell a speaker a secret, *"It's time to stop."*

Presenters get rescued from "rapture of the deep" every day—and head happily home realizing that they have snatched victory from what might have been disaster.

And all they need is a little quiet direction from a friend.

25

A true story
about Valium

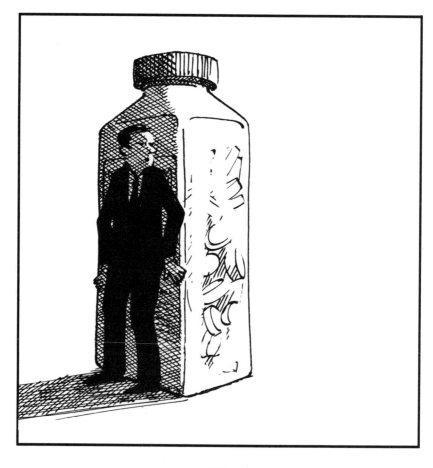

He was a senior partner in a successful corporate consulting firm in New York City. The company was known for its long hours and unrelenting pace.

"I had an experience that could be useful to anyone interested in presentations," he said, "but I'd rather you didn't use my name."

I agreed—and here's what he told me.

"I had a back problem. I also had a speech to give. It was to be in Minneapolis. So, I took Valium through the weekend before going out to Minneapolis. I gave the speech on Tuesday. I was calm. I was cool. In terms of covering the points I wanted to make, it was the best speech I ever gave. Out of the corner of my eye I saw a few people leaving—maybe ten, maybe fifteen. The speech was videotaped and I was eager to see it. I saw it. It was flat. Boring. It was *awful*. I'd covered the points all right, but I was *so* laid-back, nobody got them."

There are two lessons to be learned here:

1. Great content never saved a bad presentation.
2. Anything that makes you feel *un*natural isn't going to help your presentation.

NOTE: Now it's fashionable to swear by beta-blockers (propranolol) as prepresentation stress relievers. These are prescription drugs which reduce the acceleration of the heart. Here's a better idea: Go back and review the chapter titled, "How to get the best out of nervousness—and control the rest." You don't need a prescription to read it, and it won't fool around with your heart.

26

How to make a speech in a strange hotel.

Idea: make a copy of this chapter and take it
with you the next time you're invited
to speak in a strange hotel.

Raise your hand if anything like this has ever happened to you when you've been asked to make a speech in a strange hotel:

The scene: the night before your presentation. You're looking over the room that you'll be using the next morning. The hotel technician is with you.

"There's a light up there on the ceiling that's washing out the image on the screen. Can we just get rid of that light?

"Nope. All those ceiling lights are on the same circuit. Want to kill 'em all? Here. Take a look."

"That turns the whole room into a tomb. I don't want the audience to think they've *died* here."

"Okay. You got your lights back."

"How about if we get a ladder and *unscrew* just that *one* bulb? *I* could do it."

"I don't think we have a twelve-foot ladder."

"You don't have a twelve-foot ladder? I have a twelve-foot ladder in my garage at home."

"Besides, you couldn't do it. Even I couldn't do it. I'm not allowed to get up on a ladder."

"If we had a ladder to unscrew that one bulb, who could we ask to get up there?"

"Have to be an engineer."

"Okay, whatever it takes. Could you call the engineer?"

"Too late. He went off duty at nine. He's home havin' a beer by now."

"Forget the light bulb. Do you suppose I could have a lavaliere?"

"A what?"

"You know, a remote mike . . . a wireless microphone."

"Was it on the invoice?"

"I don't know. I'm sure it would be all right with the people who invited me here. They're sponsoring the entire convention—in *your* hotel."

"Have to charge you extra."

"Okay. Fine. I'm sure it will be *just fine*. If not, I'll pay for it myself."

"I'll see if we have one."

"Great!"

"But first, I gotta have an invoice."

"Oh, man . . . I go on at eight in the morning. That's only a few hours from now."

"Yeah, and I got another setup to do. Just let me know if you need anything else."

That's a true story (the lavaliere *did* arrive the next morning—with strict instructions not to walk away with it).

Ideas for "Strange Hotel" were contributed by a panel of 14 experts— all are speakers of long standing.

Lynette Botsford
Director of Sales
Telemundo Group, Inc.
New York, New York

Maggie Brydges
Communications Consultant
Wordbridges
Norfolk, Virginia

Louis A. Centlivre
Creative Consultant
Chicago, Illinois

Mark A. Dacey
Senior Vice President
Chicago Sun-Times
Chicago, Illinois

Abbott C. Jones
Managing Director
Ad/Media Corporate Advisors, Inc.
New York, New York

Bob Linden
Staff Executive
American Association of Advertising Agencies
New York, New York

John Lucht
Consultant
Author of *Rites of Passage—at $100,000+*
New York, New York

Lynne O'Shea
Vice President/
Business Development
Gannett Co.
Chicago, Illinois

John O'Toole
President
American Association of Advertising Agencies
New York, New York

Bill Phillips
Independent Designer of A/V Systems for Communications Companies
New York, New York

Joel Raphaelson
Senior Vice President
Ogilvy & Mather–Chicago
Chicago, Illinois

Mary Ann Rood
Director of Communications
Ocean Spray Cranberries, Inc.
Lakeville, Massachusetts

Don E. Schultz
Professor
Northwestern University
Medill School of Journalism
Evanston, Illinois

Edward C. Stephens
Professor
Syracuse University
Newhouse School of Public Communications
Syracuse, New York

You can't really blame the people who work in hotels. They're in the food and shelter business. They're also in the convention business, but—to them—that means a heavy-duty podium, a microphone that grows out of the podium, and a big screen which hovers over everything somewhere near center stage.

Anything that deviates from that antiquated norm is probably going to require a certain amount of planning—and maybe even a few harsh words—*from you.*

Checklist for a "Strange Hotel"

Here's a checklist to stick in your pocket or purse. It has been generated with a lot of help from my friends (see panel on page 132). All of these people have spoken in hotels of every shape, size, and altitude. They've weathered everything from creaky floors to crashing dishes. They're veterans of 1001 "impossible situations." Harken to their advice. It can save you from the kind of calamity that only a "strange hotel" can devise.

■ Make sure the chandelier in the middle of the ballroom doesn't overhang the screen you're going to be using for your slides or film. Either lower the screen or find another place for it. It would be nice to raise the chandelier, but this suggestion may cause apoplexy among the hotel staff.

■ Before you start, turn on your slide projector and *test for bobbing heads.* People sitting in front of your projector can create restless shadows at the bottom of your screen. Elevate the projector (often a book of matches will do it) or reseat the people.

■ Be absolutely certain that the local boy scout group isn't going to have its drum and bugle concert on the other side of that sliding partition to your right (or left). This is unfair competition—and should be changed. The same goes for local beauty contests. And Ararat Shrine dinners.

■ Get the feel of your room at least two hours before you present. Better still, ask to make a little inspection the night before. It will make you feel better about your presentation. You'll sleep more soundly. Take as many "unknowns" out of the situation as possible.

■ If you plan to display presentation boards around the room as you're speaking, check to see if the room has ledges wide enough to hold your boards upright. You'll probably find there are *no* ledges. Most hotels have never *heard* of ledges! Maybe you can push-pin the boards to the walls. When all else fails, ask the hotel manager what other speakers have done. Prepare to be creative.

■ Is there a clock that's clearly visible? If there isn't, find a place for your own timepiece where you can sneak a glance at it from time to time.

■ This is vital: make sure you have the extension number of the guy you can call when all of the A/V equipment gives one last heaving clank and breaks totally down. There's no guarantee that he will be there when you call, but it will make you feel better to have it.

■ If you've asked the hotel for easels, make sure they stand up. Most are like folding lawn chairs. They topple over just as you are revealing the most important sheet in your entire flip chart presentation.

■ If you're going to show a video, make sure the player plays your tape. There's ¾- and ½-inch. Idea: bring two tapes so you're covered either way. More to the point, make sure the player *plays* at all!

■ Be sure to check the number of light levels in the room. Is there a rheostat? Or an ON/OFF switch? Best idea: set the light level *exactly* the way you want it before you start. (Then, don't let anyone *touch* it. See Chapter 7).

■ Ask how many people are coming to your presentation. Then, have the *excess* chairs taken out of the room. Be ready for more static from the hotel staff. But empty chairs just don't do much for a presentation. They suggest that people didn't show up. Who needs to be reminded of *that*?

■ Watch those cords that snake along the carpet, extending for ten yards or more, from a piece of equipment to a plug. Ask the A/V technician to tape them *all* down—to make them trip-proof. IMPORTANT: don't hesitate to ask for *anything*.

■ Many presenters in hotel ballrooms seem to be part of the vegetation. These poor devils stand in the middle of a bunch of fake plants and wait for rain. Get out of the greenery!

■ If you're using a lavaliere with a remote, make sure you know exactly where the "hot spots" are in the room. If you don't you're likely to encounter a lot of feedback—none of which is audience-generated. Before you begin, stroll around with the lavaliere turned *on*. Sudden, sharp static in a presentation is like a buzzsaw in the brain. It *murders* concentration.

■ Before you go on, sit in the audience. Just sit there. How do you feel? Comfortable? How is the ventilation? Can you breathe easily? If the place seems the slightest bit stuffy to you *before* the presentation, it's going to be *awful* when the audience is there. Better to be cool than hot. Ventilation can make the difference between an alert audience and a droopy one.

■ Are your slides set for *rear* screen projection—or *front*? Many is the presenter who has arrived at the hotel, a few minutes ahead of schedule, only to find that the slides are positioned for *front* screen projection and the hotel is projecting from *behind* the screen. All the slides must be taken out of the drum and carefully turned around. At the last minute, it's no fun. If you *really* want to be safe, make up *two* drums; one for front, one for rear. Just make sure you have the right one.

■ If you have bar service before your presentation, be sure that *somebody shuts it down* before you start speaking. Leave the bar "open" and the temptation may be too great for some members of your audience. Never compete with booze!

■ In a large theater or auditorium, a wireless remote to advance your slides can be troublesome. Here's why: electronic interference can move the slides ahead *no matter what you do.* Those who have experienced this phenomenon say it's like riding a runaway horse!

■ Most hotel ballrooms have service hallways at the far end of the room. Unfortunately, that's where most presentations are made. So, if the hotel staff will be serving food during your presentation, you'll have a constant parade of waiters and waitresses swirling around you. Here's what you do: set up your presentation on one side of the room or the other—*away from those swinging doors with the dish-clattering traffic.*

■ Many hotel meeting rooms have support pillars. They're big and fat. Don't let the hotel put tables behind those posts. You may get some mumbles from the hotel staff on this one, but just remember—it's *your* show.

■ Expect things to get lost in hotels unless you follow them like a hawk. If you check in with A/V equipment, don't let it out of your sight until it gets safely stored in *your* meeting room. Without close scrutiny, A/V equipment can end up in "convention headquarters," lost and found, *anywhere.*

■ Ask the hotel to post signs in the lobby announcing your presentation. The signs should flag your audience . . . tell them exactly *where* to go, *when* to be there, *who's* speaking, and on *what.* (How many times have you heard people in the hotel elevator saying, "Does anybody know what floor this guy—*what's his name?*—is speaking on?")

■ Often, a platform will be hauled in so that the speaker can be seen above the audience. Good idea. But these platforms are often relics from some prehistoric age. Test the platform you have been given. Bounce up and down a little. If it squeaks every time you move, your audience is going to be laughing in all the wrong places. Ask for a platform that doesn't make funny noises, or just walk and talk (see Chapter 13).

■ Invest in one of those little flashlights about the size of a ball-point pen. You'd be amazed at how many times you'll use it. Maybe you want to review your notes offstage before you go on. Maybe that tiny little light on the podium conks out, and you're unlucky enough to be presenting at that exact moment. Maybe *all of the lights* in the room go out and you want to let your audience know you haven't panicked and run. A little light can provide a lot of reassurance.

■ Best idea: take your own A/V technician if one's available to you. But check with the hotel *first*. If the hotel equipment is run by union people, *your* A/V technician won't be able to say a word or do a thing.

■ Big, ornate ballrooms can be intimidating—especially if you're hosting a less-than-capacity crowd. A small insight for a big room: show your audience that *you* are completely comfortable in such fancy chambers. Move around. Tell them you didn't know you would be playing Caesar's Palace at this stage in your career. Use a laser pointer and flick it across the vaulted ceiling. Poke a little fun at the place and your audience will probably follow your lead. (If this doesn't work, see the tail end of Chapter 17 and don't lose a wink of sleep.)

■ Go to the head of the "wait staff" in the hotel where you'll be speaking. Talk to the person who's in charge of the waiters and wait-resses, or "food and beverage," as it's sometimes called. Here's the question to ask: What's *wrong* with that room I'll be speaking in?" You'll get some interesting answers. Examples: "We get a lot of complaints that it's too cold." "Between 10:00 and 12:00 we get a lot of take-off and landing noise from the airport. That's when the chandelier shakes." And so on. You can take action on *some* of these little "insider secrets," but even if you can't, you won't be surprised when the "secrets" occur.

Professor Edward C. Stephens of Syracuse University sums up the entire subject of speaking in strange hotels with the hard-won wisdom of a person who has suffered, survived, and still has his wits about him:

> "After all, when the hotel was designed and the function rooms were installed—nobody sat up late hunched over a design board worrying about some poor person from out of town who was going to have to show up one day and make a speech in that strange hotel.

"You have to worry about that yourself. In a better world somebody would worry about it for you, but even if you had the staff of the Queen of England, you would be better off to check it yourself."

NOTE: Professor Stephens had just recounted how the Queen (on a recent trip to the U.S.) had found herself rendered invisible by a podium elevated far beyond her regal height.

27
The Electronic Presenter

Electronics has lit up the sky, the screens, and the stages of presentation with a blazing bombardment of high technology.

Live videotape cameras show us the speaker as he or she is speaking—projected, from the rear, onto a giant screen inside the meeting hall.

The live presenter often stands directly in front of the gigantic simultaneous live videocast.

It's awesome. Faces seem carved out of Mount Rushmore. Mustaches become neatly clipped hedges. Tiny tics and twitches become monstrous aberrations. Remote pick-ups often introduce Gulliver-sized images glowering and towering over suddenly shortened live presenters.

Computer-programmed slide projectors are turned on and off by computer, from multitrack audiotape, throwing images on dozens of suspended screens of varying shapes and sizes—round ones, long skinny ones, perfect squares. Multi-channel sound wraps its resonance around us.

Meticulously scripted speeches, or artfully conducted interviews, are now shot on videotape—with original music and special sound edited in. A business executive can see himself or herself at a sales conference on a scale comparable to Clint Eastwood in *Pale Horse, Pale Rider.*

Live speeches, also carefully chiseled out of the intricate language of corporate communications, are punctuated with animated slides and video segments triggered into action by a computer-directed "storyboard." In the process, the presenter can become little more than a conjunction between electronic bedazzlements.

Anything that appears on a computer screen can now be transformed into 35mm slides, transparencies, and "hard copy" sheets. Changes can be made right on the computer console. Electronic "brushes" or light pens can alter images, adding computer-created colors and redirecting shapes, and doing it all in a fraction of the time required by archaic typeset slides.

Many corporate sales conferences are so electronically sophisticated that they would rival a Broadway musical in theatrical splash and splendor. (The British musical *Cats* is an electronic phantasmagoria of computer-choreographed effects.)

Broadway and Hollywood stars—to say nothing of Las Vegas chorus lines—have been known to appear in corporate sales spectaculars. The money is right. A lavish three-day sales conference may cost a company a million dollars to produce.

This is a live videocast on a giant screen. The presenter looms over himself—every tic and twitch magnified for all to see.

The question is: Does any of this high-tech magic have any-thing to do with your next presentation?

And the answer is: well, *maybe.*

It is unlikely that the next meeting of the Bank Marketing Asso-ciation is going to feature laser holography or the skating chorus of the Ice Follies.

This is not to pooh-pooh electronic presentation. It's here. Closed circuit television is here. Teleconferencing is here. Factory floors can be transformed into exciting electronic theaters (shows are ingeniously packaged and modulized for speedy set-up and take-down). Electronic character generation is here (large screen format for displaying resolutions, notes, documents). Dolby sound is here. Prepackaged electronic courses (audio or video cassette tapes, trans-parencies, games) are here and can be obtained on subjects ranging from "Comic Relief from Seminar Fatigue" to "Coping with Death and Dying."

But, in all truth, for your next presentation, it's likely that a careful selection of *less audacious* electronic aids would be more use-ful—and certainly less expensive.

Example: With an FM transmitter microphone clipped to your collar (it's no more than two inches wide), you can be heard through-out the hall without having to stand there like a statue talking into a static "stick" microphone. You can move around without needing to shout and without worrying about tripping over a spiderweb of wires. You're wireless.

You can change the computerized slides in your presentation by hitting a button on your electronic lectern (which can look like the flight deck of a 747) or you can ask for a wireless slide changer that lets you shoot out infrared signals that change slides whenever you please.

There are even electronic blackboards now. They don't use chalk. They use felt-tip pens. The board isn't black. It's white, and it takes notes electronically, reproducing whatever you put on the board. Some of these electronic boards will even project your notes, charts, and "buzz words" onto an overhead video screen. Many con-ference centers can supply them. If you want to buy one, you're talk-ing in the neighborhood of $3500.

Slides, as noted, can exhibit much greater brilliance—with vastly deeper dimension—when produced by computer. Transparencies and "hard copy" can then be reproduced as needed. The time sav-ings are phenomenal. And the costs aren't bad, from $60 to $75 a slide, by computer. If you've got your own computer units, you can knock out a slide for as little as $3.

None of these remarkable little A/V aids will transform you into an "electronic presenter," but they will enrich your presentation and eliminate some of the pesky irritations that have bothered presenters in the past.

When the day dawns that you want to produce, or be part of, a full-scale electronic spectacular—here are a few tips to keep in mind:

■ *The bigger the electronic extravaganza, the smaller the presenter becomes* (unless you're Liza Minnelli). It's hard to compete with laser holography that creates 3-D images which seem to hover in midair. Peter Allen was able to dance with the Radio City Rockettes as electronic skyrockets burst in the background, but it's hard for the average guy to kick that high. Sooner or later, in most presentations, the speaker must step forward and register a message. Don't let the hullabaloo overshadow you. Don't allow yourself to become a piece of static in an electronic hurricane. There must be a time when you step forward and present yourself as a living, breathing human being.

Let the video segments roll, let the multimedia images explode around you—but don't be intimidated by them. Don't become an usher in your own theater.

Electronic effects introduce presenters, help presenters make their points, but they shouldn't ever overwhelm them. The one unique advantage of a meeting is its irrepressible *aliveness*. The people are *alive. You* are alive. That's something you don't want to lose.

■ The more A/V equipment you use in a presentation, the more susceptible you become to electronic goof-ups. Computers are amazing, but they do develop glitches and hitches—they are not foolproof. Unless you can deliver your presentation *without* fancy A/V equipment, don't try it *with* fancy A/V equipment. Never go on the road with a one-of-a-kind prototype system that is guaranteed to dazzle your audience "providing everything goes right." "KISS" is the order of the day. "Keep It Simple, Stupid."

■ Don't even think about an electronic presentation unless you've got an experienced staff of audio/visual experts backing you up *every step of the way*. Electronic presentations require enormous preparation and constant surveillance. Presenters shouldn't operate anything more complicated than slide changers. If you don't believe that, take a look at some of those electronic control panels just behind the presentation theaters. They would frighten a nuclear physicist. Unless you've got a professional staff in the control room, you can be out there in a small pool of light waiting in silence for the multimedia showstopper that never starts.

■ Note from Bill Phillips, New York technician and independent designer of A/V systems for communications companies: "Presenters have a responsibility to be able to communicate to an A/V staff *exactly what* is supposed to happen, and *when.* A/V technicians are not mind-readers nor are they particularly good at ESP." Presenters should present. Technicians, working from clear instructions, should run the show.

■ Lastly, in today's attitudinal climate, it's possible to look *too* polished, *too* slick. Credibility often declines as reliance on A/V aids goes up—especially devices like teleprompters. They may simply prompt your audience to wonder who wrote the script.

■

It's okay to be partially electronic—everybody can use a bit of glitz. But, when all votes are counted and all scores are in, the presenter who is most *alive* will carry the day.

28

Are you Red, Blue, or Gray? (How to find yourself in the presentation spectrum.)

Every presenter in the world operates in one of three zones: the Blue, the Red, or the Gray. There may be some temporary crossovers, zone to zone, and presenters can *change* zones with practice— but you'll find that most presenters are *mostly* Red, Blue, or Gray.

There are variations in the Red Zone (scarlet to pink), and the Blue Zone (midnight to eggshell), but the Gray Zone is one big blob. It is like a Scottish sky when the weather turns ugly.

What we're talking about here is a presentation scale, a sort of color map for your private use in determining what kind of presenter you *are*, what kind you'd *like* to be, and what kind you *should* be.

You can also use this scale to analyze and categorize the presentation techniques of politicians, professors, TV anchorpersons, attorneys, sales people, and whomever else you have in mind. It also works on personalities from history, providing you have a perception of their presentation style.

First thing to do: Figure out the simple but strange-looking chart below . . .

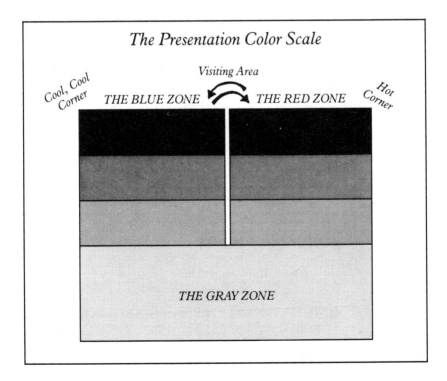

The Blue Zone Defined:

The Blue Zone is an orderly neighborhood. Things don't get out of hand here. Presentations are disciplined, organized, cohesive.

Here are a few singular descriptives for presenters who head-quarter in the Blue Zone:

> Analytical
> Logical
> Pragmatic
> Thoughtful
> Deliberate
> Rational
> Restrained
> Intellectual
> Insightful

The bluest of the Blue Zone presenters can capture your attention with their clear-headed persuasiveness. They can marshall arguments with military precision, and lead you to conclusions of unimpeachable logic.

The best of the Blue Zoners come across as being so secure in their knowledge that they are virtually unshakable. Yet there is an *intensity* about them that builds steadily. They are presenters on a carefully considered mission.

Whether true or not, you get the feeling that they are intellectual. They are most comfortable when speaking from a *very* deep data base.

As you move down the zone, into lighter shades of blue, you'll notice that the presenters change slightly—the intensity fades, the message becomes a bit more diffused, the hard edge becomes a bit dull.

The best Blue Zone presenters *cut through* to the core. This requires a certain sharpness. Not only of word but manner too.

The Red Zone Defined:

Once you're inside the Red Zone, you're going to *feel* it. The atmosphere is charged. If a Red Zone presenter is really up for it, he or she can blow the roof off a sizable meeting hall at any time.

The descriptives come fast and furious:

Emotional
Driven
Surprising
Instinctive
Charismatic
Creative
Impulsive
Daring
Disjointed

Some Red Zone presenters give new meaning to the word "volatile." They push passion to its outer limits. When they have had theatrical training, these presenters radiate a kind of brushfire emotionalism that can be effective with some audiences—disastrous with others.

The Red Zone runs on adrenaline and chutzpah. Its credo is: "Maybe you like us, maybe you don't—but you sure can't ignore us."

As the Red Zone becomes less red and eventually passes into the palest of pinks, you'll find that the presenters seem harder to describe. They become less memorable, less ardent—moving even closer to the most densely populated zone of all, the *Gray Zone*. This is where you'll find the majority of presenters. It is a place that *must* be visited—but not for long.

The Gray Zone Defined:

The Gray Zone is a safe place to be. It has been here for centuries. It doesn't change much. This is very flat country, not much color, and a tendency toward chill.

The Gray Zone lacks the heat of the Red Zone and the incisive edge of the Blue. It survives because a considerable number of people would rather be bland than risk "making a fool of themselves." This fear respects no professional boundaries. It afflicts editors and educators as well as presidents of banks.

Next time you attend a large business conference, ask yourself—just for fun—how many of the speakers you would put into the Gray Zone. The following list will help you identify them:

Cautious
Traditional
Accommodating

Compromising
Predictable
Neutral
Noncommittal
Ambivalent
Boring

The Gray Zone is the absence of color and therein we find its gravest problem. Gray Zone presenters tend to be eminently forgettable. This can be costly. It's hard to win a competitive presentation if the judges have to say, "Refresh my memory. I can't quite place her (or him)."

There's a certain irony at work here. Many inhabitants of the Gray Zone don't know they're living in the Antarctica of presentation styles.

There are two reasons for this:

1. There are so many other Gray Zone presenters that grayness begins to seem normal.

2. Being boring is something that most friends, relatives, and business colleagues don't like to chat about.

To help you place yourself on the Presentation Color Scale, let's get you oriented. Take a look at the next few pages. You'll see some of the better known residents of the Red and Blue Zones, and you'll read a few words about each just to explain, quickly, their various locations on the charts.

Then, we'll get *you* involved.

The Blue Zoners: Some representatives from past and present

The captain of the Blue Zone is Mario Cuomo of New York.

The politically astute Mr. Cuomo has everything a Blue Zone presenter needs. The purest logic. A penetrating intensity. A searching, analytical mind. And a meticulousness about control (he writes his own scripts and reads most of them word for word). Everything comes out "just so." Also, he does not hesitate to leap to the Red Zone to borrow a story, a personal experience. Then, back he comes to the sanctity of the Blue.

Henry Kissinger is right up there with Mr. Cuomo, but further from any hint of emotionalism. His thoughts are carved with a diplomat's infinite care. They move from point to point as if they were being examined under a magnifying glass before being released for consumption. He personifies the rational judgment, the informed decision, the voice of reason. He makes no effort to emotionalize his presentations. He remains aloof, intensely *cool*.

George Will speaks for the Blue Zone. Articulate, cool, precise, organized. In content and style, he rarely permits emotion to enter his presentation.

Jeane Kirkpatrick, former U.S. ambassador to the United Nations, shares a certain diplomatic kinship with Kissinger. Both are calm, concerned, deliberate thinkers—but Ms. Kirkpatrick is remarkably direct for a person so sensitive to the nuances of international relations.

In an area less deeply blue, you'll find an interesting group of journalists. *Bill Buckley, George Will,* and *Ted Koppel.* They are commentators of an intellectual bent—not terribly concerned with emotional trappings, though Buckley has his moments. Analysts, generally, are *blue.*

Moving into the lighter shades of Blue, ominously close to the Gray, we find ex-candidate for president *Walter Mondale.* Likable and industrious, Mr. Mondale never registered as persuasive. His story seemed to consist of bits and pieces of logic— and his changing strategies didn't bespeak great confidence. *Dan Quayle* fits here, light blue, but slowly turning up his intensity.

Should you aim your presentation style toward the heady stratosphere of the Blue Zone?

Before you answer, ponder these points:

■ An effective Blue Zone presentation requires a *ton* of preparation. Be ready for homework.

■ Blue Zone presentations require nimble memories. When questions are asked, they will be reflective of the presentation—probing, pragmatic, seeking more data. You must soak up information and be able to play it back on request.

■ Executives prefer Blue Zone presentations. They feel more comfortable with them. Many executives believe that emotions have no part in business. If you have CEO aspirations, you may want to concentrate on the Blue Zone.

■ Audiences are more patient with Blue Zone presentations. They allow the presenter time to build his (or her) case. Is your personality suited for this kind of pacing? (Keep in mind that Blue Zone presentations must meet timetables, too, and ramblers are not tolerated.)

■ Blue Zone presentations are generally more persuasive than Red Zone presentations—but logic simply isn't as engrossing as emotion. Mario Cuomo may get standing ovations, but *most* Blue Zoners have to settle for polite applause.

■ Nothing wrong with a dash of drama, or a touch of emotion, in a Blue Zone presentation—but the main body of the message must be hammered out of stone.

The Red Zoners: Some representatives from past and present

The Reverend Jesse Jackson, despite an obvious effort to soften his speaking style, is captain of the Red Zone.
Jesse Jackson can be an emotional firestorm. His presentations frequently feed the emotional needs of his audiences, and their responses feed a need in him.

The unpredictable *Bobby Knight*, famed basketball coach, is a highly placed resident of the Red Zone. His range of emotions is as broad as any Shakespearean actor's.

If you have ever seen *Leo Buscaglia*, the author and lecturer who is perhaps America's leading advocate of "love," you'd probably put him in the more intense shadings of the Red Zone.

Senator *Joseph Biden* of Delaware is an interesting study in terms of red and blue. He has the instincts of an orator, the blinding smile of an actor, the genial tone of a talk show host, and yet he often registers—in his presentations to an audience—as the voice of reason. Reddish, bluish . . . maybe purple.

Barbara Jordan, ex-congresswoman and now a university professor, is a presenter of engulfing power. Her voice alone gives her an emotional resonance that can control any audience. When she speaks from strong content, which is usually the case, her presentation takes on the characteristics of an incantation.

Emotionalism of a different order is what audiences perceive in television personality *Barbara Walters*. Ms. Walters brings a personal tone to her presentations, but they are always very professional—sometimes blatantly theatrical. Her style is to explore the sensitivities of others without revealing too much of herself. Nonetheless, she generates a highly emotional atmosphere.

Jimmy Carter projects his feelings, but softly. His voice lacks authority, and the audience worries about him—not much, but enough to cause emotional discomfort.

Let's put down a few additional points to remember as you consider your own presentation style, and which zone is right for you.

■ Red Zone presenters elicit a feeling of participation from the audiences that is more emotional than intellectual. Reactions tend to be visceral.

■ Because their style is more outgoing, more personal, Red Zoners involve their audiences more quickly. Important perceptions are formed on sight. Judgments are also rendered more swiftly. And the judgments are usually clearly drawn. There is seldom much "middle ground" when Red Zone presenters appear.

■ With a Red Zone presenter, content is not the only message. The presenter is an important part of the message.

■ The Red Zone speaker is high risk, high reward. Red Zone speakers make things happen in a hurry.

Now let's see what we can learn down below—in the Gray Zone.

The Gray Zoners:

The Gray Zone engulfs people, swallowing them up in sameness. It's hard to tell one presenter from another, so we won't try to identify anybody. All we really care about is *you*.

Are you in there somewhere? You could be *without knowing it.* Idea: take this quiz and find out. It's not entirely serious—but it could give you some clues:

1. When you give your presentation to your mirror, do you get a little tired of it?
2. Does your particular part of a team presentation often get cut during rehearsal? Do people tell you it's because the entire presentation is running long, and it really has nothing to do with you? *Do you believe them?*
3. When you *do* present, do you find that you don't get many questions after your presentation? *Do you sometimes find that you don't get any questions at all?*
4. During rehearsals, do you find that your colleagues don't pay much attention to you? Do they even leave the room while you're presenting?
5. Do you find that your colleagues give you very general comments about your presentations? Example: "It's a little flat." Or, "Well, you'll probably be okay when we actually do it."

6. Do you find that a significant number of people peek at their watches while you're presenting?
7. Do you find that the eyelids of people in your audience tend to flutter and fall to "half-mast" while you're presenting?
8. Does it seem to you that there's a lot of rustling, scuffling in the audience, during your presentation?

If you answer "yes" or "well, maybe" to five or more of those questions, you could be sinking slowly into the Gray. Invisibility could be next. Don't chance it. Read on.

NOTE OF THANKS: Much of what you have seen here has been strongly influenced by the research of Richard Vaughn—Corporate Director of Research and Planning at Foote, Cone and Belding Communications, Inc.

29

How to pull yourself out of the Gray Zone.

1. **D**emonstrate your proposition. Don't just say it.

- Lectures are verbal, usually dull. Demonstrations are graphics, usually interesting. Lectures *state* the case. Demonstrations *prove* it.
- Do what great coaches always do. *Show us* what you mean. Make us *feel* the problem. If you want your audience to take action about the crowded subways, demonstrate how it feels to ride on one.
- Don't *tell* us to get more exercise. Show us three exercises we can do *at our desks today.*
- If it's easy to learn a foreign language, give us some phrases to *try* on each other *in German.*
- Your appearance and style should be a demonstration of your proposition. If your subject is "How to Handle Stress"—better be cool. If you're presenting a line of hair care products, *your* hair should look great.
- Demonstration forces you to get involved. This makes you more interesting to an audience, creates "pictures" in their minds—pictures to remember you by.
- If your presentation involves a product, show us how to use it. Demonstrate its value.

2. Use audio/visual aids that give you freedom.

- Some A/V aids are anchors. They make you static, boring, gray.
- Example: Overhead projectors are widely used. They don't work unless you stand there and feed them transparencies. You become a prop for the projector. Color you gray.
- If you're going to use a slide projector, ask for a remote control that gives you freedom to move—cordless, if possible.
- Try using *two* easels—to keep concepts and categories separate and to give you a reason to move.
- Example: One easel is for objectives, the other is for results. You compare, draw conclusions—referring to both.
- *Act upon your A/V aids.* They don't control you. You operate upon *them.* If you're using boards or charts, circle key words with a crayon or felt-tip pen. Underline figures, move things around. Make them *work* charts.
- There's nothing duller, grayer, than one presenter after another standing in the same spot—using the same set. *Change the environment.* Forget the lectern. Move the table. Turn up the lights. Start from a different point. Create your own environment that enables you to move freely.

3. *Improvise* within your knowledge.

■ Nobody improvises in a vacuum.

■ The technique of improvising is based on having compartments in your brain—and every compartment is filled with *terrific* material.

■ Every compartment has a label: recent headlines, personal experiences, funny stories, vivid pictures. Use whatever compartmental categories you want—it's your own mental filing system.

■ Associate each compartment with a visual that helps you remember it. Maybe the "Personal Experience" compartment has a picture of you as a kid—doing something crazy.

■ Let your brain roam freely, scanning those compartments, plucking out whatever serves the point you're trying to make.

■ Keep making connections. Your mind is loose, light, floating. You *know* you'll make another connection; you'll hook up—move ahead—always within your knowledge, always within the parameters of your presentation.

■ Surprise people once in a while. Improvise. Make them think "How did he (or she) ever think of *that*?"

4. Don't break eye contact for more than ten seconds.

■ Think of eye contact as the electric current that keeps audiences turned on. Turn off the current for more than ten seconds and you're going to disconnect the involvement you've generated.

■ Never hand out reading material before you're finished. If you do, your audience will start scanning the material (even if you tell them *not* to). You've lost them. The circuit is broken.

■ *Glance* at your audio/visual aids. Don't study them. They're reminders, triggers—not scripts.

■ As long as you're talking to an audience, maintain eye contact—at least every ten seconds. A disembodied voice, floating over an audience, is no longer in charge. Voice-overs don't get much recognition.

■ If you deliberately give up your eye contact, have a powerful substitute ready. And make sure it gets going without delay. (There's nothing worse than waiting in a dark room for a videotape or film to roll. Continuity suffers, minds wander.)

5. Be more of your strongest strength.

■ Don't imitate anybody. Be more of what you *are*.

■ Take a candid inventory of your strengths as a presenter. What are you *best* at?

- Acknowledge your weaknesses, but don't dwell on them. They're probably less noticeable than you think. They may even be strengths.
- Ask yourself, "How do I want to be perceived by my audiences? What would I like them to say about me after I have made my presentation?" In other words, how would you like to position yourself as a presenter to future audiences?
- Complete what you have started here. Fill out the presentation analysis in the next chapter. It's short, simple, and can be *extremely* revealing. It's the next step toward getting out of the Gray.

30

Are you the presenter you *think* you are? (A self-analysis to help you find out.)

Now, the toughest question of all for anybody who has ever had serious aspirations about being a presenter:

If you were going to describe yourself as a presenter without undue modesty, what words would you choose? Give us a candid capsule of yourself as the presenter you see in your mind's eye.

Most people, when put in this position for the first time, say something like this:

> "Well, I'd just like to be myself . . . you know . . . pretty much the way I am, just me. I'd like to come across as being natural."

Fine. You're headed down the right road. The determination to protect your own personality as a presenter can keep you out of more trouble than you can possibly imagine. A few words of explanation as we proceed:

> Starting-out presenters (and a host of seasoned presenters, too)—lacking a clearly defined style of their own—try to adopt someone else's style. More often than not, that "someone else" is the *boss.*

This may be flattering to the chief, but it can be disastrous for the rest of the staff—particularly if *everybody* tries to fit into the same presentation mold.

Even if the boss is better than average, the overall impression of a staff presentation will have a certain *déjà vu* quality to it—and if the boss is *mediocre,* there's going to be an understandable reluctance on the part of the staff to rise above that level.

So, hang on to your own hard-won identity. The question now— *what is it?*

The World's Easiest Self-Analysis

There are three things (all short, simple, and self-revealing) that will enable you to clarify your identity as a presenter and help you project it more effectively.

Think of this exercise as the world's easiest self-analysis (at least in presentation terms). Let's just stroll through the three points you'll be asked to examine:

What is your strongest strength as a presenter?
- *How this answer will help you:*
   By writing down your strongest strength, you will give your presentation style *a focus* that will differentiate you from other presenters and still retain what is most natural *to you.* Also, you will find that as your strongest strength begins to assert itself more forcefully, other positive aspects of your presentation identity will emerge.

What is the weakness that you consciously try to block out or eliminate?
- *How this answer will help you:*
   It will define the weakness so that you can address it and cut it down to size. A weakness can fester until it's acknowledged. Write it down; *expose it,* and you'll find "it wasn't such a big deal." Once you get things out in the open, they become much less fearsome.

What would you like your audience to say about you after you have made your presentation?
- *How this answer will help you:*
   It will give you a perception of yourself to *aspire* to. It will encourage you to develop a self-imagery that will feel comfortable to you. And you'll have to think about yourself in terms that your audience might use. That's always good practice.

Before you begin your own self-analysis, scan the quotes on the next couple of pages. You'll see how other presenters handled the same three questions you're about to consider. Names have been deleted for confidentiality, but all quotes are exactly as stated by the presenter.

Examples: "My strongest strength"
(Do any of these direct quotes sound like you?)

- "When I'm presenting at my best, I come across with good-natured confidence. There's nothing more exciting for me than communicating with people. I let my feelings show. I figure—why not?"
- "I really know this business. I can answer any question, resolve any issue that may come up. I have total faith in my knowledge."
- "I like the way I look."

- "I can make dry details come to life. I think of them as being alive, changeable, volatile. They're so lively, I have to *catch* them."

Examples: *"My weaknesses"*
(Do any of these direct quotes sound like you?)

- "I can't edit my own presentations, and I tend to resent it when others do it for me."
- "I blush. I turn beet red."
- "I'm confrontational. I can't help it. I want to score points."
- "I find that I work harder to make the audience like *me* than I do to make them understand and appreciate the *work*."
- "I'm intimidated by an unresponsive audience. I take on *their* mood."
- "I lose the thread. I'm sailing along, doin' good, then I *unravel*. I don't know where I'm at."

Examples: *"Perceptions of me"*
(Would you like your audience to perceive you with reactions like these?)

- "You know, I think that person could really turn our business around."
- "Let's hire her before the competition does."
- "He sees things differently. He would bring us a point of view we've never had here before."
- "She'll take care of us. I trust her. She gives me a good feeling about the whole place. She sets a good tone for it."
- "I got more out of that guy than from anybody else I've heard talk on that subject. He made me realize that what I have long suspected to be true *is* right for me—and it's time I took action on it."

Finished? How to use your self-analysis.

1. *Show your self-analysis to a colleague*—your own "Stanley Kubrick." It should be someone who has seen you make a presentation (either a rehearsal or the real thing). *Here's the crucial issue: Do you see yourself, as a presenter, the way other people see you?* Usually, self-analyses are remarkably close to evaluations by the people in your audience. But not always. Example: If you see yourself as au-

thoritative and your audience sees you as combative, some adjustments—obviously—need to be made.

2. *For your next presentation, emphasize your strongest strength.* If your strongest strength is solid blue logic, be *more* of that. If your strongest strength is anecdotal persuasion, be *more* of that. If your strongest strength is bringing data to life, be *more* of that. Be *the most* of what you do *best*.

Important Possibility: Take yourself *up* the chart, but don't neglect the *possibility* of "just visiting" the Red Zone if you're Blue; the Blue Zone, if you're Red. The important thing is to know where you belong. Once you know *that*, you'll have the confidence to do all kinds of things.

3. *Make sure your weakness isn't really a strength.* "Being different" is often endearing—and memorable. "Being perfect" is often suspect. Is the problem mainly in your mind, or is it really bothersome (ask "Stanley" for the audience's view). Okay, it's a real problem. Here are some real steps to take:

(A) *Confront* it in the mirror, or on a videotape (or an audiotape). Bring it down to its *real* scale. Know what you're dealing with. It's probably *less* than you imagined.

(B) *Apply* some of the *simple* techniques in this book (and others) to control matters. The *simpler,* the better.

(C) *Concentrate* on emphasizing your strongest strength and the weaknesses will diminish or just quietly go away.

4. *Those words you'd like your audience to say about you (the answer to Question #3 on your self-analysis)—run off a dozen copies.* Keep a copy in the file folder of every presentation you make. Read it at least once before every presentation. Pretty soon the words will stick in your mind. You will find that they will help you to *visualize* and *present* yourself as you want to be perceived by your audience.

Give yourself two minutes a question. Verbalize your thoughts as quickly as you can. Eloquence doesn't count. Candor *does*.

Presenter's Self-Analysis

1. What do you consider to be *your strongest strength*, as a presenter? When you are presenting *most effectively*—what do you think is working hardest for you?

_____

_____

_____

_____

_____

_____

_____

_____

2. What is the *weakness* that you consciously try to block out or eliminate?

_____

_____

_____

_____

_____

_____

_____

_____

_____

_____

_____

_____

3. What would you like your audience to say about you *after* you have made your presentation? How do you want to be perceived?

_____

_____

_____

_____

_____

_____

_____

_____

_____

_____

_____

PART FIVE

Understanding the audience. How to get inside their heads.

A NUGGET FOR YOUR NEXT PRESENTATION:
"Audiences are sensitive to signals."

He came rushing toward the platform as if he were running for a train. He reached the speaking area, held up one finger as people do when they've forgotten something and want us to wait for them, trotted back to his seat, picked up a bulging briefcase, and hauled it down to the platform.

He opened it up and started flipping through a vast stack of papers. He was looking for his script. He found it, held up his finger again—and said—"Jerry, do you have my slides?"

A voice from the back of the room said, "Did you give them to me?"

The speaker returned to his seat, and —from somewhere—pulled out a drum of slides. He walked briskly to the slide projector, waved his drum, and looked for Jerry. "Does anybody here know how to work this thing?"

Jerry emerged from a door (he'd been looking for the slides) and took the drum from the speaker—who returned to the rostrum.

"How's it goin', Jerry?"

The lights went out. A projector came on.

Blank screen. Click. A triangle, drawn by a rather shaky speedball lettering pen, replaced the blankness.

"Hope everybody can see that," the speaker said, still puttering, "because you're going to be lookin' at it for the next thirty minutes."

Behind me, I heard a loud whisper say, "Think I'll head for the bar."

NUGGET: An ill-prepared presenter sends a dramatic message to his or her audience: "I don't think you're very important. If you were, I'd be better prepared." Audiences are sensitive. They pick up signals and react to them personally.

31

How to become one with your audience— with a little help from Jackie Mason.

What is the most useful lesson to be learned about making presentations?

I've got a candidate for you, but in order to present it to you in all of its glory (are you ready for this?), we'll have to go to the movies.

GoodFellas is a Martin Scorsese film, adapted from a book called *Wise Guy* by Nicholas Pileggi.

The wise guys are brothers, full of camaraderie, who never quite trust each other. Beneath the swagger, there is always suspicion.

I should also add that wise guys use the F-word in an awesome variety of ways—as a verb, adjective, noun, adverb, *anything*. I have tried to minimize its frequency here, not because I'm a purist or anything, but because it really has nothing to do with why we're sitting here in the movie.

This is the scene.

A bunch of the guys are whooping it up at the local restaurant. They have self-defining names—Pete the Killer, Fat Andy, Freddy No-Nose, and Jimmy Two-Times (he says everything twice).

Then, there's Tommy (Academy Award winner Joe Pesci). Nobody has ever given Tommy a self-defining name because Tommy sort of defies description. He's just your run-of-the-Mafia homicidal maniac, and he tells a mean story—which is precisely what he's doing. He's telling, in his own likably obscene way, how he humbled a persistent cop who picked him up for loitering.

According to Tommy, the cop is giving him a hard time, grilling him, insisting that Tommy "tell him something."

"Tell me something"—the cop says. "Tell me something, tough guy." Tommy, of course, isn't about to tell the cop anything—but he is getting fed up with all the cajolery, all the "tell me somethings."

So, Tommy the wise guy says to the cop, "I'll tell you something. Go f___ your mother."

Oh no! He didn't really say that, did he? A moment of silence (even wise guys can be shocked), then deep rumblings of laughter convulse the table.

What a guy, that Tommy. What a beautiful sense of humor!

And Tommy rides the crest, building his story—adding insult to incest at the cop's expense.

The place is rocking. Nonstop. The laughter has reached a point where it is regenerative—one wave creating another.

Henry, Tommy's long-time partner, is holding his sides. The poor goombah can't stop laughing. That Tommy, what a funny, funny guy. It's wall-to-wall uproar.

Then, something happens.

The director, Martin Scorsese, pulls the plug.

He drains the laughter right out of the wise guys, and right out of the people in the theater.

Tommy suddenly says, "What do you mean . . . I'm funny?"

Oh, oh.

What's with Tommy? He's not laughing. The laughter, all around the table, is dying.

One of the wise guys tries to pull it back together. "You're just funny—a *funny* guy—the way you tell a story . . . and everything."

"Funny . . . *how?*"

The laughter dies a little more. There's no thunder in it now. Just fear.

"Nah, Tommy, you got it all wrong. . . ."

Yeah, yeah, yeah—comes the terrified chorus, well aware that Tommy might blow their f___ing heads off. But Tommy is determined to become even *less* funny.

"Funny? Like I'm a clown? I'm here to amuse you—is that it? *How* am I funny?" The wise guys are shutting up now, backing off.

The laughter has disappeared, the glasses have stopped tinkling—it's eerie.

And, in the sudden quiet of the surroundings, a phenomenon has occurred.

The audience is a mirror.

The *two* audiences, Tommy's pals *and* the theater audience, have followed Tommy right over the cliff. It has happened in two minutes—starting from rumbling laughter, then moving to nervous chatter, then to mumbling seriousness, then to silent fear.

Tommy has led his henchmen *and* the audience like a masterful conductor directing a symphony.

A drumroll of laugher here. A touch of tension there. An undercurrent of fear throughout.

Let's freeze the frame a second.

Tommy's mastery of his pals has been based on the most useful law of presentation:

The audience is a mirror of the presenter, mood for mood, minute by minute. Want to know how you're doing? Look at your audience.

Of course, it must be said that Tommy is no cupcake—that, in being a wacko of the first order, he does bring a certain intimidating presence to the scene.

But the phenomenon holds true, for Tommy or anyone else who makes presentations (or likes to tell stories). Where you lead, the audience is sure to follow.

■ If you're funny, they will laugh. If you're *not* funny, and try to be, they will be embarrassed for you.

■ If you're a nervous wreck, they will be uncomfortable.

■ If you are bored, they will drift with you—perhaps dozing off along the way.

■ If you wish you were back at the office, they will wish the same.

■ If you are having a good time, they will smile and enjoy themselves.

■ If you are constantly changing moods, they will strive to ride the roller coaster with you.

■ If you like them, they will like you.

■ If you *don't* like them, it will show. They won't be crazy about you.

■ If you tread upon their toes, they will respond in the only civilized way they can—and they will withdraw their toes. In extreme cases, they will kick you in the pants as you leave.

But, generally, audiences are forgiving. They would much rather be *with* you than *against* you.

It's time to *un*freeze Tommy back at the restaurant.

The place is still quiet. Anything could happen when Tommy gets like this.

Then Tommy—ever the wisecracking wise guy—blurts out, "Almost had you there, didn't I?" He laughs. He *laughs.* Don't you get it?

Everybody blinks in amazement, then the Mafia chorus begins to erupt around the table. Everybody's into it. Wild, guffawing laughter. Tommy, what are we gonna do with you? Such a funny guy! Such a funny, *funny* guy!

Tommy, that crazy goombah, has done it again. He has led his audience into a new mood. The reflection in the mirror has changed. No more fear, just good old macho Mafia after-dinner talk.

It is worth noting, as an eternal principle of presentation, that the *heartiest* laughter is reserved for the relief of tension.

The audience had followed Tommy at every turn—like recruits singing back the cadences of the drill instructor.

The audience follows the presenter, no matter what. Actually, there's a stop beyond—if you're willing to go for it. Once in a great while, the audience not only reflects the presenter's mood, *it becomes one with the presenter.* You have seen audiences—on TV and in "live" auditoriums—that have given themselves over to a presenter. Physically, mentally, emotionally.

You can see it in their faces, read it in their body language. The presenter can do no wrong. Every line is a winner. Every story is a smash. Every little wink of the eye, every little smile, everything that a presenter *says* and *does* is relished, treasured . . . *identified with!*

The audience has been captured and rendered helpless.

Question: how many audiences have you seen in this unique condition? It is not any excessive number. In the business world, it is close to never.

In an effort to *eliminate* the gulf between presenter and audience, let us ask ourselves what is it *exactly* that you have to do.

Becoming one with them.

1. *You must be able to see them, and they must be able to see you.*

If you expect to claim the crowd as your very own, and gain from them their support, you must be able to *see* them. If you turn the lights down, you've disengaged your support system. It's hard to give yourself over to a presenter who has become part of the scenery.

HISTORIC NOTE: During General Norman Schwarzkopf's now historic presentation following the hundred-hour ground war between Iraq and the Coalition Forces, *the lights in the briefing room stayed up.* The general, four stars gleaming on his collar, used his red-tipped pointer to trace the avenues of attack. His aide hoisted bulky graphic panels on and off sturdy stands as needed. The whole thing had the precision of a military mission. But throughout this fascinating performance, General Schwarzkopf was always the focus of attention. Always in command. Always easily visible. Would the presentation of "How We Won the War" have made so many prime time news broadcasts—and become a special TV event *by itself*—if the general had shown transparencies instead of panels and worked in the shadows?

Presentations in the darkness actually *increase* the distance between presenter and audience. To become one with an audience, don't be afraid of the light!

2. *The audience must sense that you are driven by some inner force that is overpowering (for you and them).*

Once in a while, you'll see somebody whose energy and persona almost bowl you over. Invariably, presenters of such magnetism are motivated by a raging need for approval—and when they are presenting, *they are most alive.*

Recently, in New York City, a performer in a one-man show actually made that admission: "The only time I'm really alive is when I'm *up here,*" he said, and you could see the truth shining in his eyes. His name is Rick Reynolds and he is *possessed* by that attitude which obligates certain presenters to succeed. These presenters *need* audiences like most people need air. It's something in the blood, or the brain, or somewhere. But it creates a force that most audiences recognize instantly, and don't really try to resist. They know the force is going to get them sooner of later. Jackie Mason has described this need, this compulsion, better than anyone else I've ever heard.

3. *The audience must sense that you know their business as well as you know your own.*

Generic presentations are history—gone with the era that awarded contracts and accounts on the basis of the presenter's credentials. "Look at all the great work *I've done . . . I* can do the same for you." It was a leftover of the "Me" Generation.

Today, the game is won or lost on the basis of how well you understand *our* business. How quickly you can put yourself into *our* situation—absorb *our* problems and then work them out.

A company president in charge of a regional sales conference in Kansas City made this comment recently:

"For years, we've had people come to our annual conventions and give us the same presentations they gave at somebody else's convention the day before—and somebody else's the day before that. That simply won't work anymore. We're way beyond that."

Presentations now are built on the prospect's future rather than the supplier's past.

There's this hoary old line that sticks in my mind: *"Don't tell me about your grass seed. Tell me about my lawn."*

Audiences will always reflect the attitude of presenters—giving back the good *and* the bad. That's a priceless lesson for any presenter.

But audiences rarely accept presenters so *totally* that audience and presenter become indivisible. That's presentation far *above* the norm. *So, you—obviously—are going to take a crack at it!* Terrific.

Here are your keys:

- See your audience as a mirror of yourself.
- Don't ever let the darkness get in the way of you and your audience.
- Allow yourself to *need* your audience as ardently as Jackie Mason and Rick Reynolds need theirs.
- Understand your audience as thoroughly as you understand yourself.
- Keep closing the gap. Keep reducing the distance. At the end of your presentation, you and your audience see things in exactly the same light.

Jackie Mason talks about presenting to people.

Jackie Mason was on CNN's "Larry King Live" not long ago. Mason was suffering through a sitcom which starred him and Lynn Redgrave. It was "Chicken Soup," and it was not a tasty brew. Jackie knew it. Everybody knew it. "Chicken Soup" sputtered along, nothing really working.

King asked him how he kept at it. Jackie smiled, and explained. He'd leave Manhattan every week and return to his old resort hotels in the Catskills where he got his start.

"You mean you'd work up there on the weekends, then come back into New York to do the sitcom?"

"Absolutely," Mason said.

"But why?"

"Because it's what I do," Mason said. "It's the best thing for me as a person. You walk out on a stage and you feel better right away. People are there to listen to you. Can you imagine? A bunch of strangers have gathered together to hear you! You can tell them what you think about anything. You can make them laugh! You can make them think. And they love you for it. Why not—they're having a good time. You're having a good time. You're getting paid for having a good time—saying what you think to people who are there to hear what you want to tell them. What could be greater that that?

173

Nuthin'. It's perfect. It makes me feel good. It gives me pep. I make a lot of friends. And, after doin' a few shows, I feel so great that I can come back into New York and do this terrible sitcom I'm doin'. . . ."

Mason is one of those rare presenters who enjoys such rapport with the audience that it becomes a part of his performance. It is an ongoing love affair, including his jousting with the fans in the first few rows. Above it all is Mason's absolute need to be there in front of people—"having a good time." You may not have Jackie Mason's talent, but even a little bit of his *attitude* will take you a long way in the right direction—*toward your audience.*

32

A simple structure for your next presentation. It's "All About Them."

Is there anyone anywhere who hasn't been forced to write a "speech outline" or a "thesis outline" or some other kind of outline following this nervous contour?

I.
    A.
    B.
        1.
        2.
        3.
            a.
            b.
            c.
        4.
    C.
    D.
II.

Outlines can frazzle your brain. Should "History of Manchuria" be a big A or a little a?

Most of the outlines I've seen have all of the appeal of a sleepless night. They look like very long grocery lists, with each item somehow rated by how far it's indented.

Outlines can be so boring to write that professional speech-writers often write the outline *after* the script. It's true. It's a bit like bombing the harbor and then writing the strategy (just in case anyone should ask).

Also, a complicated, cumbersome outline simply cannot be remembered. An outline should help you remember the path of your presentation. It should lend itself to graphic interpretation—so that you can make a map of it.

Your presentation structure, to be of any use whatsoever, must be simple enough to be remembered. It must be simple enough so that *you'll* remember what you want to say, and *your audience* will have no difficulty remembering what you told them.

John S. Wood, commercial attaché at the United States Embassy in Mexico City, is a tall, imposing presenter who uses a speech structure that is classic in its simplicity.

I asked him to draw me a picture of the structure he uses. He said "gladly" and scribbled this sketch on his paper napkin (he did the whole thing in about twenty seconds).

John Wood, it should be noted, is a superb storyteller (dialects, imitations, everything). And a tall, funny man from the U.S. Department of Commerce is a stellar attraction on the foreign service speaking circuit. John makes a presentation every other week. It is based on simplicity of structure, sturdy content, sandwiched with humor. You can't do much better.

In point of fact, the John Wood speech structure is a personalized variation of what has been fundamental to the subject since the time of Cicero.

I. The Opening
II. The Core
III. The Close

There are literally thousands of extensions and elaborations of that basic three-point structure, but—after reviewing dozens of them—I realized that John Wood's outline was surely the simplest, if not the best, and all the others would grind this chapter to an overloaded halt.

However, with all due respect to John, I did think that *Cicero* might be worth noting.

He wrote the first handbook for orators (somewhere around 100 B.C.) and his reputation as a speaker/orator has endured for over twenty centuries. That says something for his immortality. He was no slouch at defining structures either.

Here from a little crimson book of Cicero's called *Ad Herennium (Book I)*, "On the Theory of Public Speaking," are Cicero's rules of discourse:

Cicero's Six Rules of Discourse

I. Introduction ("get attention").

II. Statement of Facts (background). Emphasis on brevity, clarity, plausibility.

III. Division (areas of agreement, disagreement, decisions needed).

IV. Proof (positions on pending matters—with supporting evidence).

V. Refutation ("destruction of our adversaries' arguments"—Cicero was tough as nails).

VI. Conclusion (the end "formed in the accordance of art"). This meant, I assume, to remind your audience of its responsibility in the matters at hand and leave gracefully.

Should anyone wish to summarize, Sections I, II, and III could be called:

■ *Understanding the Problem*

Sections IV and V could be:

■ *Resolving the Problem (competitively)*

And Section VI could be:

■ *Taking Action (gracefully)*.

Cicero, incidentally, sounds pretty stern in his rules of discourse—but scan the rest of his theories on public speaking, and you get the feeling that he would endorse John Wood's structure, particularly the emphasis on "jokes, stories, and anecdotes." Listen to this, from Cicero's pen:

"If the hearers have been fatigued by listening, we shall open with something that provides laughter—a fable, a plausible fiction, a caricature, an ironical inversion of the meaning of a word, an ambiguity, innuendo, banter, a pun . . . a challenge or a smile of approbation directed at someone."

Cicero understood audiences, didn't he? *Wake them up,* he says. Tell a story. Banter. Pun. Smile. *Do something!*

Back there, in the dusty courtyards and bustling halls of Rome, it seems only natural that there would be lively conversations around heavy tables—leading directly to presentations of one kind or another.

"You know, there's an issue here that troubles me. It troubles me greatly, and we seem unable to deal with it."

It could be about anything. Politics. Law. Education.

"We were wondering if you could give us your point of view. Tell us how you see it."

The attention centers on one person in the group.

"Of course we'd want to know why you think as you do."

The person singled out now realizes that something must be said, some response.

"Then, if you have an idea, a proposal, we'd be glad to hear it."

And so, perhaps, the presentation begins—just as it does over thirty million times *every day* throughout the U.S.

The situation suggests a graphic structure that could be appropriate for your next presentation.

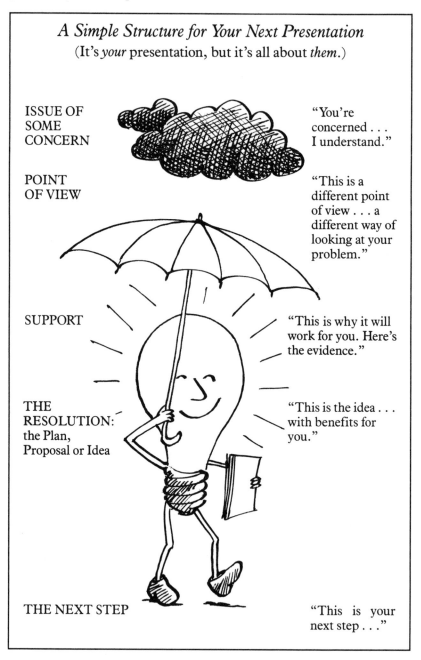

A Simple Structure for Your Next Presentation
(It's *your* presentation, but it's all about *them*.)

ISSUE OF SOME CONCERN — "You're concerned . . . I understand."

POINT OF VIEW — "This is a different point of view . . . a different way of looking at your problem."

SUPPORT — "This is why it will work for you. Here's the evidence."

THE RESOLUTION: the Plan, Proposal or Idea — "This is the idea . . . with benefits for you."

THE NEXT STEP — "This is your next step . . ."

Every part and parcel of that presentation concerns the audience. It *starts* with an issue of concern to the audience, and *ends* with "the next step" towards resolution of the issue. From start to finish the presenter is the guide—presenting his or her views, data, plans, ideas, processes—*but always talking in their (the audience's) terms.* Audiences invariably believe the best presentations are *all about them.*

The "All About Them" Presentation Structure

- *Start* with an issue of direct concern to the audience (it could also be an opportunity).
- *Provide* them with a different point of view, a different way of looking at *their* problem.
- *Back it up* with evidence.
- *Offer* a resolution (an idea!). Could be a proposal, plan, package, product. Mention the benefits.
- *Suggest* the next step to take. It should be as specific as possible.

The structure, "All About Them," may sound like a lot of homework for *you.* Not as much as you might suppose. Presentations do require audience analysis, and digging. But what you are really doing is applying your *knowledge strategically,* so that every bit of it relates directly to the self-interest of your audience.

"All About Them" can be used on any subject for any audience, because all audiences—probably even back in Cicero's day—are sitting there wondering, *"When is the presenter going to start talking about me?"*

33

What to wear
to a winning presentation
(when you're the presenter).

What you wear, when making a presentation, is one of the strongest components of what you communicate.
Here's why:

- Your clothes—or, more specifically, what you choose to wear—are pure, *nonverbal* communication. Clothes communicate almost instantaneously, as quickly as the eye can telegraph a snapshot to the mind.

- Clothes provide a self-portrait of *you*. You are what you wear. Fashion has drummed this concept into our minds—and it has achieved a certain credibility.

- Clothes are universal. Everybody wears them. Outside of a nudist camp, you won't find many audiences totally disregarding the importance of clothes.

Thus, you can't dismiss or pooh-pooh the relevance of clothes to your presentation effectiveness. They're *very* important.

What you wear tells us, your audience, two fundamental things:

—your perception of *yourself,*
—your perception of *us.*

Let's start with you:

For most people, clothes are a deliberate indication of lifestyle and attitude. Shirts and blouses speak volumes. Colors make announcements, sometimes loud and raucous—sometimes shy and muted.

Shoes talk. Wingtips say one thing; sandals, another. Scarves, jewelry, eyeglasses—they all make their own presentations of your taste and personality.

How do you see yourself? Your clothes give us, your audience, our very first clue. Your clothes communicate your aspirations for yourself. Unless you are standing behind a podium that covers up everything except your head, your audience is going to notice your clothes.

After all, you're *presenting* yourself—and clothes are part of the portrait.

Many presenters don't consciously think about what they're wearing—and that comes across, too. Color them gray, rumpled, diffident, unconcerned with the vagaries of passing fashion.

Here's the point: whether accurate or faulty, perceptions are going to be made—and your clothes will con-

tribute. You don't want to give your audience the wrong perception before you've even spoken a word.

Your style of dress should be an extension of your strongest strength.

Example: If you're a designer or interior decorator, why not show us your understanding of color and texture by the way you dress? Dress can be a demonstration of special talents as well as a projection of a special personality.

Another example, more subtle: If you're an analyst or financial consultant, why not wear an outfit that is nicely coordinated—that comes together naturally—just as the pieces of a deal or transaction fit together in your mind?

Will your audience make this subtle connection, or is it *too* subtle, *too* subliminal? Even if most of your audience doesn't make the precise connection between a well-coordinated outfit and a well-ordered mind, they'll see you as successful—and that's not half-bad. Audiences relate success to dress.

There is absolutely nothing wrong in selecting clothes that strengthen the perception that you want to project. *Who says that presenters must blend into the woodwork?*

Before we go any further with this, there's something you should know about audiences:

Most audiences tend to be suspicious of presenters who show up in unfamiliar garb.

If you're not known for your unique wardrobe, it's not wise to appear on the scene in black leather and heavy metal.

If you're not Willie Nelson, you're probably well advised to leave your headband at home and get a haircut (or at least a trim). If you're not Joan Collins, beware of cleavage. Celebrities can be a bit scandalous (it's expected), but strangers in strange outfits are simply regarded as oddities.

Let's see if we can construct a rule for at least *most* of the time:

Dress in a manner that projects your strongest strength, but don't *shock* your audience (unless you're famous and people love you for your eccentricities). As John Wood of the U.S. Department of Commerce says, "You must blend in with your audience, but you must also be memorable."

Another thing (perhaps the most important thing): you should be comfortable. You should feel good about what you're wearing.

NOTE: Disregard all of those courtroom dramas you've seen. You know the ones I mean. Courtroom attorneys seem to think that a subway mugger poured into a pinstriped suit will register on the jury as a pillar of the community. A mugger in a Wall Street suit invariably looks like nothing more than a very uncomfortable mugger.

Don't dress to project a personality that isn't yours. You'll just be miserable.

A few other tips to improve how the audience perceives you:

1. Take the stuff out of your pockets that make them look stuffed. The eyeglasses, the wadded-up handkerchief, the airplane ticket to Phoenix, the grocery list, the taxi receipts, the notepad from the hotel, *all that stuff.*

2. Remove the objects from your clothes that make noise. The coins that jangle. The pills that clatter in their little plastic vial. The keys on their chain. Some presenters walk across a stage or platform and sound like a pick-up truck from the Salvation Army. Your clothes can create *audio* impressions as well as video.

3. Some presenters use their clothes as "props." A tie loosened at the collar, a coat removed and tossed across a chair—such touches of theatrical business can communicate intensity, informality, a shirt-sleeves approach.

A woman, hands in pockets of a very chic designer outfit, can register poise, sophistication, thoughtfulness.

Using what you wear to help create desired perceptions is simply utilizing one of your best means of communications.

Clothes don't just cover, they *communicate.* They don't just protect you, they project you. They present your perception of yourself.

What about the other half of the equation? What about *your* perception of *them*—the people out there in your audience? What do your clothes say about *them?*

The answer is short and simple. It is so unsophisticated that it probably predates the invention of fashion.

We tend to like people who, on special occasions, get a little bit dressed up for us. Nothing splashy. Nothing flashy. "Just a little bit" dressed up.

Your presentation to any audience is one of those special occasions. By dressing up a notch, by dressing appropriately but with obvious care—you're showing your audience that you think *they are important.*

They look at you and they *see* that you want to make a good impression. That's a nice form of flattery. Presenters aren't the only people who appreciate a little praise.

NOTE: When someone in your audience peers at you and whispers, "Hey, that must be the speaker," you've probably dressed just right.

Now, nobody's expecting you to rush out to Gucci's and spend a fortune before your next speaking engagement—or put your paycheck into a lush new wardrobe—but it certainly won't hurt you to wear your nicest, most becoming sports outfit to a presentation you're going to make at LaCosta, the Greenbrier, or the local country club.

It certainly won't hurt you to wear your newest, best-fitting business suit to that executive staff meeting you've been asked to brief.

Compliment your audience by what you wear. Let your clothes communicate that you think your audience is important. Yes, you got "a little bit dressed up"—and you hope it shows. After all, *they're worth it.*

That's a perception that any self-respecting audience will applaud.

34

Palaver:
Is it helpful, harmful, or just hot air?

It's fashionable to be *anti-meeting* these days. Most people tend to think there are too many meetings, or they last too long, or they're badly handled. All of which has considerable merit, but there seems to be one part of most meetings which is seldom, if ever, criticized.

Let's call it the *palaver* section.

There's *harmless* palaver.

—"Boy, are we ever glad to be here today and have this chance to get acquainted. We have admired your company for so long . . . and we have so many things in common that . . ." Palaver, palaver.

—"Did you see that football game on TV yesterday? Wasn't that some kind of game? How 'bout that last quarter?"

Then, there's the weather, the traffic, the weekend. It's all harmless palaver that may, in fact, be useful in some localities. It's just part of the culture.

Self-conscious palaver is something else. It doesn't serve any useful purpose. It simply articulates the presenter's self-consciousness—and the audience doesn't really give a damn.

—"Gee, thanks a lot, Charlie, for putting me on the program right behind that fellow from L.A. I don't have any films or videotapes like he did—all I've got are some sheets of paper. But I'll try to make this as painless as possible for everybody."

This is the presenter being self-conscious about being badly prepared. The expectations of the audience aren't enhanced by this kind of talk, but it is essentially the presenter covering his own sense of inadequacy.

Here's another case of self-conscious palaver:

"You know so much more about this subject than I do that I feel sort of silly getting up here and . . ."

The presenter is telling us that he (or she) is on shaky ground.

Phil Hoadley, a corporate banking executive of long experience, told me that a presenter who admits to knowing *less* than his audience is letting himself in for a *massive* dose of stress. It figures. The presenter has deliberately cast doubts on his own credibility.

And, finally, there is the type of palaver that is important to the presenter but causes needless concern for the audience:

"I think I feel a little indigestion coming on.
What do you say we take a break and I'll take a
bromo . . ."

This is telling the audience more than it really needs to know. Now, the audience will begin to worry about the presenter and forget about the presentation.

One final example:

"We have been on such a roller coaster here lately
that we're lucky to be here."

What roller coaster? Lucky? How come?

Palaver can provoke nervousness about the presenter. Yet presenters often feel compelled to reveal what's bothering *them* before they even begin to consider the needs of the audience.

Without further palaver, here are five suggestions for dealing with it:

1. If you feel that you must warm up your audience with a layer of palaver, get *one* person to do it—the first speaker. An audience doesn't have to be *re*warmed before every presentation. Once is enough (some meetings turn into *pure* palaver).
2. Be conscious of palaver. It's the filler, the guff, the platitudes, the "necessary words" that aren't really heard.
3. Resist the urge to chatter, self-consciously—to make excuses, or make amends for your inadequacies. It will simply draw attention to them.
4. Don't tell your audience what's bothering *you* if it really has nothing to do with *them*. Once you tell them that you're in trouble, they'll be troubled—distracted from the purpose of the meeting, and there goes your presentation!
5. Try an opening line for your presentation that goes right to the heart of your presentation. One of the most effective presentations in recent memory started with these three words: *"Information Reduces Risk."* Everything thereafter related to that singular thought.

Don't get me wrong. Palaver has its place, but it's not as harmless as most presenters think. And it consumes a lot of precious time.

If your presentation is running long, or seems slow—or any of those other complaints that are frequently made about meetings—the problem could be palaver.

The audience is much older—
or much younger—than you.
Either way,
the Age Gap can be trouble.

"That kid can't be more than twenty-five years old—and he's up there telling *me* how to sell my cars. He's never run a dealership—never had to meet a payroll—never worked a used-car lot. What can he know? I'm supposed to let him spend my advertising budget? *He's just a greenhorn kid!*"

> *—An automobile dealer in Wichita watching his advertising agency present the spring advertising campaign.*

"Who is *that*? She's got to be fifty—maybe even fifty-five, and *she's telling us* about the trends in retailing. She reminds me of my Aunt Jane. I expected somebody like me—you know, *tuned in.*"

> *—A magazine staffer listening to a market research consultant present lifestyle trends affecting the market place.*

The two presentations are occurring simultaneously—hundreds of miles apart.

The young business school graduate presents his agency's recommendations to a group of veteran automobile dealers in Wichita. Each dealer contributes a share of the advertising monies, so the dealer's involvement is intense, to say the least.

The market research consultant with twenty-five years of experience presents her company's findings to an editorial staff meeting in New York City. The average age in the conference room, *excluding the speaker,* is about thirty.

Both presenters are encountering the same problem.

They are talking to audiences who were expecting a presenter of a very different age—and, because of that age gap, the presenter's authority is being questioned.

It happens every day. It is not unique to any business, or any region of the country. And as more and more companies "restructure" their staffs, the middle levels are dropping away—being eliminated—leaving the bright, eager "young Turks" and the seasoned, tradition-oriented "mature executives." Often, they confront each other.

Resentment usually stays below the surface, simmering, yet coloring the discussion. And it creates a tension in audiences that can become a sort of self-induced guilt blanket. (Everybody *knows* the presenter's age isn't going to change just because it makes the audience cynical.)

What's to be done?

Here's a distillation of suggestions and insights from presenters who encounter the Age Gap problem almost every day:

1. *How you dress* is very important in situations where your age could work against you. If you're *older* than your audience, wear your least conservative outfit (that doesn't mean you have to come on looking like the latest creation from Paris—but it *does* suggest that you pick one of your livelier numbers from your current wardrobe). If you're *younger* than your audience, wear your *most* conservative outfit. This doesn't mean "somber," but it *does* suggest *seriousness.* You don't have to look like Daddy Warbucks, or a female version thereof, but it won't hurt to show them that you think this meeting is *extremely* important.

The point here is simple but sensitive: ***Don't encourage*** ***negative stereotyping by what you wear.*** **Besides, for some of the more enlightened members of your audience,** ***attitude*** **is more important than** ***age***—**and, for them, dress can be a mirror reflection of how you think about things.**

2. *Consider the age of your language.* If you're *older* than your audience, go easy on the nostalgia and references to personal history. "Back when I was getting started in this business . . ." is an automatic tune-out for most audiences, particularly younger groups, no matter what the rest of that sentence turns out to be. Previous affiliations with now-defunct companies needn't be glorified. "I used to be national sales manager of the Hudson Motor Car Company," isn't going to impress many people.

George Burns can say, "You know, used to be—when me and Gracie were playing Peoria . . ." and the audience will howl. But listen carefully and you'll notice that he always relates his recollection to something that is happening *now.* The past is interesting only to the degree that it affects the future. Besides, audiences *love* George Burns. Who else could puff on a monstrous cigar, sing off-key while shuffling through a small dance, and make us believe he's really a Casanova?

If you're *younger* than your audience, be careful of those phrases like "you guys" when addressing the whole group. Playful and affectionate though it may be, it can make a mixed audience of mature vintage *cringe.*

"You know" is another youthful phrase that irritates older ears. When used between every unfinished thought, "you know" becomes a ceaseless, shamelessly inarticulate reminder of the age differential. After a while, audiences may be tempted to say, "*No*, I don't know."

Don't let your language contribute to negative stereotyping. Listen for it when you hear yourself on tape—then do some self-editing on your next presentation.

3. *Keep in mind the one inexorable law of human nature that's working for you.* Whether your audience is quietly older or brashly younger than you are, here's the thing to put firmly in the front of your head when you get up to speak:

They are far more interested in themselves and their problems than they will ever be in how old *you* are.

Once you have accepted that snippet of psychology, your tactics become clear (and pretty easy):

■ Address their problems as *quickly* as possible and apply your *full* knowledge to the solutions. Do your homework. Don't let them think, for one moment, that you're giving them a "pat" presentation. "Generic presentations" simply won't work on audiences who think they're special. Show them that you have worked hard to help them, *really help them*, and the Age Gap will evaporate.

■ Don't patronize their age bracket. Don't give them the feeling that you're on the outside looking in. Just don't mention age *at all.* It's irrelevant. Once you get into answering their needs, it doesn't really matter how old you are, how tall you are, or whether you have had a slight stammer since childhood. What matters is how effectively *you help them.*

There are a few other points you may want to keep in mind, and no audience in the world will dispute either one of them:

■ Experience is a teacher that's hard to beat, and the only way to get it is to *live* a few years . . . usually quite a few. That's a nice little credential for presenters who have accumulated some hard-earned living time.

■ The future is usually reserved for the young. This may be unfair, but that seems to be the system. And the future holds a certain irresistible allure for almost everybody. That's not a bad break for youngish presenters who represent, for better or worse, *the future.*

Moral: Accept what you are, but don't give your audience any excuses to apply negative stereotyping. Actress and author Ruth Gordon used to ask this question: "How old would you be if you didn't know how old you are?" That's how old you want to be when you present yourself.

36

What audiences
know
(without being told).

Very few audiences have more than a modicum of knowledge about presentation technique. They have probably never heard of *group dynamics* (and couldn't care less). "Body language" is something that remains fairly fuzzy in their minds. And speech pathology is a course they *didn't* take, or even consider, when they went to school.

Yet, in some strange, mysterious way, audiences *know* more than presenters ever give them credit for. Audiences have a sixth sense that flashes sharp, clear signals to their brains—and the signals are invariably accurate. *Never underestimate the sensitivity of an audience.*

1. *Audiences know how you feel that day.* They'll read your energy level within the first ninety seconds. If you get up in the morning and don't know exactly how you feel, you'll find out pretty quick. Your audience will detect your feelings *and play them right back to you.* If you're grumpy, watch out! (*Personal Aside:* I call my ninety-two-year-old mother every day. The moment she picks up the phone and says, "hello," I can tell what kind of day she's had.)

2. *Audiences know if you don't like them.* Everything you do will seem slightly reluctant to them. Or confrontational. Almost every question becomes a problem. Voices get thin and edgy. A presentation where dislike simmers below the surface is *not* unlike the Titanic heading out to sea on a cold night.

3. *Audiences know when you've memorized your presentation.* The act of memorizing instills the fear of forgetting.

Once the audience realizes that you're reciting lines you've memorized (everything sounds like it was chipped out of granite), they'll start to worry if you're going to make it through to the end. Every pause will present the unsettling possibility that you have forgotten your lines. Moral: *don't memorize.* It's hard on you. It makes audiences uneasy.

4. *Audiences know when you're lying. They know when you're bluffing.* Eye contact crumbles. Voices grow thin. Your colleagues squirm. The moral: don't even *think* about lying. It alienates audiences like nothing else.

5. *Audiences know when you're giving them a sales pitch.* Something inside of them says, "This bird is trying to sell us a bill of goods." Contrary to all popular sales folklore, audiences don't like to be sold. They like to be entertained, helped, even *taught*, but I never heard an audience say, "Gee, I hope somebody tries to sell me something today."

6. *Audiences know when you've given up on yourself (they'll think*

you've given up on them). Recently, in a new business presentation for a $75 million national advertising account, the creative director—presenting a crucial part of the agency's effort to win the business—said "I've got this thing so screwed up I'll never get it straightened out." This was uttered as a sort of aside to himself, but it was loud enough for the audience to hear. Now, this kind of candor isn't a big confidence builder for an audience expecting to be dazzled. Can't blame an audience if they hunker down and expect the worst. This, of course, makes the presenter feel like he's been abandoned at sea.

Moral: Even if the power goes off, the slide projector explodes, or the audience refuses to crack a smile at your funniest stories—plow ahead. Keep your poise. Keep your energy level up. Don't throw in the towel. Ovations are often awarded to those who survive.

37

Questions that often float through the minds of audiences.

Audiences do a lot of daydreaming and talking to themselves. That's because many presenters don't do a good job of registering decisively on an audience's consciousness. So, the audience asks itself a lot of questions.

Here are some that you have probably asked yourself, sitting out there in the audience. But the main point to keep firmly in mind is that these are probably the very same questions that audiences have asked about *you.*

IMPORTANT: Every "he" could be a "she" in the ten points below, and vice versa (but you already knew that).

1. *"Is this presenter alive?"* A good way to consider this question, realistically, is in terms of The Pickpocket Test. Pickpockets, you see, are the only professionals in the world who make their entire livelihoods from watching body language. If somebody walks briskly and seems alert, the pickpocket will stand aside. If the "victim" walks slowly and seems uncertain of where he's going, the pickpocket moves in for the hit. *Many presenters would draw pickpockets like flies.*

2. *"Am I glad I came?"* This question is usually asked shortly after the presenter gets underway. If the answer is "no," the next question is, "Who talked me into this thing?" This is generally followed by a long, low sinking feeling that the next ten minutes will stretch into infinity.

3. *"Is this presenter a phony?"* If there is the slightest suspicion that the answer is "yes," a string of silent questions will be hurled at the presenter. "Who is this guy really trying to help—him or me? How much did he get for coming here anyway? Does he even know I'm here?" And so on. It is not wise to be regarded as a phony. Sometimes, it is not even safe.

4. *"Does this presenter really have an idea I haven't heard before?"* Or is this an old record being played at a new speed? Am I hearing something new, or am I hearing something that *sounds* new?

> *Herb Zeltner,* marketing professional, asks this question: "What's the burning issue here?" If there is no "burning issue," the presentation is likely to fade quickly.

5. *"Is this presenter giving me everything he's got*—eyes, face, body, brain, personality, energy—or is this person just passing through town?"

6. *"Have I nodded my head at least once* in recognition of the

inescapable truth of what that presenter is saying?" Is there the slightest kernel of truth here—or am I getting a hot blast of hype and drive?"

> *Jane Maas*, advertising executive, put this point into words that have a rich and classic ring: "Preserve me from presenters who ramble in ever-widening circles until they disappear from your consciousness."

7. *"Am I really getting the point—*or do I just *hope* I'm getting the point?"* Is there a point to get? If the person sitting next to me whispered, "What's this guy trying to tell us?"—could I provide a nice, clear answer in two sentences or less? Or would I start out with, "Welllll, you know . . ."?

8. *"Does this presenter have a persona* that I will remember a year from now?" How about a day from now?

9. *"How much longer is this thing supposed to last?"* This question is accompanied by coughing, shuffling, and watch-glancing. The most memorable quote ever uttered on this problem came out of the mouth of a marketing whiz named *Fred Lemont*:

> "I'd like to have all presenters *wired*—so that when they go on for too long, I can momentarily stun their tongues into silence."

10. *"Will I be quoting anything this presenter has told me—*or passing along his views to my colleagues?" Have I taken a single note? Has *anybody* raised a pencil? If no one has written anything down, chances are nobody is really planning on remembering anything. *Not* a good sign.

This little list makes a pretty good checklist for the next presentation on your calendar. It also makes a pretty good checklist for *you* when you're looking into the mirror, rehearsing your next presentation.

38

"Who wants to get hit by a truck?"

The group of twelve settled into their chairs for what would undoubtedly be a pleasant presentation. Marie Claire* was known for her years of service at the company, and for her mothering attitude. Marie Claire was something of an institution.

She was also the manager of creative services, an elusive title meaning she managed the budget for such things as art supplies, production services, audio/video equipment, and—most importantly—creative personnel . . . writers, art directors, and others striving for success in the uncertain world of sales and marketing. Many of those people were seated before her now.

For some reason, Marie Claire seemed uncharacteristically tense. Her voice sounded like it had been strained through a carrot shredder. It didn't take long to find out why.

Her subject hit the audience like a meteor that had been lobbed up like a softball. "Just a modest budget reduction," she said huskily. The audience would have to find ways to "stretch supplies"—an "essentially creative" task, she explained. They would have to operate leanly, cut time that was nonproductive (she had never thought much of "staring out the window" in the face of onrushing deadlines). Economy was good for the soul, she said. It produced not only harder work, but better work.

Marie Claire was ticking off a laundry list of budget cuts, serving them up in a graphic and remarkably positive fashion. She seemed better now, animated in a sharply edged way, returning to her theme that cutting costs was good for creativity. Therapeutic, she said. She finished on that note. *Therapeutic.*

The first question whistled through the air like a bolo knife. "Are you *telling* us about these cuts, or are you *asking* for our opinion?" A softly defiant murmur rose in the room.

"I'm telling you what I have been told," she said. "Cuts must be made."

"But what about all this other junk you're giving us," another voice asked. "Do you really believe that we can be more creative when we've got less to work with? You don't expect us to buy that, do you? That's b____t."

Marie Claire could not bring herself to repeat the word. "Call it what you will," she said, "but if you want to work here in the foreseeable future, you'd better be ready to change your attitude. This place is going to work more economically in the future, and the work

---

*Not her real name. But everything else is true.

201

is going to improve as a result. That's my mission—and yours as well. At least, it better be."

There. Everybody heard it. A bare-faced *threat*. Silence settled in, the questions faded. Slowly, one by one, the employees got up and left the room. Marie Claire gathered up her presentation materials. It was going to be a long day.

What have we learned?

Presentations where the audience is taken to task *never* work out well. Fear is a lousy motivator. People who must work under "do it or die" pressure usually turn into a mass of tightly strung piano wires. They jangle on each other's nerves. What used to be teamwork and pride begin to foul the forces that have threatened them. Attitudes turn. Atmospheres change.

I have never seen an effective presentation where the presenter gets into a truck *loaded with complaints* and slams into the audience. It happens more often than you might guess. It happens in places where it would have been considered unthinkable a few years ago.

IBM scolds its own.

IBM, for example. Always ahead of its time in terms of hiring people and keeping people, IBM recently decided to read the riot act to its own employees.

"The tension level is not high enough in this business—everyone is too damn comfortable at a time when the business is in crisis," fumed the CEO.

"I used to think my job as a [sales] rep was at risk if I lost a sale. Tell them theirs is at risk if they lose one," the CEO continued—speaking bravely *through* the supervisors of his company.

The tirade went on and on, duly reported by the *Wall Street Journal, Business Week,* and others. Letting anger take over, the CEO drove a truck full of grievances into his employees.

IBM is a company which has had a more clearly defined corporate culture than any other major firm in recent memory. "We will not let you fail" was the positioning battle cry that promised every customer that IBM was behind them. That was back in the '60s. Employees responded with the energy and pride inherent in that compelling promise.

Now, the call goes out to the supervisors to ride hard on their people—fire the ones that don't show enough tension.

Of course, customers and prospects will see the fear. Fear is such a palpable thing. The *fear* of being fired is a very different feeling than the *responsibility* of never letting a customer fail. One wears you down. The other bolsters you up.

A presentation that hammers its audience is going to lower morale and generate fear.

When you lose respect for your audience, you have lost your audience. That goes for Marie Claire. And the chairman of IBM. And any other organization that whacks its employees from above.

Never slam an audience.

Presentations must be essentially positive. That doesn't mean they have to be sugar-coated or superficial. It simply means that the audience must walk out of that room feeling *more* capable, not less. They must be more conscious of the *strengths* in them than the weaknesses.

They must go home and want to tell their wife, husband, kids, whoever is important to them, that the boss has put more faith in them to do a *bigger* job rather than less faith because they're doing such a *stinking* job.

Presentations that slam the audience are dumb.

They make everybody feel rotten—except, perhaps, the presenter. And any presenter who feels better after telling people they're a bunch of lazy louts may be simply tranferring the blame rather than taking it. Next time, the people may just get up and leave the room *before* the presentation is over. Who can blame them? Who wants to get hit by a truck?

39

The Man
in the Box

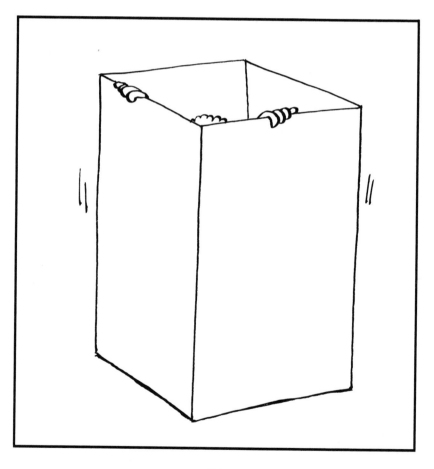

A young advertising man named Jim Wise gave one of the best presentations on making a presentation I have ever seen.

He's an art director, and when I saw him deliver his presentation, he was working for an agency in Atlanta, Georgia.

Here's how I remember it:

He moved quickly into his proposition: To really communicate with an audience, you've got to escape from the everyday routine of your own life and get inside the mindset of your audience.

Fair enough. His audience settled back to hear about it. But, like most outstanding presenters, Jim had a surprise for us.

He reached into his pants pocket and pulled out a roll of white tape. He kept on talking.

"You know, every one of us lives inside a box."

Suddenly he's on one knee. He begins to peel the tape off of the roll. With an art director's sense of style and proportion, he starts to form the outline of a box on the floor. He's using the tape, gently but firmly pressing it onto the carpet—*enclosing himself within the box.*

He talks as he works:

"Our boxes, for each of us, are the individual routines of our lives. We get up at the same time every day, brush our teeth with the same toothpaste, eat the same breakfast, read the same paper, take the same route to the same job, stare out of the same window—and probably say the same things to the same people. You know something? Your world becomes your box."

He stands up, still within his box—neatly formed on the floor. He looks down at the bars of white tape.

"You've got to get out of your box."

He steps out of his box and starts to walk around. He's looser now, the words seem to flow more easily. The dynamics inside the room change. The room itself seems bigger.

He proceeds to tell us how he looks at the world through another person's perspective.

"If I'm trying to understand a writer, maybe someone I'm working with, I'll sit down and try to *write* something—to see how it feels to fill up a page with words, or express a thought that I had only *pictured* in my mind before."

He then tells us about getting married and, on occasion, having an argument with his wife.

"Now I try to see it from her point of view (which isn't always easy) and when that doesn't work, I say to myself, 'How would Elvis Presley deal with this situation?'"

A funny thought, but the principle is serious.

Most of us operate, day after day, within the self-imposed confines of our own boxes. Presentations suffer from parochialism—from the rantings of "soapbox orators" who never bother to find out what their audiences are thinking.

Before you tell somebody else what to do, spend a little time inside that person's world.

It's not hard to do.

■ If you're going to make a presentation to an audience of stockbrokers, call your own broker and ask him or her if you can spend a few hours soaking up the atmosphere of a busy financial center. Listen to the calls come in. Where do the problems come from? Watch the stock prices change and see if you can pick up the patterns of the day. Note the language of Wall Street. See how it *feels* inside the pressure cooker of a broker's office.

■ If you're going to talk to a grocer's association, spend a morning in a supermarket—watching the manager, asking questions, sensing trouble spots.

Or, at the very least, get on the phone and talk to three or four store managers, "How's business? Where's the competition coming from? What's happening to produce prices? How do you see the future?" Tell them you're making an important presentation to the grocery industry. They'll talk to you.

Get out of your box and find out what's happening in all those other boxes, especially those boxes where your audience lives. Remember—they'll be evaluating you and your presentation from inside *their* boxes. Better know what it's like in there.

The young art director was finished with his presentation. He carefully removed the tape from the floor, but the symbolism of it stayed—indelibly imprinted where extraordinary presentations always leave their mark . . . on the memory of those lucky enough to have been there.

40

The audience needs
a break—but when?

If you receive a message like this, sort of mashed and desperate looking, you've been presenting too long without giving your audience a break.

There are other "give me a break" signals, and you should have no trouble detecting any of them.

Recently, I attended a one-hour and forty-five-minute talky, tedious drama *presented without a break.* About forty minutes into the tedium *(Aunt Dan and Lemon),* I started watching the audience, sketching the postures of bored people enduring life without a break.

Head down, right hand over eyes. Then, head down, left hand over eyes.

Examining glasses—squinting through lenses, as if they were at fault, responsible for what he sees, how he feels.

Head being held by hand, as if the head had lost consciousness.

Glasses off, arms crossed, right leg propped on back of chair, then the left leg gets the chair.

Hand rubbing something out of eye—trying to erase the scene, trying to stay awake.

One finger at temple . . . what does all this mean?

208

Head looking reso-
lutely away from
stage—refusing to
be involved. Hand
protecting brain
from damage.

Deep, heavy sighs—
"How much more
can I endure?"

Pulling on ear,
resisting what he's
hearing.

Knuckles rapping
quietly on the chair.

Arms crossed, legs
crossed, head low
on chest. Trapped.
Besieged.

It's amazing how tolerant and polite audiences are. They can survive a lot of pain, but in an audience that needs a break, you can always detect the ceaseless body movement, the nervous fidgeting, the shifting of weight, the scuffing of shoes, the restless discomfort of needing to be "released"—to take a break.

When things get too insufferable, audiences often resort to more direct means.

■ Someone will shout out, "How about a break?" Others will chime in, reluctant to be the first complainer, but more than willing to join the chorus.

■ One by one, they get up and leave. They don't say anything. They just leave. Everybody knows where they're going.

When the audience is doing everything from writing "desperation notes" to trooping, one-by-one, out of the meeting room, you—as the presenter—have a duty to perform.

Call a break. Let the poor devils go.

But you know it and they know it: *you have waited too long.* It's always best to anticipate the needs of an audience rather than to respond to them once they have become urgent.

There is a rule of good sense to be observed in most cases: Give your audience a break every half-hour. A break doesn't have to be more than five minutes, but it should be strictly adhered to.

> *SUGGESTION:* When you call the break and give
> your audience a specific time at which to return,
> appoint someone in the audience to be responsible
> for getting everybody back on time. This does some
> interesting things. It makes that person feel impor-
> tant. It creates a little good-natured fun. And it
> removes the "herding" job from your shoulders and
> allows you to do other things (more about that in a
> minute).

The idea of a break every half-hour has many precedents. Most television shows don't last over thirty minutes. Many sporting events are broken into halves—a National Basketball Association half, for example, has twenty-four minutes of actual playing time. Most plays and musicals are broken up into two or three acts (except for the tortuous *Aunt Dan and Lemon*), and you seldom find a show that runs much over two hours.

If people get uncomfortable sitting for long stretches of time at Broadway hit shows and professional sporting events, what does that tell you about your presentation?

No offense intended—but you owe those people a break. It's just good manners. "Oh, oh"—says the presenter—"I'm not so sure I want to do that. I have been allotted a certain amount of time and I've got an enormous amount of material to cover." Or, "If I call a break, I'm liable to lose my audience." Or, "We're usually running so far behind schedule, there's no time for breaks."

> *Here's the point:* the minute you start to worry about
> yourself—how much *you've* got to cover, how late
> *you* already are, whatever—thereby ignoring the
> condition of your audience, you're headed for deep
> trouble. Audiences invariably put *their* needs ahead
> of *your* needs. It's not even close.

"Breaks" can be very useful for *you* as well as nice little rewards for your audience.

"Breaks" give you a chance to take a reading on how you're doing. If your audience has been unresponsive, ask a few people for their off-the-record comments. Maybe something's happening you didn't even know about. (They're worried about a management change, they're concerned about a possible client loss. Who knows? But, after you're informed, you'll be better able to cope, and the more you know about your audience, the better.)

Taking a break will give you a chance to do something about any nettlesome problems you've noticed. The room is too hot. The room is too cold. The ventilation sounds like a thrashing machine. Lights are flickering. You can, at least, *ask* if anything can be done. (It's always better to get it fixed during the break, not during your presentation. Maintenance people on stepladders are tough competition.)

Well, here they come—your audience trooping back from the "break." Maybe you've made a few editing changes based on the comments you've heard. Maybe the room is functioning better. Maybe one or two of your colleagues have made some insightful suggestions.

One thing's for sure: *Your audience looks better* (maybe they got good news when they made those phone calls). Most important, they're grateful to you and ready to give you their undivided attention. You've got a better chance now. And that encouraging realization should be good news for *you.*

"Don't tell anybody I told you what I'm about to tell you. . . ."

When you call a break, your audience will scatter— some to the phone, some to grab a smoke, some to visit the rest rooms.

The following tid-bit concerns the rest room group.

If you want to hear how your presentation is *really* going, hurry to your appropriate rest room. Slip into a stall and listern for the sound of voices. The voices will belong to your audience, and they will say *exactly* what they think of your presentation *thus far.* "Well, what do you think?" one voice will ask. "Okay, but I wish there were more specifics," the second voice replies. Or, "It's too damn slow." The voices depart and so do you, knowing *exactly* what you must do to your presentation. This goofy idea works in *both* rest rooms (or so I've been told).

41

How to eliminate audiences and start reading faces.

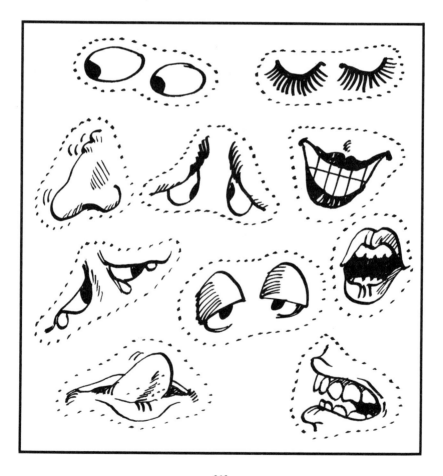

Professional golfers don't really see the hazards that terrify run-of-the-mill golfers.

A huge lake in front of the green? Forget it! Let's concentrate on the ball going in the hole.

That's the way it is with professional presenters, too. They don't really see the audiences when they're presenting. They concentrate on individuals. They strive to connect one-on-one, one person at a time.

This eliminates the audience hazard, reduces nervousness, and vastly improves communication.

There's something else about professional presenters that you should know. They look at individual faces a bit differently than ordinary people do. They see eyes, ears, mouths, foreheads, and other aspects of facial geography in terms of what they suggest or symbolize to the presenter.

You've heard of body language.

Let's examine facial language—and see what you, the presenter, can learn from it.

FACIAL LANGUAGE

Furrowed forehead means problems with acceptance.

Same for eyebrows.

Any placement of the hand over face is a signal of apprehension, hesitation, suspended judgment.

213

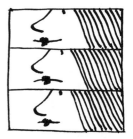

Final verdict registers in eyes first.

Eyes are the best indicators of interest. May range from "riveted" to asleep. This man is glazed.

Also a good indicator of interest. Ends of mouth up—agreement; down—disagreement; straight—judgment pending.

"When is that presenter gonna start talking about *me?*"

Type A—Intense, eager, concerned, fretful (typical new business prospect).

Type B—seeking entertainment, diversion (typical luncheon club member).

Your audience: daydreams easily.

Retains nonverbal impressions. Forgets 90 percent of what he hears.

Is extremely time-conscious (except Type B).

42

Body Language:
It can sound an alarm
without making a sound.

Body Language: A knotty case that *could happen to you.*

You may never meet this person. But it's possible that he or she may show up at some kind of interactive meeting where you are the presenter—and that person will be important to the outcome of your meeting.

Let's say the person is a man—in his mid-forties, well dressed, an executive—sitting on the aisle in the third-row center. He may never utter a word. In fact, it's possible that you didn't even notice him until your presentation was almost over.

Then, you become extremely conscious of him. He has arranged himself into a body language that is disturbing. It sends out signals. And the signals are like warning flags, waving silently in the wind.

This one person's case of body language is well worth examination, since he's giving off some signals which are easily recognized—and can usually be fixed. Let's see what this fellow looks like.

Who is this man and why is he avoiding you?

He's probably a nice person—sitting there in one of those funny wraparound desks you find in old classrooms. But his body language, for all of its indolence, is sending out signals that you, as the presenter, must be able to read.

This man has checked out of your presentation. He's there, but he's gone. Not only has he mentally excused himself, he is physically retreating. The body language couldn't be clearer.

Everything about him is leaning away from you. Even his head is averted. His eyes are open, but they aren't making contact. His body is slumped, sort of draped backward over the desk. He has wrapped himself up in his own limbs. One arm protects the chest, grasping the other arm that is thrust into a pocket—out of action (you'll notice his notepad has been abandoned—another distressing signal). His legs are crossed, defensively. He's given his feet over to the presentation and withdrawn his brains. What else? Glasses are off—apparently he doesn't need them anymore, but his wristwatch is evident, exposed just under his drooping head. Resignation, that's what it is. He's sitting there, all self-constrained, waiting for the presentation to be over.

How on earth could this man be dangerous to you? Because other members of the audience are aware of his attitude, and it could be catching. Or maybe he's the boss of the group and they think he's giving them his opinion of the presentation. He's creating a cloud, a negative presence, and the dynamics in the room could be turning against you. One person's body language can do it, particularly if that one person carries a certain influence. *What should you do?*

How to cure a bad case of body language.

In treating a bad case of body language (like the man on the aisle in the third-row center), you've got to bite the bullet and assume that *you're* the problem. Or at least a sizable *part* of it. Maybe he disagrees with your point of view. Maybe he's heard it all before. Maybe he feels left out. Maybe you never really addressed *his* problem. Maybe he thinks you stole his thunder. Whatever the reason, fair or unfair, his body language and facial language are telling you exactly how he feels at that precise moment.

It is time for some rather intense sublety. He won't appreciate it if you suddenly zero in on him. Don't patronize him. But you can begin to work on eye contact with him, reducing the distance, showing your concern. Once you make any kind of connection, get any kind of response, you can ask him if you've covered everything he needed to know. Give him time. It will take him a few seconds to rouse himself. Let your concern show. If he remains unresponsive, don't give up on him (*never* give up on an audience). Back off, move on, circulate. Don't let one person pull your energy level down. But don't hesitate to return to him. You're not angry. You're not pushing. You're not confrontational. You're *concerned*—genuinely interested in him. (Maybe, just maybe, you even *like* him.) Ask him what his experience would suggest. Stay with the eyes (it's your strongest avenue of access), inviting him to contribute. Once he changes his body language, straightening up, shifting toward you, you'll feel a difference in the entire room. The cloud is lifting. The meeting is moving forward again.

There's an old saying from somewhere, "People lie—body language never does." Infallibility may be pushing things a bit—but it certainly won't hurt to keep your eye on the guy in the third-row center.

43

"If you don't give me a list . . ."
(Audiences just love "do" lists.)

It was break-time. I had been presenting to a group of bankers in New England—and the first half-hour of my presentation was over. There was another hour to go.

People were lining up at the coffee table, picking up doughnuts and bowties, then moving into little clusters of conversation.

A young woman of about thirty was nipping into a chocolate doughnut and trying not to spill the cup of coffee she had just filled. She was standing by herself, and I decided to do a little research.

"Give me your honest opinion," I said. "How am I doing so far?"

She smiled pleasantly, munched on her doughnut, and thought about it. I could tell from her nice, open expression that she was going to tell me exactly what she thought.

"Well, good," she replied. "Maybe good *plus*."

"Any suggestions?"

"I'm finding it a little hard to take notes," she said. "I think people like to be given *lists* of things, don't you?"

"Yes, I suppose." I had never really thought about it.

"Oh, yes. If you don't give me a list, how can I write my report? If I can't write my report, how can I prove I was here?"

She sipped her coffee. Everything was under control.

"An audience like this—most of us anyway—are expected to write a report to our superiors. You know, just to prove that we were here. Without notes, it's hard. We need lists."

She was so sure of it, so logical, so *right*. Tell people you have six things for them to do and they will instinctively pick up their pencils and start writing. It must be a carryover from high school. Or some kind of deep-rooted association of lists with matters of substance. A list, no matter what it says, communicates nonverbally—"Here's something you'd better remember."

Suddenly, after this young banker had explained everything to me, it all became quite clear. If you don't give your audience an itemized list or two—they may subconsciously think you're not giving them anything worth writing down. It becomes an excuse not to listen, an opportunity to daydream (which most audiences love to do anyway).

There are additional rewards in this wisdom about "lists." If you have ever been told that your presentations lack content, put in a list or two. You'll find that in making the list you'll compress your information and it will indeed become more substantive.

Mention the *number* of items on your list. It's magic. Note-taking will accelerate like crazy. You'll *feel* the activity in the room—bodies moving forward in their chairs, pages of notepads being flipped, papers being rustled in the search for pencils and pens. The place comes *alive*.

Help them as much as you can. Orchestrate the ritual. Maybe you write the items on a blackboard or a flipchart (this gives your audience extra time to make their notes as you're guiding them through your list). Or maybe you create a "build"—which is nothing more than a series of slides, each slide adding a new item to your list.

Caution: Don't hand out lists. This gets people involved in reading instead of being led by you. It's often difficult to get their attention back.

After learning the importance of lists to people seeking knowledge (and having to report to their bosses), I vowed that if I ever wrote a book—I would pepper it with lists of all kinds. You'll find one in almost every chapter.

44

Nerve Endings.
(Insensitivity can overpower
any subject.)

There's a pearl of presentation wisdom that says audiences react to "personal affronts" more quickly than individuals do. It's true.

An individual may shrug off an insensitive remark, thinking that it was inadvertent and, besides, it was no big deal. ("I was the only one to hear it, and maybe I took it wrong.")

When that same remark slips into a formalized presentation that is heard by a *crowd*—the reaction cuts through the room and becomes an offense against the organization, or the locality. It cannot be pardoned or ignored. *Everybody heard it.*

The presenter might just as well pack up and catch the next plane out of town. The message has been doomed by the presenter's violation of a highly sensitive nerve ending.

How many of these seemingly trivial but utterly destructive errors have you heard (or maybe even committed yourself)?

■ *A sarcastic reference to the city you're visiting.* Let's say you've been invited to Buffalo to address a local business group. It's snowing. You've had a terrible time getting to Buffalo. Planes were delayed. It was murder. You get up to speak, cast a sorrowful glance at the falling snow, shake your head, and say, "Well, here we are in beautiful downtown Buffalo." The audience smiles and cringes simultaneously. You move into your message. *The audience isn't hearing it.* They *live* in Buffalo, have *homes* in Buffalo, do *business* in Buffalo. They were probably even *born* in Buffalo. They *love* Buffalo—and they are sick of people taking pokes at Buffalo.

Presentation Ethic #1: Don't knock the town you're in. People are extremely sensitive about where they live. They *like* it. Wherever you go, to make a presentation or simply to conduct business, it's a great place. You're *delighted* to be there. And it shows because *you mean it.*

■ *An unflattering reference to a specific age group.* Picture this (it happened): A marketing director gets up to report to her management on future plans. She speaks of broadening the sales program to include consumers from fifty-five to sixty-five years old, noting—in passing—that these more mature individuals may dilute the "youthful image" of the product—but "older people" have vastly increased buying power.

Sitting there in the audience is a vice president of the corporation *who just turned fifty-five.* He prides himself on his youthful waistline, attitude, and sex life. He hates anything that makes him feel "old." This presentation has just alienated him from the presenter and shattered any chances of the program being approved.

Presentation Ethic #2: Do not make editorial references to age. If you must mention specific ages, beware of stereotypes. People over sixty are not necessarily "senior citizens." People over forty are not necessarily "middle-aged." These terms can put you in a deep freeze, and no presentation—no matter how brilliant—can pull you out. Here's a little something to keep in mind: *You never know how old people are.*

■ *An unappreciated greeting to someone in the audience who is having a horrible year.* This happens at sales conferences all the time. The sales manager rises to greet his audience. The room is teeming with salespeople. They are brimming with optimism and bright expectations. The sales manager's gaze falls on Charlie (everybody knows good old Charlie). The manager's words of encouragement boom out to every corner of the room:

"We're particularly glad to have Charlie with us for this conference. It's been a tough year out there in Charlie's territory and we're all rooting for Charlie to get a lot of good ideas during this conference so he can go home and do the kind of job we all know he can do."

Charlie, meanwhile, is withering. He wants to crawl under the carpet. Then, just to finalize the awkwardness, the sales manager shouts, *"Right, Charlie?"* Everybody looks at Charlie. Charlie smiles a smile that only an executioner could love.

Presentation Ethic #3: Don't draw attention to poor performance no matter how worthy your intentions. One person's morale is never lifted by words of encouragement that identify the individual as a loser.

■ *The misplaced use of "contemporary colloquialisms."* Our language has been liberalized. There's the F-word, and the A-word, and the S-word, and words that defy definition. They just sound ugly. Most of the words are adjectives (especially the F-word). Their meanings may be hazy, but they communicate a certain defiance of polite society. Recently, I attended a new business presentation involving a prospective client for a marketing organization. The client was a huge service organization. In the old days, it would have been called a public utility.

The prospect had sent seventeen representatives to the presentation.

After the first break, an account executive rose to address the elusive issue of "corporate culture." As his enthusiasm grew, his language became a bubbling brew of "contemporary colloquialisms." There were all the conventional four-letter words, plus some five-letter varieties you don't hear very often (genitals get a lot of attention in today's vocabulary of swearwords). There was one man in the audience, about sixty I'd say, whose body actually convulsed a little every time he heard one of those words. I watched him carefully. It was like somebody grazed him every few minutes with an electric prod. His body language attempted to cover these jolts he was receiving (he'd cross his legs, cover his face, slouch in his chair—nothing worked).

He just physically *recoiled* from the language he was hearing. He, of course, was the senior representative of the prospect's contingent.

Later, when the business had been awarded elsewhere, I asked the account executive why he used so much salty language.

"Oh, they love it," he said. "They talk just like that all the time."

Yeah, I thought. All of them *except one*.

Presentation Ethic #4: Watch your language. What may be colorful and contemporary to you may be offensive to certain members of your audience, and they may be the very ones you want to influence. If you don't hear it on network television (please notice I didn't say "cable"), don't use it in your presentation. As far as I know, the use of blue (or purple) language has never helped a single presentation.

■ *A seemingly casual touch, on the arm, the neck, the waist, wherever, to show a sense of cooperation and mutual involvement.* When the presenter *touches* a member of the audience, red lights flash through the heads of all others in the room. "What's going on there?" When the presenter touches a member of the opposite sex, clanging bells join the flashing lights. A touch, innocent though it may be, can carry implications that far transcend your message. *Besides, most people don't like to be touched.* It can be patronizing, or demeaning. (I used to have a boss who would wrap his arm around my shoulder and clasp me to his chest. He was about 6'5" and it made me feel like Charlie McCarthy.)

Professional Ethic #5: Outside of shaking hands, don't *touch* your audience. Don't invade their "private zone"—which is the area within twelve inches of the face. Yes, there are television game-show hosts who *kiss* everybody. That's different (I find it equally nauseous, but it *is* different). Game-show hosts are regarded as "members of the family" and family members *do* kiss occasionally. Presenters like

225

you and me aren't entitled to deliberate physical contact. That's taking unfair advantage of our role as leader, teacher, presenter. We can be touching emotionally, intellectually—but, please, do not touch.

■ *A defensiveness that incites you to criticize the criticizer.* You've made your presentation and you ease into the question/answer section of the meeting. Part of your recommendation is under fire—and it's a part that you tailored, very carefully, to the specifications that your audience gave you. You really took great pains to make it fit what they told you were their requirements. Yet they're *questioning* it now. One person in particular won't leave it alone. You've had enough. You blurt it out, "Look, it just so happens that you're the one who asked for that feature. I didn't want it. You're the one who *made* us do it."

Suddenly, the criticizer is being criticized. Suddenly, the presenter is the prosecutor—"not my fault," he implies, "*your* fault!" The audience has been put on the defensive. The presenter has destroyed his own authority by shifting responsibility away from himself. It's a no-win situation. It's also curtains for the presenter's proposition.

Presentation Ethic #6: Don't turn the tables on your audience. They can criticize *you.* But if you criticize *them* for criticizing *you,* you've lost them. You can reason with them, but you can't ridicule them. It may be tempting at times, but what you'll gain in gratification—you'll lose in votes.

■ *An irritating tendency to forget the names of key people in your audience.* People don't like to be called "Harry" if their name is "Tom." Names are very personal. They were given to us by our mothers and fathers. If you ask a person what she thinks of a particular subject, and you call her "Martha" when her name is "Marlene," she's going to get the impression you don't really *care* what she thinks about the subject. And if you call a person "Malcolm" when his first name is really "Forbes" (as I did for almost an hour), the rest of the class is going to start to giggle. Your authority flies right out the window.

Presentation Ethic #7: Get a list of the names and titles of the people who will be in your meeting. Say the names out loud at least ten times each so that you connect the right first name with the proper last name. If it's a conference room, have nameplates identifying seat locations (this will eliminate all the confusion that usually starts with, "You sit there—no, I think over here would be better").

If it's theater-type seating, have nameplates that stick on and peel off easily (not the ones that *pin on* and make holes in your clothes). Of course, the best solution is to *know* everybody's name and greet them instantly—by name. This requires names *and pictures* well before the presentation date. The logistical requirements of knowing names *and* faces before a first meeting can be demanding (especially if it's a large group), but if you've got names, pictures, and a reasonably good memory—you'll be the hit of the day. People notice it when you use their names. They may not say anything, but they're impressed. They remember you—and, if you're lucky, they remember *your* name.

■ *Not knowing what to say about smoking.* In a meeting room, where you have ten or twenty people involved in a presentation, what happens when somebody takes out a pack of cigarettes and casually lights up? These days, *everybody* notices. Some people don't mind. Some people sort of resent it but don't say anything. And a few people *fume*. If those who resent it and the few who fume happen to be customers or prospective clients, or other guests of importance and influence—you've got a real ticklish situation. Here's the rule:

Presentation Ethic #8: As a presenter, you *never* smoke. If you're the world's most compulsive smoker, you steadfastly refrain from smoking at your own presentation. If your team of presenters is hosting an audience of important guests, nobody on the team smokes during a presentation. If one of the guests lights up, you act like you don't see it. But here's the point that may be tough for some smokers to accept: *even if a guest—an "outsider"—starts puffing away, the presentation team doesn't smoke.* The reason is simple: the audience isn't going to *like* you any better because you smoke (unless you're soliciting a congregation from the American Tobacco Institute), but somebody may simply "tune out" if you or any of your colleagues fill the room with smoke. Violate a nonsmoker's "space" and the presentation is over. You have committed a "personal affront" to the sensitivities of some people.

■

None of these eight sensitivities *sound* like presentation-busters. But all of them *are*. They rattle people *emotionally*. They stick in the craw. They make you so memorable (in a negative way) that your subject becomes *instantly* forgettable. Beware of the exposed nerve ending. It may not seem dangerous, *but* it can be lethal.

45

Test your mettle
as a presenter.

What would you do?

1. You are seven minutes into your presentation to an executive review committee. Things appear to be going well. Suddenly the chairman of the committee gets up and heads toward the back of the room. He (or she) goes to the coffee urn and pours a cup of coffee, then starts browsing through the Danish pastries. He isn't paying the slightest attention to your presentation and everybody in the room is conscious that "the boss" isn't listening. *What would you do?*

Recommended Action: The continuity of your presentation has been broken. If "the boss" isn't with you, nobody else will be with you either. Might as well tell the chairman he's got a great idea and invite everybody to have a cup of coffee and be back in five minutes.

2. You're in the midst of a presentation of ten people. It's 11:00 A.M. The door opens and it's the head waiter (your meeting is in one of the large hotels in town). The waiter announces that he is there to take luncheon orders. He whips out his order pad and looks expectant. *What would you do?*

Recommended Action: If you're near the end of your presentation, tell the waiter to return in five minutes (or whatever amount of time you'll need. *Be specific* about the time). If he gives you an argument, don't get angry. Be prepared to call a break. You'll find that most audiences are concerned about food. It's hard to compete with it, particularly around mealtime.

3. It's 2:10, and your meeting was scheduled to start at 2:00. Everybody is there *except* the highest ranking officer. People are starting to get restless. It's your meeting, you're the presenter. *What would you do?*

Recommended Action: Turn to the *next* highest ranking officer and ask that person if you should start or wait. Keep your voice low, but loud enough so that everybody in the room knows what's happening. And knowing who's responsible for the decision is especially important if you're presenting to a client, customer, or prospect. By quietly consulting the next-in-command, the decision is "theirs," and nobody will be mad at *you*—particularly when the highest ranking officer comes thundering in twelve minutes later and says, *"Who started this meeting?"*

4. You're sailing along, nearing the end of your presentation. A

questioner raises a point. You try to answer. Somebody else jumps in, cutting you off. Before you know it, a verbal battle breaks out between the questioner and the interrupter. They're really going at it, back and forth, and you're left on the sidelines. *What would you do?*

Recommended Action: Let them thrash for a few minutes. Some audiences *need* to argue amongst themselves (it makes them feel better). Once the battle starts to subside, step back in and take control. Be prepared to articulate the areas of agreement and move briskly back on track. Humor is often effective when a presentation veers wildly out of control. Ed Rosenstein, an exceptional market research analyst and presenter, would drop to his knees, clasp his hands together in mock supplication, and shout above the din, "Please, God, where did I lose control?" When an argument is broken by laughter, it's generally a good time to steer the group right back to your subject.

5. You're the first presenter after a big, elaborate lunch. Your audience is full of food—and wine. A person sitting up front is on the verge of being drunk. He's certainly tipsy. He won't shut up. He keeps interrupting you, asking what is essentially the same question *over and over. What would you do?*

Recommended Action: Answer the question. Stay calm. Try to rephrase your answer each time you respond. Don't laugh at him. Don't be sarcastic. Keep answering the question as best you can. Eventually, one of the man's colleagues will tap him on the shoulder and whisper, "Let's go get a cup of coffee." If you are a guest in somebody else's organization, *let them take care of their own.* This is terribly important. The moment *you* start to discipline the mischief-makers, you'll lose the sympathy (and admiration) of your audience and *you'll* become the culprit.

6. You're making your presentation, moving along smoothly, when you realize that you are looking into a *sea of glazed eyeballs.* Your audience has drifted away from you and you don't have the faintest notion *why. What would you do?*

Recommended Action: If you have lost your audience, and you don't know why, call a break. Ask your colleagues for their observations and suggestions. Obviously, there has been a breakdown in interest. Do the obvious: *change.* Change the presentation area—give your audience a different set to look at. Change the subject—move along to your next topic. Change the presenter. Maybe just a new face and a fresh voice will bring the audience to life. The worst thing to do is continue in the same style, on the same subject. Your audience will turn to stone. Most presenters can sense it when an audience has

lapsed into daydreaming. At this point, you've got little to lose—
change!

7. You're on a roll. All systems are performing perfectly. You're
showing a 16mm film and the film snaps. The projector makes that
awful sound of loose film slapping against metal. Your audio/visual
technician gets busy, struggling to splice the broken film. He is flus-
tered—and the situation looks bleak. It could be a long wait. The
audience looks at you, wondering how you're going to handle it.
What would you do?
Recommended Action: In this case, it's very important to know
what *not* to do. Here are some *"don't dos"*:

■ *Don't* get mad.

■ *Don't* just stand there.

■ *Don't* start rattling off jokes that have nothing to do with the
situation.

Here are five things you *can* do:

■ *Declare* a five-minute break and see how long it will take to
get things going again.

■ *Go on* to something else that doesn't require broken-down
equipment. Hope that repairs can be made in the meantime.

■ *Open up the meeting* for questions or discussion of the material
covered to that point. A trifle risky, but probably okay if the vibes
have been good. If they haven't, maybe you can clear the air.

■ *Tell a brief story* that relates to the situation. If you're not
good at telling stories, try the following.

■ *Say something like this:* "Have you ever had a day when everything you tried went bad? When, no matter how hard you worked,
things got *worse*? I have days like that all the time. Do *you*? Well, our
audio/visual engineer is having one of those awful days. Let's just
hang in there with him (or her) for another five minutes and show
that we understand." This plaintive plea puts the audience in the
shoes of the person in the control room or wherever the unlucky A/V
engineer happens to be, and probably keeps things reasonably peace-
ful for about five minutes. The last time I heard a speaker use those
words (or something like them), the audience not only settled down,
it applauded.

8. You're presenting to a group of executives known for their
toughness. You're moving into your proposition, and the audience is
looking good. Then, with no advance warning, the chief executive
officer says—in a brash, gruff voice—"I've read your material, and I
think you're full of crap." A hush settles over the room, and the CEO

looks you dead in the eye, waiting to hear what you've got to say. *What would you do?*

Recommended Action: You don't do what you feel like doing. You conquer the urge to grab your easels and slide drums and stalk out the door. You look *him* dead in the eye and say, "Okay, fair enough. Tell me where you had trouble and let me see if I can help you." You meet *rudeness* with *helpfulness.* You diffuse the hostility—keep yourself under control—and concentrate on the issues. If you're patient and helpful—and he's abrasive—eventually, someone will say, "let's get on with it." Chances are, the CEO is just testing you anyway. So regard it as a little corporate game-playing and not a challenge to your character or professionalism. Keep cool. It'll pass—and you will survive the situation with honor intact.

46

"Hold that temper!"

This is a cardinal law of presentation:

Never, ever lose your temper. There are tons of reasons, but here are the main ones:

1. *You are probably being tested.* People who lose their tempers are not in great demand. If you get angry, under a heavy barrage of questions or a storm of unsolicited comments, you are not likely to be invited back. The person in the audience who's taunting you is probably testing your flame-out level.

2. *Presenters who lose their tempers are regarded as "out of control."* Self-control is mandatory these days—in all aspects of human conduct. I don't care whether you're a minister or a Wall Street tycoon, you'd better be able to control yourself. A wildly careening temper marks you as *uncontrollable* trouble. Therefore, you are socially and professionally *untouchable*.

■

There aren't a whole lot of temper-taming techniques (which is probably just as well). Take these two precautions and you should be all right:

■ When you feel your temper heating up, tell yourself you're being tested. Repeat, please, after me, *"This is only a test. This is only a test."* Think of it as a fire drill. Bells are ringing, but you are going calmly to your station. Tempers react most violently when they sense that something really *important* is being suddenly violated. "This is only a test" will help you put things back in proportion.

■ Write down, word for word, the two most infuriating questions you're likely to hear. Put the *questions and your best answers* on an audiotape and play them back until you can listen to them without getting upset. This will do two things: it will take the shock factor out of the hottest questions imaginable (all others therefore move down the temperature scale) and it will help you answer questions rationally that would otherwise have you on the brink of rage.

Anger casts a pall over a presentation that is impossible to dispel. "Cool it before it heats up, or banish it before it starts."

47

"Hey— you've drawn a *crowd!*"

$\mathbf{M}$ost presentations are to groups—from ten to twenty people, gathered around a table or loosely assembled, theater-style.

Let's assume something good about you.

Let's assume that you have gotten so effective at presenting to groups that you receive an invitation to present to a crowd.

So, what's a *crowd?* Fair question.

I have always maintained that a group was any gathering of *less* than fifty people—and a crowd was anything *over* fifty.

But let's take no chances on arbitrary definitions. Let's be definite about you and what you've been asked to do.

You've been invited to address a gathering of five hundred people. That, no matter how you look at it, is a crowd.

What are you going to do differently, now that we've multiplied your usual audience by a resounding *fifty-fold*, more or less?

First, let's admit that there *are* differences—in general atmosphere, presentation skills required, and certain communications limitations that the sheer mass of a crowd imposes.

A relatively small group (twelve or less) is a lot easier to "get started" than a crowd. Think of the small group as a *car*, idling, eager to get in gear. A crowd of five hundred people is more like an aircraft carrier. It's harder to get it going, harder to turn it around, and it's always got all kinds of activity happening on deck—planes landing, planes taking off, planes getting hauled and hoisted about. Being the speaker before a crowd of five hundred is not unlike being the captain of an aircraft carrier.

If you've attracted a crowd of five hundred, you're going to be up on a platform somewhere, not unlike the bridge of a ship. You're elevated, separated from your audience. That's *one* difference from presenting to a group.

You're also going to be farther from most members of your audience than would be the case with a group of ten or twelve people. You're not going to be able to involve yourself as easily—either physically or philosophically. Distance does that.

Since you're up above and farther away from your audience, you're going to be limited in several technical respects. Eye contact is going to be difficult, and probably impossible with people sitting in the back. That's an important consideration and requires some adjustments in technique (more about that in a minute).

Also, participation by members of the audience may have to be minimized or sacrificed. People are not as eager to participate *individually* in front of a crowd. (In fact, they often like the anonymity that a crowd provides.)

Still another consideration: crowds—like carriers—have all kinds of activities going on most of the time. People coming in, going out, shuffling, and hustling about. Think of any convention you've attended lately. Constant hubbub.

So, a crowd is different from a group in significant ways.

Now, let's get back up to the bridge where we can calmly administer the resolutions to these difficulties.

Presenting to a *group* is a one-by-one process. You speak to the people individually. Presenting to a *crowd* can't be done on a one-by-one basis. There are just too many people. But a crowd can be regarded as a single entity, a single unit, like an aircraft carrier. It's *yours*. Yours to understand. Yours to control. The crowd is not five hundred people. It's *one* entity—and you got it!

If you'll accept that concept, the solutions to our previous difficulties will appear immediately:

■ *Your mission is to keep an eye on the crowd*, maintain contact—not to establish individual relationships. That means you demonstrate your awareness of everybody by letting your eyes rove into all four corners of your audience as well as the heart of it.

■ *You move*, physically, to increase your exposure to the entire audience—as well as to demonstrate your sensitivity to all of them. Also, movement by you generates alertness in them.

■ *You project your voice and yourself more forcefully*, just because you've got more space to fill and it's going to take more energy to get things moving your way.

■ *You don't get upset if you notice a few people sneaking out*. They will probably be replaced by a few people who will slip in the side door. Crowds are restless creatures.

■ *You don't try to operate all of the A/V aids by yourself*. Captains don't go down and fire up the engine room. Make sure you've got back-up systems if your slides jam or your video segment fails to show. Nothing inspires confidence and authority in a speaker like a great audio/visual technician.

■ *You remember your crowd psychology*. People react much differently in crowds than they do on their own. They join the flow. This means that once you feel a surge of approval from a crowd, it's likely to gather momentum. By the same token, if a crowd drifts away from you, it's hard to turn it around. Crowds are like aircraft carriers.

■ *There are Type A crowds and Type B crowds.* Type A crowds are intense, eager to learn, critical. Example: The Young President's Organization. A Type B crowd is there to be entertained, or for the social satisfactions.

Type B crowds are more likely to be interested in the meal than the speaker. Example: The Rotary Club. Do your audience analysis. Know which crowd you're talking to. Lighten up for the Type Bs. Knuckle down for the Type As.

■ *Keep your presentation within an hour*—shorter if possible. The reason: you're working without the benefit of truly focused eye contact. That limits your ability to hold attention for long periods of time. This is where electronic audio/visual techniques find their most useful niche. They can enlarge the image of the speaker (often, to horrendous effect) or they can create attention *around* the speaker that doesn't rely on close eye contact.

One final point about *you* and crowds.

Crowds are flattering. Not everybody can draw a crowd. *You did.* So, step up and take command. *The crowd is yours.*

48

Your best chance
to work a miracle.

It's the night before your big presentation.

You have just run through your final rehearsal for a group of randomly selected colleagues.

The response has been polite. The tone has been considerate. The comments have followed this general pattern:

> "Well, I'm sure it will be just fine when you actually
> do it tomorrow."

This usually means, with the politeness ironed out, "It didn't do much for me. Maybe the *real* audience will get something out of it."

There's also the comment that comes from a candid "Stanley Kubrick" at the end of a dress rehearsal for a crucial presentation.

> "Look, it's one hell of an effort—but it's not going
> to win. It's not going to get us past the competition.
> It's got a lot of good information in it, but it simply
> isn't connecting. It's not strong enough—as a pre-
> sentation—to carry the day."

You sense that Stanley is right.

You sense that everybody is right.

You also realize that it's midnight and your presentation is scheduled for ten o'clock tomorrow morning.

You've got to work a miracle. Overnight. *How do you do it?*

First, let us dispense with the "don'ts."

1. *Don't junk everything you've got and start over.* This is always disastrous. You'll drive yourself crazy. Your head will be a jumble. It's too late for new game plans.
2. *Don't stay up the rest of the night and feel guilty.* Don't sit there and tinker with your presentation. Don't worry it to death.
3. *Don't call up and cancel.* Cancellation is another word for capitulation.

So much for the "don'ts." It's time for some heartfelt "dos."

1. *Do start thinking positively.* Tell yourself you not only *can* carry the day, you *will.* The reason: You're not going to trash your work, you're just going to turn it a bit.
2. *Put a simple idea in your head.* Here's the simple idea:

"I'm going to put the words 'you' and 'your' into my presentation as many times as I possibly can."

All of a sudden, things are looking up. You've got a positive attitude. You've got a simple, straightforward strategy. You can sleep.

Next morning, the strategy becomes blatant, overt. You're going to inject some blatant, overt references to your audience's self-interest.

"Now, let's look at it from *your* perspective . . ."

"Here's what that means to *you* . . ."

"What's in this example for *you*?"

"Here are some things that *you* can do . . ."

"How can *you* profit from this?"

Want a role model for this strategy? Try Louis Rukeyser, the amiable moderator of *Wall Street Week*. Listen to him:

"Now, what should our viewers do? Would you advise them to buy or sell?"

"Can you give our viewers a few stocks that you think will do well in the months ahead?"

"What exactly does that mean to the individual investors in our audience?"

Rukeyser is always bringing it back to the audience, always pinning it down, always making it more useful for the viewer.

That's *your* strategy, too. You're simply turning your message toward the needs of your audience.

"Now, let's relate that to *you* and *your* situation."

The more times you add the word "you" or "your," the better. You'll see it in the response of your audience.

49

Ten points to pin to the wall before your next one-on-one.

$\mathbf{M}$any sales representatives do nothing but one-on-one presentations.

You have to be *good* to make your money this way. And you have to be resilient.

I interviewed over fifty professionals who do one-on-ones for a living. Every day. Three or four presentations a day.

Here are ten highlights of what they told me.

1. *Once you've made a date, confirm by mail immediately.* The confirmation should be no more than one page and should look more like a nice, simple *poster* than a letter. Computer graphics always help. This one-sheeter reserves the date, blocks out the time (when you'll start, when you'll finish), and nails down the subject. You may want to *suggest* the agenda, but only with a few fast-scanning bullet lines.

Here's the point: This page of *who, what, when, where* is mainly for the secretary or assistant of the person you're going to contact. Its purpose: to make sure the time (and your authorized right to it) is clearly marked on *everybody's* calendar. But the key person, at this stage, is the gatekeeper . . . the secretary.

2. Working like a reporter, *build a profile of your prospect.* Using $3'' \times 5''$ cards or a small notebook (or a PC), you begin to accumulate *everything you need to know* to address his or her self-interest. Ask for annual reports, recent speeches, brand share figures, the best trade magazines, press clippings, whatever. Most of this "intelligence" can be obtained by calling the PR department, the local newspaper, or even the library.

IDEA: Ask the secretary, for starters, what kind of presentation your prospect favors. Then, do it *immaculately.* Example: maybe your audience of one prefers a nice, unhurried question-and-answer session. On the other hand, maybe your presentation should be short, sweet, and to the point—with just a few questions at the end. Maybe this one-on-one should be purely facts and figures. Maybe it should be strategic. Whatever it should be, take another look at that chunk of time you've been given. Make sure your mode of presentation fits your block of time.

3. *Visualize your objective long before you make your presentation.* Your objective may be to simply "get by" this presentation so that you can get to the next level. Fine. That's a worthy objective. *Visualize it.* You can hear your audience saying, "This is an interesting presentation. I'd like our Finance Committee to see it." You can hear the words as you see your prospect smiling and leafing through your

leave-behind. Or, maybe you want to actually *close the sale.* Visualize it. You see it happening. It's right there—a moving picture in your mind. You're shaking hands over the figures that you have scratched on a price sheet. You're saying, "Delivery date will be the first of the month—guaranteed." You hear the words, see the responding nod of agreement.

What we see in our minds is usually what happens. Attitudes, visualized, become actions. One thing's for sure. It can't hurt.

4. *If you can work it, it's often wise to get the prospect out of the office.* One veteran of the one-on-one wars told me, "You don't want the guy sitting there next to the telephone, with all of the in-boxes full of memos to be read, and interruptions just waiting to happen. Find an excuse to get him out of there."

What kind of excuse? There's always breakfast, lunch, dinner, and golf. But a simpler lure is the attraction of a brief (but stunning) A/V presentation which you'll set up "just down the hall." This requires a bit of prearrangement with the secretary, but most organizations have conference rooms scattered about. You can set up your A/V without being rushed, and have everything ready to roll when your audience walks in. This gives your visit the atmosphere of an "Event." Always helpful.

NOTE: Conference rooms bring a kind of "welcome neutrality" to one-on-one environments. As one wise, old presenter told me, "In the prospect's office, I'm an outsider. In the conference room, it's a more balanced situation."

5. *Make it pristinely clear to the prospect what's expected of him or her.* This is a key point, often ignored—according to my one-on-one experts. You've got to brief your audience on what's going to happen, how long it will take, and what's expected of the listener. Take nothing for granted. Assume nothing. Here's how you might set it up:

> "This will take about ten minutes. The subject:
> How to reach a growing market of twenty-five mil-
> lion consumers that rarely sees or hears the media
> you are now using. We've got a special proposal for
> you to consider—it was created just for you. Then,
> we've reserved the last five minutes for your
> questions."

That takes exactly twenty seconds to say, but it *defogs* the meeting. It announces what's coming—the expected participation of the audience—and how it will end. There's no confusion about where the meeting's going—and you, the presenter, have gently suggested that all questions be held until the finish.

IMPORTANT: Whenever somebody thinks, "I don't know what this presentation has to do with me," *it's over.* Make everything clear *up front.*

6. *Have something tangible to keep you and your prospect on track.* This can be any kind of portable A/V equipment that you control. Maybe it's a tabletop flip chart. Maybe it's simply a printed deck of 9″ × 12″ cards. Maybe it's a strip film projector with a small TV-type screen. Maybe it's a brochure that's been designed for one-on-ones.

You don't read from this audio/visual aid. You *know it* by heart! It merely brings a focus to the meeting, and by watching the facial language of your audience, you can tell what's touched a nerve and what hasn't.

IMPORTANT: If you hand out any kind of literature *before* you're finished, you can forget about *ever* getting the attention back. Hand out your handouts *after* you've said your piece. Why compete with your own material?

7. *Keep reading the body language. Don't be afraid to call an audible.* In one-on-ones, body language is decisive. There's no chance of conflicting signals. You've only got *one person* to watch! Watch the blink rate of the eyes. If it increases to the degree that you're conscious of it, you've got a confused audience on your hands. Better pause and review the high points. If you've got a person who can't seem to get comfortable, pick up the pacing and move on to the next topic—it may be more compelling. If you've got an audience that keeps looking up, gawking around, seeking out the source of every little sound, you've got a concentration problem. You're off the mark. Nothing to lose by changing course. If you've got a head that nods agreeably and a mouth that smiles every so often, everything is turning out just as you visualized it!

NOTE: When questions arise, *your* body language comes into play. You may be listening with your ears. But, to your audience, you listen with your *eyes.* Make sure they stay fastened on the questioner every second!

8. *Often, an appropriate pause will tell you whether your audience is really involved or not.* Many successful one-on-ones will deliberately leave a gap in the presentation to see if the audience will jump in to fill it.

> *Example:* "This was an idea that intrigued us, but we didn't know exactly how to make it work in your operation . . . [PAUSE] . . . then we thought of the small parts factory you just acquired in Omaha."

An *involved* audience will probably leap into the pause. People who are excited about ideas usually can't wait to talk about applying them. But if the idea hasn't caught fire, the listener will leave the pause unoccupied.

This opportunity to participate can tell the presenter a lot.

A. The audience is excited, anticipating what's coming.

B. The audience has mentally checked out, and is perfectly content to let you finish.

Either way, you've received a useful signal.

9. *Close specifically.* Don't make it difficult for your audience to deal with your presentation. Suggest something specific—and easy to do.

> *Example:* "We recommend you give this idea a test
> under simulated working conditions for ninety days
> and see if the savings warrant permanent installation
> in your Omaha plant."

Obviously, you've outlined the test and detailed the costs. You've covered all bases. Most important, you've made the matter easy to decide.

Proposals that are specific are always more successful than those that are open-ended.

Many presentations close with questions such as, "Well, what do you think?" or "How does that sound to you?" If the prospect is rushed and under heavy pressure, those questions sound like *work*. They sound like heavy-duty deliberation. For a stressed official, nothing could be *less* appetizing.

Nail it down. Make it simple. Take the work out of it. That's how you *close* a one-on-one.

10. *Have a letter ready to be mailed to the prospect immediately following the presentation.*

This is a *must*. You have written a warm, friendly letter to the prospect long before the presentation *but you have not mailed it*. Reason: it has a few little "finishing touches" to be added. A few little openings to be filled. Those openings will be filled with references to what actually happened during the meeting. Maybe you'll strengthen some of your answers to important questions. Maybe you'll beef up one or two of your key arguments. Maybe you'll add something personal that you learned in the meeting.

The final letter will be up-to-the-minute in its comments, and everything will be related to the prospect's self-interest.

The letter will have taken you quite a while to write, but it will sound like you sat down and wrote it right after the meeting. It will make a big impression. It will make your presentation *stand out*. It, of course, will be delivered by special courier to arrive before quitting time. This has all been worked out *in advance*.

Five plus five equals 100 percent

If you do one-on-one presentations, you probably use at least five of these ten points. Terrific. Now, try the other five. Who knows? You could increase your effectiveness by 100 percent!

50

A guide to "relationships"— the hot new word in making presentations.

Come with me for a minute to Phoenix, Arizona, where one of the biggest names in computer systems is having its annual sales convention at a place called The Pointe at South Mountain. It's 110° in the shade. It's late July. And I'm hearing a lot about something that makes me vaguely antsy.

"We don't really think about making presentations. We put them into a much larger concept. We concentrate on building relationships."

That was about the gist of it, from everybody at the luncheon table. What's more, it had been a theme throughout the convention.

"What *makes* a relationship?"

Recently, "60 Minutes" did a segment on the singing star Aretha Franklin. She was being interviewed by "60 Minutes" regular Ed Bradley. The subject: *relationships.* Whose? Hers. It was very heavy going.

Finally, realizing the interview was fogbound, Ed asked softly, "Tell me, Aretha . . . what *makes* a relationship?" To which Franklin earnestly replied, "Ed . . . if I knew *that,* I could retire for life."

One suspects that Franklin could retire for life *without* knowing the meaning of relationships, but the utter hopelessness of their exchange made this chapter almost inevitable. No subject could be *that* baffling. And if the answer could enable us all to retire for life, we'd be crazy not to look for it.

"Building relationships" is one of those word combinations that reminds me of cotton candy. You know you're into something, but you're not exactly sure what.

It's one of those subjects that a company like AT&T will advertise lavishly, showing hundreds of people gushing happy talk into an endless variety of telephones, and nobody watching will know exactly what's going on. Gee, how could you miss it? They're *building relationships!*

But if the computer industry is excited about it, and AT&T has millions of dollars invested in it, and "60 Minutes" (see box) is trying desperately to find out what it really *is*, then it behooves us to dive in.

Remember, we're heading toward some finite moment of truth in the world of *presentations*, so don't think we've flipped out and started quoting soap opera.

It begins with two people

Let's start with the way most people think about relationships. Two people—trying to get along. For lack of a better place, let's pick up on Ed Bradley's question to Aretha Franklin: "What *makes* a relationship?"

Distill all the books, tapes, and videos on relationship marketing, relationship selling, and relationship strategies, and you'd probably come up with a version of the following:

First, sensitivity. You've got to have some sensitivity to the other person's feelings. How *you* feel has to matter to *me* before we can have a decent relationship. What are the words? Let's try a few—easy on the emotion:

> "Look, I understand how you're feeling. I know what it's like to feel the way you do right now. I've been there."

What next? Somewhere, there has to be willingness to help. More than that. There has to be a willingness to *extend* yourself on the other person's behalf.

> "I've been thinking about your problem. I've really been trying to come up with something. I think I've got an answer. I want to tell you about it and see what you think. Just hear me out on this. I think it will work for you."

The words are sounding pretty good, aren't they? Nothing heroic, but it sounds like a couple of people trying to find each other. What else do we need? A genuine interest in what happens to the other person. Something like this, perhaps:

> "Look, I want to know how things go for you. I want to be a part of what happens."

So, we've oversimplified. But it's a subject that can stand it. Maybe a relationship boils down to something as simple as this:
- *Empathy.* "I know how you feel. . . ."

- *Exceptional Effort.* "I've really been trying. . . ."
- *Equity.* "I want to be a part of what happens. . . ."

Or, in the final analysis, maybe there's a sobering parallel on a different plain:

- Courtship
- Marriage
- Real life

It's that "real life" you've got to be careful about.

Back to the speaker's platform

If we have come anywhere close to *defining* relationships—choose whatever sentiments or analogies you like—it is safe to say that there is *plenty* of room for most presenters to start building a few.

Tell you the truth, I don't think the idea of "building relationships" even crosses the mind of a person about to make a presentation. It just doesn't occur to him or her. What *does* occur? Well, maybe something like this:

> "This script looks okay to me . . . triple-spaced, just the way I like it . . . I'll read it through a few times . . . see if I can get the hang of it . . . underline a word here and there . . . try not to stumble . . . answer any questions that come up . . . smile . . . and sit down. . . . Let's see, I should be back in the office in time to make some phone calls and dictate a letter or two."

Does that sound like any boss you've ever had? That's a prespeech stream of consciousness that's *got to be* repeated at least a million times a day if we can believe *Business Week* that there are thirty-three million presentations daily.

Now, let's apply a bit of relationship building. We're going to add all those E's: *empathy, exceptional effort, equity.* Same presenter as before—only the attitude has changed. Let's tune up our stream-of-consciousness monitor. . . .

> "From this moment on, I'm in their shoes. I'm *them.* I look into their faces and try to read them. I ask myself what I would want to hear if I had their jobs. I try to be sensitive to their feelings. I'll try to give them one idea they can actually use in their jobs—if not today, *tomorrow.* I really want to help them. I expect to see these people again. This pre-

How presentations help build relationships.

1. *Empathy*
"I know how you feel
. . . I've been there."

2. *Exceptional
Effort*
"I've really thought
about your problem
. . . I think I've got
an answer."

3. *Equity*
"I want to be a part of
what happens . . ."

Presentations keep relationships going. As Yogi Berra says,
"it's not over 'til it's over."

sentation of mine is just the beginning of what could be a great relationship for them—and for me."

Would this attitude make a difference in the presentation? It would *transform* it! It would arouse the audience, and prompt waves of applause for the presenter. Providing, of course, that adequate preparation had been done reflecting the new attitude.

Six significant changes

It's easy to pooh-pooh pompous words like *relationship building,* but there's substance inside that stuffy exterior. Enough substance to bring about some significant changes:

1. Presentations would no longer be tedious tasks to be over and done with. They would be *the first step* in developing a relationship that could endure for years.

2. Chemistry and tone would become more important to presentation. If presenter and audience were going to see each other again—perhaps frequently—the personality of the presenter would get a careful rating. Dull, lifeless speakers wouldn't score well on the relationship meter.

3. No presenter would get away with a superficial understanding of the audience. To spark a long-term relationship, the presenter would have to immerse himself or herself in the concerns of the audience. When the presenter says, "I know how you feel," the audience would have to believe it.

4. The presenter must really have an idea the audience can use—not just an idea that hasn't found a home. Relationships grow on big, flowering ideas.

5. The presentation would require countless follow-ups. Not just a cheery phone call or two. Letters, reports, suggestions, offers to help, unexpected initiatives. Relationships need *reinforcement.*

6. Presenters would have to state, up front, that they want a long-term relationship. This isn't just "a speech" to be made and forgotten. This isn't just a shot in the dark. This is a relationship at the moment of creation. This concept will dumbfound some audiences. They've never heard such a thing. But, when they stop to realize it, it's a rare compliment.

"60 Minutes" was wrong. Relationships aren't baffling. But they aren't easy, either. Relationships, be they personal or professional, require a lot of tending. Making a sensitive, sincere presentation is just the start.

There's always "real life" to follow.

51

"The Deadly Game"— competitive presentations and how to win them.

Should you read this chapter?

Even if you *aren't* engaged in competitive presentations, there is no way this chapter can hurt you. But you should know what you're getting into.

Give a weak presentation to your Rotary Club and you'll probably sit down to a polite patter of applause. Give a weak presentation in a competitive situation and you may lose the budget that you *thought* was yours, the contract you had so diligently pursued, or the public office you had dreamed of holding.

If most presentations are porpoises out for a playful romp, competitive presentations are barracuda—waiting to knife through the waters and attack.

Competitive presentations take place in courtrooms, boardrooms, conference rooms, nominating conventions—wherever presentations serve to determine who wins and who loses. It's exciting, nerve-racking. And if that kind of thing appeals to you, you could be a *player* in "The Deadly Game."

Isn't it strange how the wisest words of wisdom sound sort of crazy when you first hear them?

Consider this quote from a young CEO of a growth-minded company in St. Louis:

"We want to start getting invited into new business presentations so that we can learn what it's like to lose."

Anybody who's ever been involved in competitive presentations would say "Amen!" to that.

Sustained success in competitive presentations is always preceded by a certain imprecise period which athletes like to call "learning how to win."

Sports analogies abound, but we really don't have to know that expansion teams don't win championships in their first year in the National Basketball Association.

All we really have to know is that competitive presentations, by their very nature, have a component that other presentations *don't* have: namely, competitors who want to carve you up for lunch.

It is no longer you and the audience, eye to eye. It is you, the audience, *and all those other guys.* Competitors. Hungry to win.

Competitive presentations, at maximum levels of passion, bring three little words to mind. They are not "I love you." They are "The Deadly Game." Stakes are high. Performances will be evaluated.

Competitive presentations have become a way of doing business in everything from architecture to waste disposal systems.

Considering the importance of competitive presentations (a $100,000,000 contract may be on the line), it's curious that so many blatant mistakes are repeated over and over again.

Four Mistakes You May Have Made

Mistake #1: No attention is paid to the competition. This mistake is usually covered by a comment that goes something like this: "We'll just do our thing, you know, and we won't concern ourselves with those other people." This is like Sears refusing to acknowledge the existence of Walmart—or Pepsi ignoring the tactics of Coke. It's suicidal. Yet it happens all the time. Many organizations involved in competitive presentations won't even bother to find out who their competitors *are.* Be not dismayed. We'll come back with a solution (or two) in a few minutes.

Mistake #2: "They don't understand us. I just have the awful feeling that they don't understand us at all." This is the lament of the prospect, the organization asking for help. Is it a serious grievance? You betcha. Every company in the world thinks of itself as *unique.* It may not *be* unique. It may not be able to *articulate* its uniqueness. But the belief is there—waiting patiently for some kind of evidence or proof that the uniqueness *is* understood. If the evidence never surfaces, never comes across during the presentation, the prospect will frame the question that spells disaster, "How on earth can you *work* for us when you don't even *understand* us?"

Mistake #3: The presenter ignores the prospect. The presenting company talks on and on about its humble origins, its proud history, its winning ways, its mighty management—and doesn't even come close to the prospect's situation. Keep in mind that the prospect is the one with the problem—or the opportunity to be seized. The presenter is there to supply the answers, prescribe the cure, suggest the strategy, or do whatever must be done. The audience sits there—awaiting the moment when the issue will be met. It never happens.

Mistake #4: All hell breaks loose when it's too late to save the day. It's midnight, the night before the final presentation, and confusion is written on every face. "How in the devil are we going to pull this thing together," the general manager yells, "and why does it *always* happen this way?" Everybody, it seems, was "too busy" to really give this project the concentration it deserved—and (under the breath), "I thought the general manager was on top of this." At 3 A.M., everybody goes home. The next morning, the presentation goes on as scheduled, and every member of the presentation team looks like he or she was fired out of a cannon. The presentation looks much the same.

Clear-cut mistakes, like those just described, are never allowed to stand—at least not in this book. So, let's go back and deal with each mistake as fully as need be.

Four Solutions You Can Use

Solution to Mistake #1: Appoint a CIA. Simple as that? Well, almost. CIA, in this instance, stands for Confidential Information Agent. This person is going to do everything within the law to find out what your competitors are *most likely to do* in a competitive shoot-out with you.

Your CIA may have been a reporter at one time, or a researcher, or a free-lance writer. These people know sources—like business libraries, and trade journals, and public-relations staffers of industry associations. With a few discreet phone calls, your CIA should be able to tell you the names of your competitors, how big they are, where they come from, and who their clients are. "Basic stuff," you say. "Of what earthly interest can that be to me?"

Well, let's dig into it. From the client roster of your competitors, you can pretty well visualize the *case histories* that will be wheeled out against you. By looking over the names of those who hold exalted positions in the ranks of your competition, you can figure out who your presenters will have to beat. Then, you can make sure that *your* people "match up" well against *their* people. Professional football and basketball coaches do this sort of thing all the time.

By now, your CIA has probably compiled a kind of "scouting report" about your competition. It is predicated on this unremarkable fact:

Every single one of your competitors was chosen for a reason. The names weren't pulled out of a hat. Some

pragmatic study of possible candidates was made, and every name, including yours, has one or more reasons for being selected. If you know those reasons, you can tailor your presentation a lot more competitively than if you're just "flying blind."

Here's a suggestion that can't possibly hurt you and might just help you win it all. . . .

From the "scouting report" compiled by your trusty CIA, make up an analysis of your competition. Nothing complicated. Just haul out your yellow pad and hand-print a heading that looks like this:

COMPETITOR	MAJOR STRENGTH	MAJOR WEAKNESSES	UNIQUENESS

List each competitor on the left (include yourself at the end). Fill in the next two columns from your hard-won knowledge of your competition. When you get to the *uniqueness* column, you may pause—understandably. If you don't know what a competitor's *uniqueness* is, study your CIA background information. Look for quirky details.

Example: if one of your competitors is located in Albuquerque, and all the rest are in the Chicago area, you can assume that Albuquerque has a *uniqueness* that is terribly compelling to the prospect. And if the prospect is headquartered in Chicago, the desired *uniqueness* is unlikely to be geographical. It's something else, something potent which you'd better know about—and you'd better be able to counter it in your presentation.

What about those other columns?

By analyzing the competition's strengths and weaknesses, and comparing them against your own, you'll know where your vulnerabilities *really* are.

CEOs have a nasty habit: if you've got a vulnerability, a weak spot, that's where they will aim their heaviest artillery. It never fails.

Far better to shore up the weaknesses *before* you go into a presentation room than try to survive after you're inside.

Solution to Mistake #2: To understand their uniqueness, understand their craziest problems. When a prospect says, "I don't think they understand us," they are *really* saying, "They don't have the foggiest notion of all the crazy problems we have to put up with. . . ."

Here's the way to get a handle on what bothers them: make absolutely certain that you get a thorough briefing long before the final presentation. If possible, get away from the phones and the crises at the offices (yours and theirs). This very private meeting should be for you (and your team) exclusively. You don't want your competitors hearing the answers to your carefully thought-out questions.

Talk informally to the people who manage the prospect's company—and keep in mind that you are being evaluated on *all* contacts with the prospect, not just the final presentation.

Make sure that your questions reveal some insight. Questions that could be answered by any basic reference source are *wasted* questions. "How many employees do you have?" That's a *wasted* question. "In what product category do you see your greatest sales growth in the next five years," is an insightful question that can give you something to work with.

Take a genuine interest in them (listen with your eyes!). Explore all of their problems, but focus sharply on the ones that they perceive as being unique to their business. (If they will let you use a microcassette recorder, use it—but move it out of view. Don't leave it out in the middle of the table to remind people that you're preserving every word.)

Once you have a bead on the problems that they hold to be unique, never mention your product or service again without relating it to one of those unique problems.

As soon as your prospect perceives that his or her problems are equally disturbing to you, and that your role is to relieve the frustrations of those problems, you will be accepted as someone who *understands*. You are, in effect, *one of them*.

Solution to Mistake #3: Follow the cardinal law of competitive presentations: address their *self-interest first, last, and always.* You don't win competitive presentations by ignoring the prospect. You don't win with off-the-shelf presentations. You don't win by having three sets of slides for three different business categories. ("Well, I think we'll try Drum C on these guys.") Winning presentations make the prospect say, "This presentation *couldn't* have been created for anybody else. It understands us so well. It addresses *our* needs from start to finish."

SUGGESTION: For information on *structures* that follow the cardinal law of competitive presentations, take another look at Chapter 32.

Solution to Mistake #4: Appoint a shepherd. The old problem of doing everything at the last minute is always a crusher. And it's usually due to the lack of a shepherd.

A story may be in order here. A *true* story.

There was a man named Andrew Kershaw who ran an advertising agency called Ogilvy & Mather. I always thought he was brilliant, but he *did* shake people up.

Every Monday morning Andrew conducted the Executive Committee Meeting of his agency in New York City. And every Monday morning he would have a list of blue-chip companies who were in the process of selecting a new advertising agency. Each blue-chipper on the list had indicated an interest in Ogilvy & Mather. So, Andrew would read the list—rather matter of factly, I always thought, considering the luster of the companies. Then, he would say—

"Are there any companies on this list that we absolutely must have? Are there any companies here that anybody feels passionate about?"

Maybe a third of the corporate names would elicit some comment from the people in the room. Then, Andrew would say—

"All right. Fair enough. Who wants to be a shepherd? Pick your prospect. By shepherd, I mean taking full responsibility for the presentation and doing everything humanly possible to win the business. I'll make sure that you have the total cooperation of everyone you will need."

You have no idea how this announcement could quiet down a room of ambitious achievers. Expressions changed from wry good humor to utter seriousness. The gauntlet was down. Andrew was waiting. And, in Andrew's eyes, he or she who hesitated was not likely to be a good shepherd.

The person or persons who spoke up at that moment were full-fledged shepherds from that moment on. Here's a partial list of the responsibilities shepherds had to tend (in addition to their regular jobs):

—Immediate selection of the presentation team.

—Formulation of a tight working schedule, including all available weekends before the final presentation.

—Researching the prospect, people and products, successes and failures.

—Analyzing all research. Deciding if new research was needed. If so, helping with its design.

—Establishing the point of view that would distinguish the team from all competitors.

—Theming the presentation, allotting times for each presenter.

—Polishing the presentation (and the presenters).

—Conducting endless rehearsals (and lowering the boom on those who didn't show).

—Dealing with fragile sensitivities, particularly *creative* sensitivities.

—Making all decisions, including the calling of "audibles" during the presentation itself.

—Following up the presentation with all kinds of clever reinforcements and reminders.

—Winning the business.

In other words, the shepherd was in total command until the ultimate verdict was rendered.

Of course, it was always expected that you-know-who would win. Andrew Kershaw didn't like to lose. With the shepherd system, it didn't happen often.

"You gotta have a scorecard."

Maybe it's just the nature of the beast, but competitive presentations seem to provoke mistakes of all kinds. (In addition to the four mistakes and solutions discussed so far, see the panel headed "Blunders that can blow your chances.") And almost every mistake can cost you points. *Real* points.

That's because competitive presentations usually have some kind of scorecard where criteria can be established and points can be registered.

These scorecards are completed after each presentation and then hauled out again for consideration in the final selection process.

PERSONAL ASIDE: I have taken part in hundreds of new business competitions—sometimes as a presenter, sometimes as a consultant for a client involved in a competition, and sometimes as a member of a selection panel. I have seen so many scorecards that I tend to score everything—menus, theater programs, grocery lists.

No two scorecards are exactly alike. Some are easy to understand. Others are written in dense jargon. Some blabber on and on—

SCORECARD

(Typical score sheet used by companies seeking
new suppliers via competitive presentations)

STRICTLY CONFIDENTIAL _____

(Company making presentation)

NOTE: Answer each question below on a scale of 1 to 10; 10 being the highest score.

1. Do they have a good grasp of our business? Do they really understand the *uniqueness* of our business?

2. Is there something *different* about them that *matches* up with our current and ongoing needs?

3. How would you rate the quality level of their product?

4. Do they have a process in place that assures us of the best possible product for the money?

5. Do they have an organization structure that guarantees the level of service we require?

6. Are they the kind of people we can work with?

7. Do they have a *balanced* team? Are they strongly staffed in all the disciplines we will need?

8. Was their presentation well organized and pointedly directed at our needs?

9. Did they answer our questions to your satisfaction?

10. Do they have the hardware and the physical facilities that we require to handle our business?

11. Is the management solid? Does it have a long-term point-of-view?

COMMENTS   TOTAL SCORE

_____

_____

_____

_____

_____

Name: _____

like insurance forms. Others are neatly tucked into one page. Formats vary. But, in truth, they all cover the same ground.

The scorecard shown in this chapter is prototypical—born of many, many scorecards—but eminently usable in very specific situations, such as your next competitive presentation.

The criteria are listed in order of their usual importance—although some questions may carry greater weight than others, depending on the prospect's industry and competitive position in that industry. I didn't attempt to do any scientific weighting of the various criteria. But this scorecard, as it stands within these pages, will help you right away.

IDEA: Make a copy of the scorecard shown here for each member of your presentation team. Ask him or her to fill it out (candidly and carefully) after your next rehearsal. Then, compare the sheets. Discuss scores and comments. Probe for weaknesses.

If you find that everybody scores your presentation right up there at the top—*Hey! Go with it!*

If the scores leave something to be desired, don't despair. In the next three minutes or so, you'll find some *point boosters* that could raise your morale—to say nothing of your chances when evaluation day rolls around.

Seven Point Boosters

■ *Watch for an "out of body experience."* This often happens when a presenter is *reading* something to the audience. The presenter's concentration just drifts away. Presenters who experience this sensation say it's like seeing yourself or hearing yourself from a great distance. They say they get bored with themselves.

SUGGESTION: Take the reading material away and let the presenter *talk it.* This may produce some minor mumbling and grumbling, but you'll notice a welcome difference in the concentration level.

■ *Go back and "plant some flags" in your presentation.* Familiar advice (see Chapters 14 and 48), but it will *always* work. A "flag" draws attention to the material that will win points for your team. Example: after you have outlined your recommendation, you simply say, "Now, let me apply that idea to your bottom line. . . ." Right away, you're scoring points.

■ *Articulate the key phrases you want the prospect to say about you when the selection committee is picking the winner.* Write those phrases down, word for word.

> Example: "They've got a strong point-of-view.
> They've shown us what to expect from them. But I
> think they're good listeners, too."

Write it all down and make copies for your presenters. By articulating what you want *them* (the prospect) to say about *you* (the presenter), you'll be more likely to seed those attitudes throughout your presentation. P.S.: I stole this technique from lawyers who use it to win points with juries.

■ *Next time you go through your presentation, tune out the voices.* What do you see? If you're picking up a lot of meaningless gestures, weight shifting from one foot to the other, lazy eyes, little or no decisive movement—you've got a team of presenters that's bored with the material, or lacks confidence in it. Inevitably, the audience is going to be bored with *them.* Put the presentation on videotape and freeze-frame on the bad body language. Then, ask the presenter what's happening. Is the material weak at that point? If so, fix it—or expunge it. If the material is strong but the presenter simply isn't concentrating, tell the presenter to get with the program—or words to that effect. To underline your seriousness, put a sign on the wall of your rehearsal hall, *"Watch your body language!"* Point to the sign when necessary. Make it a decisive gesture.

■ *Look at your leadoff presenter in a new light.* If your leadoff presenter is gray as ashes, tell him or her to "redden up a bit." (See Chapter 28.) If that doesn't work, try a little motivation:

> "You're our leadoff presenter. You know what that
> means? It means you've got to step forward and fill
> up that room. You've got to invade all of the little,
> private thoughts and conversations that *were* going
> on—and you've got to create a *new* consciousness of
> what's happening in that room. And you know
> what's happening? *You* are what's happening. You
> are filling up that room with your *authority,* and
> your *enthusiasm* for what you're about to say. You
> command your audience—by your poise, by your
> presence—to put everything aside *except you.* They
> can't resist. They can *feel* the change that you have
> created in the dynamics of the room—and they *know*
> that something *great* is about to happen. They have

given themselves over to you. And now *you* can feel it. Not many people can generate this kind of tension. It's a rare phenomenon. But *you* can do it. That's why we made you our leadoff presenter."

If your leadoff presenter reacts to this impassioned plea with a glazed expression, try rearranging your batting order.

■ *Have a little quiz. How many of your presenters know the full names of the people who will be in your audience?* Most presenters will flunk this test. That's your signal to distribute, *very* quickly, a list of the attendees to every presenter. Then, it's time for a game of *association.* Associate each name on the list with a recognizable physical characteristic. Mr. Bergsman is sort of triangular, a big bottom, cavernous chest, and a pointed crew cut. Mr. Bergsman is an ice*berg.* What silliness, you say. Maybe, but that's how memory wizards work. Make the word you want to remember into a visual that sticks in your mind. Sit there with your team and discuss the names and physical characteristics of each person who will be in your audience. Then, try the quiz again. Names are like gold. Nothing attracts like a name. "Hey, he knows my name!" Up goes the score.

■ *Are you closing like a breath of fresh air?* Does the audience know *exactly* what to do? Have you laid a solid foundation for the action you are asking them to take? Is every doubt erased? Is every gap closed? Is everybody comfortable? Okay. Make the next step seem as natural as taking in a breath of fresh air. There's no reason *not* to do it. And there's every reason *to do* it. *That's* the perfect "close."

Next time . . .

Every competitive presentation, *even the ones you lose,* help you to win.

The reason: you've been forced to clarify your mission and put it into someone else's frame of reference. In the process, you've gotten a better grasp of your market. You've been into the fiery pit of presentations. You've presented under great pressure and come out alive. You've played "The Deadly Game" and learned that you can compete.

Objectivity is great but . . .

In competitive presentations, objectivity can be a steep and slippery slope. It is desirable—who can be against it?—but what we are *really* talking about is what best serves the interests of the various factions on the selection committee.

Recently, I heard a quote which has lodged itself in my brain: "It's not that people are against you, it's simply that they are for themselves." This is a bit of wisdom to keep in mind as you prepare your next competitive presentation. You may be the person to win the business, but if you do, it will not be because you took a pragmatic and balanced view. It will be because you crawled inside the heads of the "jury." You looked through their eyes and saw a very *sensitized* picture, with some areas brightly inflamed. Your presentation soothed the areas of inflammation. Created a comfortable atmosphere *inside their heads*.

Objectivity will enhance your reputation. Sensitivity will win you the business.

Blunders that can blow your chances

(Actual quotes from prospective clients—describing presenters who floundered *and lost* in new business presentations.)

- "They had no energy. They *read* everything. It was tedious."
- "Their case histories had absolutely no relevance to our problems."
- "They talked endlessly about *themselves.*"
- "I couldn't read the visuals. Everything was set in mice type."
- "They fumbled the questions. They even contradicted each other."
- "They just rambled on. Nobody seemed to have any sense of time."
- "There were a lot of *empty* words. Just bull, if you ask me."
- "I don't think they had ever been through the presentation before. It never quite came together."
- "The light blew out in their slide projector—and they seemed totally nonplussed."
- "They didn't seem to have any sense of their own identity, let alone ours."
- "At the end, they just seemed to run out of gas."
- "They didn't seem to enjoy themselves. So, we never got comfortable with them."

PART
SIX

How to deal
with questions

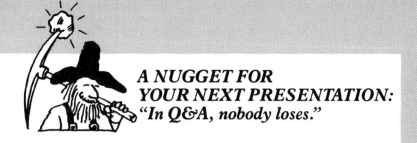

A NUGGET FOR YOUR NEXT PRESENTATION:
"In Q&A, nobody loses."

If you're into Q&A, and somebody is giving you a hard time, it's perilous to say, "I just don't agree with you on that." You can feel the tension rising. Confrontation fills the air. *Somebody is going to lose. If you win, you lose the questioner. No good.*

NUGGET: When you hear a dissenting voice, listen to it carefully. Listen to the dissenter with your *eyes* so that he/she feels that you are giving the opposing view *serious* thought. Then, never disagree openly. Ease into it. "Let me add something to that . . ." Or, "There's another factor to consider here." Disagreement may work on "Crossfire" and other TV talk shows. But in real life, it's far better when *nobody loses.*

52

What "no questions" really means.

You have just concluded a resounding summation of your main points, hammered home your theme one last time, and thanked everybody for being so gracious.

You're finished.

Applause ripples around the room.

You stand back and wait for the first question.

Nothing.

You survey the audience expectantly, waiting for the first hand to go up, the first questioner to start a spritely dialogue.

Quiet. *There are no questions.*

You say what everybody says in this awkward situation, "Well, I guess that means I *answered* all your questions." The room titters. You sit down or slither out a side door.

What does "no questions" *really* mean?

There are a variety of interesting possibilities, but "no questions" rarely means the audience is totally satisfied. It generally means that there's something wrong somewhere. What are the possibilities?

■ *You have gone at it too long.* Your audience is exhausted. You've overwhelmed them. They haven't got the energy to ask a question. They're eager to move along to the next meeting, catch a train, find the nearest bar, or watch a ball game. They don't want to hear any more about your subject—and they'd probably strangle the first person who said anything that even *sounded* like a question.

■ *You stepped on a sensitivity somewhere along the way.* You didn't mean to. You just said something that alienated the whole crowd—and they *tuned out* at that point.

It doesn't take much to "freeze" an audience. Just say something chauvinistic to the League of Women Voters. Or crack a lame joke about the local football team. Hit a raw nerve and your audience will abandon your subject, and dispense with questions. (See Chapter 44 on "Nerve Endings.")

■ *Your audience has already made up its mind* to cast its vote elsewhere. This happens. You were invited to present—but the outcome was a forgone conclusion. The winner was already in the clubhouse. When this happens, you'll probably hear about it later. Don't let it throw you. Competitive presentations aren't *always* what they seem.

■ *You never quite reached them.* Some audiences listen attentively but the presenter never really connects with their daily lives. The subject remains abstract, distant, theoretical. An eloquent presentation about "the indomitable sea lion" as a symbol of inspiration is going to be lost on a bunch of factory workers who have just been fired. They'll listen. They'll watch. They may even applaud. But the speech won't elicit many questions.

■ *They got muddled in the middle of your presentation* and couldn't muster the energy, or the interest, to stay with you until the end. By the time you had finished, they didn't really know what you were talking about. Bewildered audiences seldom ask questions. They don't like to admit they didn't understand it, and they won't struggle to make sense out of it. They just sit there. Quietly.

■

Some audiences simply don't ask many questions. Oriental audiences regard questions as a form of criticism, so you won't get a lot of questions at the Nippon Club. But, for most audiences, the asking of questions means that you have whipped up enough interest to create a desire for more information.

"No questions" usually means what it means in a courtroom. "You're excused. You can leave now. We're through with you."

That's not what an effective presenter wants to hear. But now at least you know some good, hard questions to ask about your next presentation:

■ Is it too long? Too heavy with detail? Have I told them *so much* that I have obscured my main point? Have I saturated their brains with information they don't really need? Have I *suffocated* them?

■ Am I stepping on any sensitivities that could override my subject and turn off my audience? Have I said something that cuts too close to the bone?

■ Is my subject of no earthly interest to these people? Have I selected a subject that interests *me* but is a yawner for them?

■ If it's a competitive presentation, had the winner been selected before you even had a chance to tell your story? (Nothing you can do about this. Just keep your poise and give it your best shot.)

■ Am I talking above their level of interest? Is my message too theoretical, too fancy? Does it simply fail to talk their language?

■ Is my message absolutely clear? Do I have any gaping disconnects in my logic? Will my audience drop through the holes?

Don't be afraid to ask tough questions of your presentation to make it more provocative to your audience. If *you* are your toughest questioner, your presentation will generate plenty of response.

53

Questions that top executives like to ask— and some suggestions that may save the day.

If you find yourself in a presentation to a group of top executives, particularly chief executive officers and/or presidents, there are certain possibilities, or likelihoods, that you'll want to keep in mind:

■ Top executives frequently ask questions that they have asked before and, in fact, *know the answers to.* So, why do they ask? Answer: they want to know if *you* know. Evaluation of employees, consultants, and advisers goes on all the time. It is a continual, almost automatic, activity for most top executives—and it can save a lot of time in the evaluation process if the executive knows the answer to the test question. This doesn't mean it's an easy question. It's probably a question of considerable importance to the executive, one that he or she asks regularly of different people to get a deeper understanding of it.

Suggestion: Do a bit of detective work. Ask some of the CEO's aides if there is any particular question, or series of questions, that comes up frequently these days. What's the subject of greatest concern? You will undoubtedly get a question related to that concern—even if the question has been expressed before.

■ Top executives often ask questions that are (A) of transcending scope, or (B) of almost impossible precision.

A. "Can you give me an idea of where your recommendation fits into our five-year corporate strategy?"

B. "Do you have a month-by-month cost comparison of this operation with our plant in Atlanta? What's the pay-out plan on each installation?"

Executives like to say, "What are the *implications* of this?" They also like to say, "What are the *key figures* here?" You've got to be ready for both ends of the spectrum.

■ Or, the question may fly off into some totally unpredicted but astonishingly pertinent area. "Where did you people ever get the idea that the consumer really gives a damn who makes her grocery sacks?" The best executives think through the minds of their customers. It's not a bad channel for the presenter either.

■ Top executives can also be caught thinking their way through a thickly complex issue, and articulating it in the form of a thickly complex question. Example: "If we were to make an analysis of our corporation in terms of its corporate identity before and after the merger, how much of our total communications budget should we allot to clear up the confusion that I strongly suspect exists?"

Now that's tough. A hypothetical situation requiring some highly problematical assumptions.

There are a good handful of ways to deal with convoluted questions of that kind:

1. Ask to have the question repeated so that you can be sure you understand it. (As the question is repeated, you'll probably find that it gets shorter and clearer. But it may also change in emphasis if not in meaning. Your mission here is to gently help the executive think his or her way through the troubling issue and then provide your best answer.)

2. *You* repeat the question as you understood it (that will probably prompt the executive to clarify *your* clarification and you will have more time to consider your answer).

3. You request a few minutes to think about it. The question may just go away.

4. If you really *do* understand the question, relate it to a similar situation in your experience. This will provide an answer to the question, but won't lock you into any specific action until you can obtain more facts.

If there's a CEO in your audience—and that person is the boss of everybody else—the sooner that CEO asks a question, the better it is for you. It will send a signal to the others that will clear the air—and get *everybody* participating.

54

The "short form" list
for answering questions.

Let's say you have just made a stimulating, substantive presentation to a group of anywhere from ten to fifty people.

More than likely, you'll get some questions.

Whether you get questions or not, *you should always be ready for them*—because Q&A, as it's called, is where presentations enter "the real world." The mood changes. The audience shifts from passive to active and begins to close the gap, if there is one, between *your* proposition and *their* immediate situation.

You should have a pretty clear idea of who's going to ask what questions and what you're going to say in response. That's not always precisely predictable, but if you've done your audience analysis—and you know your subject from *their* point of view—you're going to find that answering questions is not only satisfying, it's sort of fun. It's nice to be asked for your wisdom.

There are "long forms" for dealing with questions raised by cost-cutting managements at budget review sessions, and there are "short forms" for shorter presentations dealing with less complex subjects.

Since it may be some time before you are called upon to justify your department's cost allocation to the budget review committee, let's look at the "short form" which will help you at almost any presentation where questions are likely to arise.

The "Short Form" Process for Q&A

1. *Anticipate the questions you are likely to get. Write them down on yellow tablets,* leaving about six ruled lines or empty spaces between questions. You'll find the questions will come easily to mind if you know your audience. People ask questions about the issues of greatest concern to *them*—their positions in the organization, the problems affecting them *that day.* Sales managers ask about sales promotions. Corporate communications directors ask about images. Personnel managers ask recruitment methods. And *everybody* asks about costs. If you've done your homework, you'll be able to anticipate at least *70 percent* of the questions you actually get. The president of the United States does even better—*85 percent,* according to recent reports. Of course he's got a staff of experts trying to figure out what's bothering each one of the White House correspondents on any given day, especially days when press conferences are held.

2. Once you've got all of the likely questions written down on

your yellow tablet, see how many you've got. *If you have more than twenty questions, chances are high that your presentation is a little loose and needs to be tightened up.* Maybe you should answer some of those anticipated questions within the body of your presentation.

NOTE: The process of anticipating questions is a superb exercise for testing the strength of your presentation. Questions which elicit more detail are *good*. Questions which point up gaps and holes are *bad* (better answer those in the main part of your presentation).

3. Once you've got your anticipated questions down to a manageable size (under twenty), *go back and answer each one—as best you can—out loud, into a microcassette recorder.* It's no big deal. No pressure. You're not making a speech. You're just giving the recorder your best thoughts on the questions you're likely to hear.

4. *Now, let's listen to what you said.* Play your answers back to yourself. Impressed? This is where your yellow tablet gets into the act again. In a different color from the questions, make notes under each question that will strengthen each answer. Pertinent facts. Vivid phrases. Maybe even simple, little sketches to help you remember the fresh points you want to add to your original answers.

5. Using your yellow tablet of questions, your notes to yourself (written after hearing your first cassette), *answer the questions one more time on a fresh tape.* When you listen to the second cassette, you'll notice a stronger content to the answers *and* greater assurance in your voice. If you're happy with the second tape, use it as a way to keep engraving those strengthened answers into your memory. Maybe you listen to it when you're driving to the site of your presentation— or while you're eating breakfast that morning. Pretty soon you feel as confident about your Q&A session as you do about the more formalized part of your presentation.

6. *What do you do about the 30 percent of the questions that you probably won't anticipate?* If you don't know the answer, say so. Write the question down and tell the questioner you'll have an answer for him or her in a specific length of time (twenty-four hours always has a nice ring to it). By writing the question in plain view of your audience, you demonstrate to the questioner that you *too* think the question is important. If you don't have a detailed answer for the unanticipated question, there's nothing wrong with a short, crisp answer. Most busy people prefer brevity. A "yes" or "no" is often more responsive than a reply that drones on forever.

7. Write, at the very bottom of your yellow tablet, a nice, clear summary of your proposition—including "the next step."
Example:

> "Research shows this company is associated with
> old, established products that are no longer grow-
> ing. I propose that we investigate the acquisition of a
> small company in the health-care field. The next
> step is a thorough, discreet analysis of the three
> companies I have suggested."

It's just one paragraph; no more than three sentences. But it's the *heart* of your presentation. Keep relating your answers to it. Use it to keep questions from wandering too far afield. Make sure *the core* keeps coming through. In Q&A, you're always working your way toward that succinctly worded summary statement.

A Far-out Idea That Works

Include a few far-out, "extremist," questions on your list. And have some good, serious answers ready. That way you won't be shocked into silence when a few sizzling firecrackers land at your feet:

> "Is this all you have to show us? We like to see *lots* of alternatives."

> "Those are big city ideas. We do things our own way around here. Have you checked with the merchants down on Main Street?"

> "Your plan sounds good. Now show us how you can cut the cost to us by 25 percent."

The secret to answering questions is being ready—anticipating and preparing. The seven steps in this "short form" will help you do that. There's one more thing that will help you. It's attitudinal rather than technical. Think of it this way: *Every question you get is an immediate expression of interest in your presentation.* There's no way in the world that can be bad.

55

How to handle questions that are really suggestions.

Snapshot: It is the delicatessen convention on the boardwalk in Atlantic City. Various companies representing delicatessen products are having their sales meetings in the committee rooms of the flamboyant Trump Plaza.

Low-salt salami is up for discussion in one of the meeting rooms. It's a new product and salami salesmen in the room are excited about it. The presenter of the new item is a young manager, in his late twenties, and he's using a big chart to point out the specifications of the product.

Suddenly, one of the more mature salesmen (he looks like the Willy Loman of the salami trade) has a question. He holds his hand high and waves it around.

"Hey, why don't we list the ingredients on the side of the package and put the calories on there, too?"

"Interesting, Charlie, but we've already printed up an inventory of labels in these new, iridescent colors and we didn't consider labeling calories."

"But I watch the young people in the stores these days and they really read those labels. They want to know about calories and chemicals—they're really into it. Especially on a new item like this."

"Well, I'm going to see how these labels work first, Charlie, then maybe we'll get into calorie-labeling or something of the kind."

" . . . just thought I'd ask."

That was that. I watched Charlie sag into his seat, hands covering the lower half of his face as if to stop himself from saying anything else.

He listened as the next product was introduced (new baked ham loaf), then slipped out of the room.

I figured Charlie wouldn't be asking many more questions. He had the look of a man who might be visiting the casino, or the bar.

■

Granted, the manager handled it badly. But maybe we can learn something from what happened:

■ Charlie wasn't asking a question. He was offering an *idea.* Questions are frequently used to express ideas. They often get adopted more easily. *But the presenter has to know an idea when he or she hears one.* A question that has a concept in it is likely to be an idea.

■ If it really is a good idea, tell the group it will be reviewed with the package designer in terms of feasibility.

■ Tell Charlie you'll get back to him *by a specific date* with the decision on his idea—and thank him in front of the group.

This little docu-drama at the delicatessen convention isn't going to win a Pulitzer Prize but it does make a practical point.

Many questioners aren't really seeking answers. They're seeking *approval*.

Sensitive presenters can detect the difference. There's much at stake. Charlie's important. And his idea just might be a world-beater.

56

Never incur the wrath of a talky crusader.

Certain kinds of audiences bring out certain kinds of trouble. If you're ever asked to speak at any kind of "open forum"—be ready.

I call them *crusaders*. Self-appointed messiahs. Leaders of unlikely causes. Speakers whose names never appear on the program.

Then, suddenly, they're there. On their feet. Speaking. The subject could be anything. And it could be a very worthy subject—or a wacky subject—or an explosive subject. The only thing we can be *really* sure of is this:

It is not the subject of the meeting. If may be an offshoot of the subject of the meeting. But it's really another meeting.

Before trying to figure out what to do about this singular phenomenon, we should realize what is happening.

A person is speaking on a subject which is of *overriding* importance to him or her. Overriding, in this case, meaning overriding *you*. Remember, we're talking about *crusades* here. Therefore, *anything goes.* Robert's rules of order do not hold in this meeting. The crusader does not observe parliamentary procedure. Even fair play is not required, or even relevant.

The target is the audience. The objective: to grab a little share of mind. Or maybe a few lines of publicity. It's a long haul, this struggle for mind-share—and the crusader is patient, but *not* when holding the floor of someone else's meeting. Then, as we said, anything goes.

What are you, the legitimate speaker, going to do?

Well, the last thing you want to do is *destroy* the crusader. The person who has stolen your platform can easily become a martyr in the eyes of the audience. And it can happen with a few shouted words: "Sit down. You are out of order here. This is not your meeting." A few words like those, spoken dictatorially, and you can feel the group shifting beneath you. Whiplash, you *don't* need.

Some suggestions for a sticky situation:

■ *Anticipate the problem.* Before the meeting even begins, scan your audience with one or two associates who know exactly who's supposed to be there. People who interrupt meetings are generally recognizable. They interrupt meetings *all the time*. So, before your presentation starts, know who's out there. If there's an interrupter in the house, and you know it, you're not going to be surprised when the strange voice rings out in the middle of your strongest sentence.

■ *Have a secret aide.* Before your meeting gets underway, ask someone in your audience—someone who knows the problem and has considerable poise—to speak *for the group* should an interruption occur. The words would be reasonable, rational. "There are many here, I'm sure, who agree with your point of view. But we have a limited amount of time, and our speaker has less than twenty minutes to complete the subject we asked her (him) to talk to us about. After that time, I suggest that you join me for coffee. I'm certain others in the group will want to come, too. Yours is an important subject, but now we must give our speaker the time we promised her (him)."

It is always better to have someone from the audience deal with the uninvited speaker than you. If you try to do it, you become much more vulnerable, not only to the crusader—but also to the wavering loyalties of the audience.

■ *When all else fails,* you may have to settle things yourself. Be crisp. Be decisive. Don't let yourself be intimidated. Give the interrupter the feeling that *something* has been derived from the effort. Maybe you say something like this: "Look, I simply don't have the authority to do anything for you. I wish I did. But I do know someone in our organization who could help you and your cause. I promise you that I will write that person today—spelling out your subject as clearly as I can—and I will send you a copy of that letter. Everybody in this audience can be witness to that promise. How about it? Let me finish, and I will do what I can—but I need the next twenty minutes to cover what I was asked to present."

This will sound eminently fair to the audience, and should enlist their support even more strongly. And who knows? It might even make sense to the crusader.

One other thing: you must do whatever you promise to do. Never incur the ire of a talky crusader. Crusaders may not fight fair, but they fully expect you to.

PART SEVEN

Learning from
those who cast a spell
and stay with us forever.

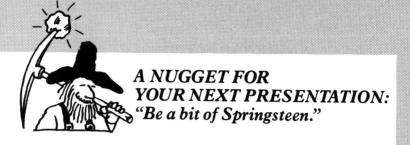

A NUGGET FOR YOUR NEXT PRESENTATION: *"Be a bit of Springsteen."*

Bruce Springsteen is one of America's master presenters. He presents ideas, attitudes, himself. In a recent article on Springsteen, *Newsweek* described the singer's presentation style as "a complete commitment to the immediacy of the moment." Precious few of life's experiences allow *you* to approach the kind of commitment that Springsteen makes in every performance. Presenting is one of those rare experiences.

NUGGET: Put a bit of Springsteen in your next presentation.

57

The most electrifying presentation I have ever seen.

I shall never forget it, no matter how old or how jaded I become. It lasted only five minutes, but it changed my life.

He was a young man, no more than twenty-five or twenty-six. He stood up before a small group of his coworkers, neatly dressed, but slender almost to the point of fragility.

I can see him now—maybe six feet away from me, tall and thin—talking quietly, but with almost tangible intensity.

"I have what is politely called a health problem," he said. "I have had it since I was a child. I started losing weight. One week I lost twenty pounds. The next week I lost fifteen. The doctor said I would never gain those pounds back again.

"The doctor gave me one of these." He walked over to a nearby table and carefully removed a hypodermic syringe from its case. The barrel was empty. He reached into a sack and took out a blue vial. He punched the needle into the top of the vial and drew the plunger upward. It was then that I noticed his hands were shaking. I thought he was nervous, trembling from the experience of making a presentation before his peers.

He returned to the center of the room. He held the hypodermic instrument up for all to see. "The reason I am shaking so badly is that I haven't had my insulin injection yet today. I usually take it when I first wake up—about seven o'clock—and now it is ten. I'm late. But I wanted to show you exactly what I have to do."

He bent his right arm at the elbow and made a fist. I felt frightened for him. He positioned the needle halfway up his arm, then pushed it into his vein just above the elbow. Silence.

"There," he said quietly. "It's really quite simple. Quite easy. Look." He extended his right arm and it was shaking slightly, but not nearly as uncontrollably as before. "I guess I am a little nervous," he said.

He went on to tell us how diabetes had changed his life. "I probably look at life a bit differently than you do," he said. "I see each new day as a gift, a bonus—and this needle is my friend."

His quiet, intense voice never faltered. "If you have diabetes, or have ever wondered about having it—I'd like to talk to you, to tell you what it's done for me. I don't think you'll fear it anymore."

The young man sat down. The audience was silent, stunned. Suddenly, my personal problems didn't seem nearly as serious. Then, there were murmurs of agreement, understanding. There was a feeling that we had shared something almost therapeutic. I felt *different.*

The "picture" of that young man with the syringe poised above his arm is forever imprinted on my mind, and his quiet affirmation of life is an integral part of it.

In a presentation, things that are personally important to you always come across with great impact.

You don't need notes or a script if you're talking about life and death matters. Especially when they're your own and they apply to *everybody.*

58

"Tell me about *you*."
The dynamics of Donahue.

Watch Phil Donahue "work" an audience for sixty minutes and you will see an absolute master of crowd control. Some people might call it group dynamics, which is the term to use if you're a behavioral scientist. Donahue is *not* a behavioral scientist—at least not formally. He's a sort of synthesizer. He presents controversy, but manages his audience so adroitly that explosions seldom occur. He's an inquiring father/confessor in a labyrinth of volatile possibilities. Donahue has his own style which might best be described as conversational earnestness—but he's never too earnest to smile when a guest or member of his audience gives him a verbal poke in the ribs.

When Donahue had two life-term inmates from the Rahway, New Jersey, state prison on his show (via satellite), he professed surprise that the inmates would favor the death penalty. The more talkative of the inmates said, "Why, Mr. Donahue, I'm sure you've been surprised a lot of times by what people say on your show."

Donahue laughed, probably thinking of all the people who *have* surprised him by some wacky comment—but you also got the feeling that Donahue would say something unexpected but perfectly appropriate if *he* were sitting behind bars down in Rahway with absolutely nothing to lose.

That's the thing about Donahue. He seems able to identify with *everybody*—whether it's a life-termer in Rahway or a housewife from suburban Chicago. He gets inside of people's heads and ventilates their feelings, but he does it in such a way that you feel he's really learning a lot. His curiosity seems boundless. He swings off of one person's opinion and into another, knowing full well that the feminist from Highland Park isn't going to agree with the criminologist from the big city. He hovers over both sides with the same fair-handed style: "Let him make his point, Mrs. Jones . . ." His objectivity may be a bit suspect, but his manners are impeccable. He may tilt to one side of an argument or another, but he is never overbearing.

Though he is always well briefed by his staff, he gives the impression that he is really warming up to his subject. Gradually, artfully, his point of view emerges. Often, it is a melding of the best arguments from each side of the issue. It may become more clear-cut, more dogmatic, but it never loses the sound of moderation. When he sees heads nodding, he shares the credit with his audience. "Isn't that really what we're talking about here today?" he asks. Heads nod more vigorously.

When he breaks into somebody's long-winded argument, he'll say, "Excuse me, I want to get back to your point in just a minute—

but first we've got to take a break." When he returns, he may come back to the windy person in the audience, or he may not, depending on the way he wants the program to flow. He's like a judge on the move, swinging from defense to prosecution—treating each side decently—not patronizing anybody. All the while he is seeking opinions, thrusting the microphone like it's some prized award for having a coherent or colorful point of view.

Donahue is a remarkable blend of intensity and good humor. He is everybody's oldest brother. He's the one who takes charge in an argument, giving both sides their due—or he could be the thatch-topped, youngish-looking uncle who obviously loves everybody and doesn't want anybody to go away mad.

When a person disagrees with Donahue, Phil may look a little quizzical, shaking his head in good-natured disbelief—then turn to one of his guests and ask, "Does that make any sense to you, Mr. Rothenberg?" Generally, Mr. Rothenberg agrees with Mr. Donahue. In a courtroom, this might be called "leading the witness," but on "The Donahue Show," it's sort of "All in the Family."

When Donahue talks, he may stumble a little—but not in such a way that you ever feel sorry for him. It's likable stumbling. His intentions are good. Never the bully, he has the same quality that James Stewart has. He's just too darn likable to do anything wrong. And he's really interested in each and every one of us. When he says, "Tell me about *you*," doggone it—he really wants to know.

Watching Donahue—Picking Up Pointers

1. If you're presenting a subject to a group, keep the dialogue conversational. Don't let intense feelings burst into flames. Keep the subject moving around the room.

2. Clarify carefully—credit merit. Respect your resisters. Be a good distiller. "Isn't *this* what we're really trying to say here . . . ?"

3. Make an honest effort to get everybody involved. Reach out to them.

4. Protect the soft-spoken and inarticulate. Don't let the big talkers clobber the people who can't get their thoughts out. Direct traffic.

5. Have a good time. But demonstrate that you're really involved in this subject—and that the truth is going to serve, perhaps even *save*, them all.

59

Cats and circuses and
stone-cold meeting rooms.

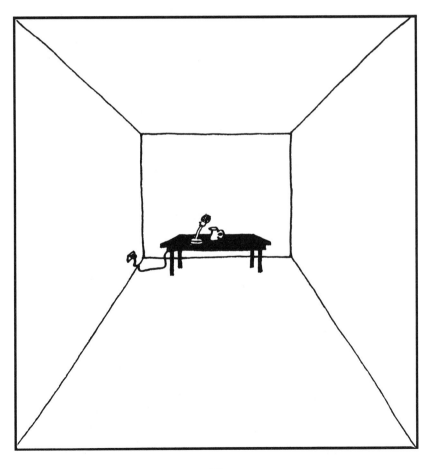

Many presentation rooms are stone-cold dead. They look like they should be roped off and preserved *as is.*

They usually have marble windowsills. And heavy tables that were carved out of petrified mahogany. Often, there's a little spidery lectern up front—like the vocalist uses in church.

The very idea that an interesting presentation might occur in one of these dreary rooms is hard to imagine.

A wake maybe. An interesting meeting? *No way.*

These heavy-handed rooms don't do much to inspire a lighthearted presenter.

And what kind of an organization would specify a room like this in the first place? What kind of corporate culture *prefers* mausoleum decor?

Never mind. What about *you?*

> What in the world are you going to do if you find yourself scheduled to make a presentation in one of these chilling chambers?

Woody Allen would probably come in and hand out colored balloons. Or play a little Dixieland. But—is that really *you?*

More to the point, would your audience really *like* it?

One by one, they might just topple over in their high-backed, leather-tufted chairs. Too much excitement.

First thing for you to do is ask your host if you can bring in the audio/visual material that you normally use. The host will want to know what you've got in mind.

If it sounds like more than the organization can handle, you may want to hold off on the video wall and the telestrator for another day.

Still, you don't want to be left looking out from behind that spidery little lectern.

Here's what I say:

> *The very least you can do is make the room look like something's about to happen there.* Put a slide on the screen and let it burn itself into the brain of the audience. It could be the theme of your presentation: "I'D LOVE TO KISS YOU, BUT I JUST WASHED MY HAIR." (This, incidentally, is my favorite quote of all time—from Bette Davis in

Cabin in the Cotton.) Or, maybe it's a completely
unexpected photograph: See the photo labeled
"Who *is* this man and what is he doing here?"

Already you've got a bit of theater started. It's not *The Will
Rogers Follies*—but it's not dullsville, either.

Now, you can put an easel or two at various points in the room.
(See if you can splash some light on them from the ceiling.) Maybe
there's a video monitor up front with its red light flashing. Maybe
there's a display of products covering up those somber windowsills.
Maybe there's a computer screen that's aglow with the organization's
logotype.

This room, which looked so lifeless before, now looks like
something might happen there. People are going to show things,
mark on things, engage electronic equipment that's ready to roll.

Things are going to happen here.

Would you *dare* have some stereo playing—softly, softly—as the

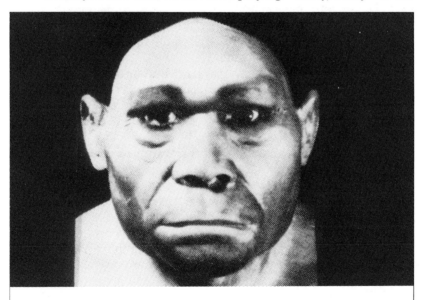

Who *is* this man and what is he doing here? He is on the screen as
your audience enters the presentation room.
Is he the competition? Is he an account executive and you are talking
to a bunch of creative people? Only *you* know the answer—and you
will get a laugh when you reveal it. In the meantime, your audience is
intrigued. Something is going to happen!
P.S. Actually he is a Neanderthal man.

audience arrives? Maybe you would *if* the music held some special meaning for your audience.

A little meaningful music never hurt anybody.

Not Guns n' Roses—but music to give somebody the feeling that folks are *alive* here. It's not going to be another one of these meetings that was recently described in *Business Week:* ". . . meeting after meeting where nothing ever gets decided."

Dressing up a room to show that something's going to happen does something else:

> It indicates that the presenters have really prepared
> for this meeting. They've worked on it—put some
> imagination into it. They're *ready.* It's probably
> going to have a beginning, a middle, and an end. It
> may even end on time. What a revolutionary idea for
> a meeting!

This chapter has a couple of delightful assignments:

—*Go see* Cats. When you walk into the theater notice how your senses react. There is no curtain. And the set overflows the stage, into the audience. Suddenly you're in the middle of a gigantic collage of things where cats hang out. Barrels. Trash cans. Big inner tubes. Cellars. You feel like you're in somebody's back alley. And you say to yourself, "What on earth is going to happen here?" You're eager for things to get going. This is going to be *really* something. *See if you can build just a little of that anticipation into your next presentation.*

—*Next time the circus comes to town, gather up an armful of kids and go.* You've been before, but look at it in a slightly different way this time. Study it *before* the show starts. Notice the way it titillates you. Is somebody really going to dive from that tiny platform up there at the top of the tent? What's that huge, silver cannon going to shoot this year? Two men and a woman? An eighty-year-old man? A dog from China? Everywhere you look there are props that make you think this is really going to be something.

When was the last time you had that feeling about a meeting you were supposed to attend? When was the last time a presenter really captured your imagination before he or she even started?

When was the last time you really *looked forward* to a meeting?

Next time you have an important presentation to make, get the audience involved *before* you present yourself. Put some *Cats* into the mix.

PART EIGHT

Afterwards—Some things
to think about
that will make your
next presentation
even better.

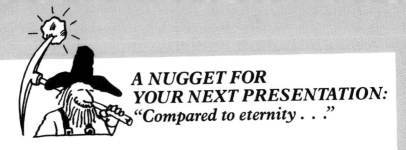

A NUGGET FOR YOUR NEXT PRESENTATION:
"Compared to eternity . . ."

My daughter is a social worker in Evanston, Illinois, and her caseload is demanding and draining. She tries to help people with their problems—and sometimes she's successful and sometimes she isn't. But she's seldom down in the dumps. I asked her how she maintains her professional poise, how she handles the disappointments that can seem like disasters. Her answer struck me with such force that I had the words framed. It's a marvelous quote for "after the presentation," when you may feel sort of dubious about your efforts.

NUGGET: "Compared to eternity, it's really small potatoes."

60

The art of
compassionate criticism

Criticizing the presentation of a close friend or business associate can be like hopping through a bed of hot coals. As Dr. Seymour Hamilton, a professor in Calgary, Canada, and a former presentation coach of political candidates, told me: "You want to tell them how bad they really are, to *help* them—but you don't dare. It's too sensitive."

Presentation is such an intricate melding of personality and message that it is often difficult, if not impossible, to make a helpful criticism of the message without deflating the personality. And a candid comment about the *delivery* of the message can cast a cloud over the message itself. ("If I can't work up any enthusiasm for this crazy idea, maybe I shouldn't be the one presenting it.") It's tricky business, the critiquing of presentations, but here's a simple little process that works. It works not only on the criticism of presentations but on almost any kind of creative effort:

1. *Find something good to say about it.* There must be something. The top football coaches don't haul a player out of the game and berate him for what he's doing *wrong*. They start out by telling him what he's doing *right*. Presentation is fueled by self-confidence. You have to keep that confidence alive, refueling it, before you can stand a chance of fixing the problems.

2. *Characterize the presentation before you criticize the presenter.* Give the presenter your impression of the *total* presentation before you get personal about the flaws of technique and delivery. Was it an "entertaining" presentation? Was it an "analytical" presentation? An "eminently reasonable" presentation? How would you characterize the presentation in a word or two? It doesn't have to be favorable. It could have been a "discursive" presentation. Or, maybe even a "disturbing" presentation. Whatever its effect on you, describe it.

This will give the presenter a general "environment" in which to place your more specific comments later on.

3. *Keep the focus of your critique clearly on the future.* "We're talking about your *next* presentation, and how we can help you make it the best one of your life." Presentation style is hard to change. It becomes ingrained, a part of behavior, as habit forming as a golf swing that has stroked some very good hits. By critiquing the presentation *now*, you aren't knocking what has worked in the past, you are simply offering suggestions for the future. Keep the emphasis of

your critique where it does the most good—on "the next presentation."

4. *Be specific.* A criticism that "it just didn't seem very interesting" isn't going to help the presenter. You'll probably get a look that says, "You're a big help . . . how about telling me what I can *do* about it?" So, you tell him or her. "Use some examples from your own experience." "Make your gestures broader—think of yourself as a traffic cop." "How about starting with a question that addresses the problem head-on?"

Most presenters don't really need to be told they're deadly dull—it doesn't do much for the ego. But they'd probably appreciate it if you told them exactly how to get an audience off their duffs and actively engaged in a presentation.

5. *"Make it useful for everybody."* It's a lot easier to accept criticism if you feel that you're not the only person on earth who's got those same problems. Maybe, just maybe, what you've learned will help somebody else. The great coaches say, "Look, let's learn from each other." And it works beautifully.

Example: A presenter gets up and seems hesitant, tentative. Why? She's embarrassed about being short. "Only five feet tall," she says in a shy voice. Somebody else says, "I feel the same way because I'm so darned tall." Out of this exchange comes a realization that can be useful to everybody. *Being different is only a problem when you make the audience feel uncomfortable.* If you present with self-assurance and authority, nobody is going to fret about the fact that you're five feet tall—or whatever distinguishes you from other people. They'll admire you for what you are. That's a discovery of universal value that came out of one presenter's experience.

61

Good news:
You'll never get a
bad evaluation.

To make a presentation and not get an evaluation is like running the Melrose Mile without a timer's clock. It is like playing baseball without a batting average—shooting a round of golf without a scorecard.

You've got to get an evaluation of your presentation if for no other reason than to know that you were in the game. A presentation that doesn't warrant an evaluation probably didn't make *any* impression.

Whoa! Before we get too dogmatic, let's define the field of play.

There are all kinds of evaluations—from a polite round of applause to a computerized form with grades, ratings, and multiple-choice answers.

Iron-clad rule: Whatever its configuration, wherever it comes from, welcome your evaluation with open arms! Clasp all kind words to your bosom and be thankful (same thing goes for unkind words, only it's tougher to do).

There are two reasons, basically, for going out of your way to obtain some valid kind of evaluation from your audience:

1. It's just human nature to want to know, *need to know*, how your audience felt about you.

2. An honest, constructive evaluation can be enormously helpful to you as you get ready for your next presentation. You'll have some idea of what worked and what didn't (that's why the more specific evaluations are always the most valuable).

In talking to program directors throughout the land, I have discovered that audiences register their evaluations in patterns of behavior that are sensible and frequently surprising:

A. There are the people who will come forward after a presentation and thank you for your effort. That's not easy for some people to do, so you want to let them know that their kind words mean a lot to you. Tennessee Williams said, "Why do people begrudge you a bit of praise?" When praise comes your way, *soak it up!*

Seldom, if ever, will people approach the presenter after a presentation and say critical things. Occasionally, a suggestion will be made, but generally in a positive way. I've never heard anyone say, "That was a *rotten* presentation. I was bored silly. Why don't you find a new subject to talk about?" It's quite possible that evaluations of that severity are warranted, but they aren't made—at least not face-to-face—right after a presentation.

B. The people who have harsh things to say about a presentation usually register them in a *non*-face-to-face manner. If something that you said really *galled* some members of your audience, look for a written response—usually at the back of the room.

Chuck Kelly, an advertising executive in Minneapolis who is always a program chairman of at least one noteworthy organization, says, "People will write what bothers them and leave it at the back of the room. The comments are more likely to be emotional, sensitive to something that was *touched upon* in your presentation rather than to the main subject. Written comments, left behind, will probably be subjective rather than objective." Heated comments, it would seem, are more likely to be dashed off on the spot. But you know the rule: *welcome all forms of evaluation with open arms!*

C. Then, there's another group you should know about. These are the members of your audience who will take the time and trouble to fill out a form that has been dispatched to them after your presentation, or was picked up at the presentation and carried home. These forms can be demanding (there's a fairly simple one on the opposite page). Some organizations send out questionnaires, some don't, but here's the point:

Since time has elapsed between the presentation and the filling-out of the questionnaire, answers are likely to be dispassionate and thoughtful. This kind of evaluation, requiring recall, is going to put your presentation into a larger context than an evaluation made on the spot—and is likely to be more useful. These are considered judgments.

D. You've detected the gap, of course. What about those people who don't come forward, don't leave notes at the back of the room, don't take the trouble to fill out questionnaires.

They just get up and leave.

I've given these people a name: "The Movie Crowd." Here's a snapshot:

Have you ever watched people coming out of a theater after seeing a movie that you are waiting to see? You search their faces, seeking a clue—some slight reaction to the film they just saw. They reveal nothing. They just amble along.

They're not chattering happily. They're not muttering *un*happily. They're not storming the box office. They're just leaving.

One day, it came to me. A presumption on my part, but it seemed unarguable: *"Well, I guess they got their money's worth."*

PRESENTATION EVALUATION

Name of presenter _____

✔ Please rate the presentation on a scale of 10 (highest) to 1.										
	10	9	8	7	6	5	4	3	2	1
Relevant to my needs:										
Strength of material:										
Persuasiveness:										
Learn anything new?										
Delivery:										
Audio/Visual:										

Comments, reactions: _____

_____

_____

_____

_____

Signed: _____
(optional)

Welcome whatever your audience says about your presentation. You'll be better for it. Feel free to copy this form for your next presentation.

That blinding flash of obviousness has helped me at presentations ever since.

"The Movie Crowd" shows up, in varying numbers, at all manner of presentations. They come in, listen, *and leave.* They get their money's worth.

On the evaluation scale (ten being "ecstatic"), you can figure that they gave you a five or six. You take it, *gratefully* (remember the rule).

Be particularly thankful when you get an evaluation that reflects some thoughtful effort, but keep in mind that *all* evaluations can be helpful. Even "The Movie Crowd" is telling you something. And the more feedback you get, the better you're going to be.

62

Compliments, countercompliments, and presentation diaries.

I've never known a presenter who could refuse a compliment.

Compliments are confirmations of success. There's nothing like a little positive reinforcement at the end of a presentation. Pumps you up. More importantly, it gets rid of those irritating suspicions that you bombed.

Granted, Chapter 61 instructs you always to get a written evaluation from your audience. Good advice, except there are some situations where you can't quite do it.

If you're speaking at a sales conference, for example, and things are running on a tight schedule—you're not going to have time to pass out evaluations, even if they take only a few minutes to fill out. Maybe the sponsor of the meeting will mail your evaluations to you at a later date *if* all speakers are evaluated by some marvelously efficient process.

Then again, maybe *compliments* will be the only measure of your success. That suggests you should know something about them that you can actually put to use.

1. If you don't get *any*, you didn't exactly "knock them off their chairs." When nobody says anything positive, it may be because nobody could think of anything positive to say. Trouble in River City.

2. If you've made your presentation to fifty people and over 10 percent of them come forward with compliments, you can go home singing a merry tune. The people who complimented you are probably speaking for a lot of people who enjoyed your presentation but were feeling a bit bashful that day.

3. If *less* than 10 percent of the people complimented you, you're in no position to uncork the champagne. The situation is *not* wildly positive. But you shouldn't head for the nearest bridge either. No reason to do anything rash. Maybe the *audience* was having a bad day.

4. There is simply nothing to *counter* a good, face-to-face compliment. It would be useful if there were "countercompliments." It might be tough on the ego, but a "countercompliment" could clear things up in a hurry. I mean, if somebody looked you in the eye and said, "That was the dreariest half-hour I've ever spent," you'd know where you stood. You could even balance the "countercompliments" against the heart-warming compliments and *rate* yourself. But, as we discovered in Chapter 61, most people just disappear into "The Movie Crowd"—faces focussed on nothing more than the nearest exit.

5. Since the present system, imprecise though it may be, is not likely to change—and compliments are destined to remain the chief

measurements of your success—maybe we should examine a few. Here's one that crops up frequently, for many presenters:

"Interesting presentation. You certainly gave us a lot to think about."

Now, that sounds like a nifty compliment, doesn't it? Accept it *instantly*. If it's meant as a compliment, *take it as a compliment!*

Later, however, you may want to give this compliment a little scrutiny. The truth of it is, most audiences don't want a lot to think about. They're up to their ears in things to think about.

They're looking for answers they can apply *immediately*.

The more you give most audiences to ponder, the less likely they are to take action.

> So, "a lot to think about" usually translates into, "What was that all about, anyway?" Any compliment that suggests the audience has been left on the horns of a dilemma should be accepted graciously but without much optimism. Most members of the group probably don't have the foggiest idea of what you want them to do.

6. Unless you're some world-class celebrity, you can take the compliments you get at close to face value. For someone to take the trouble to make a comment—when remaining silent is so easy—the sentiment is probably genuine. Praise is seldom lavished on a ho-hummer. Why bother?

That means fewer compliments, but a higher level of believability. Some compliments are so genuinely heartfelt, so honestly stated, that they will stay with you for a lifetime. Here's a compliment that's hard to get, doesn't have a lot of glitter, but it can make you feel like you just won the lottery:

"That was great. You took the time and trouble to really understand us."

When somebody expresses that feeling, the compliment takes on an entirely different tone. There is *awe* in it. As if it had never happened before (and maybe it hasn't). You can feel the gratitude. Sometimes, it's related to business:

"That was great. You took the time and trouble to really understand our business."

How many people that you know *really* understand your business? Not many, I'll wager. Most presenters never get close to really understanding the problems of a particular audience. It takes too much time, too much work. Far easier to talk about the presenter's achievements than the audience's deeply felt needs.

A compliment that says "you went out of your way for me" means that you have done something quite rare. You have recognized the *uniqueness* of an audience and made a unique contribution in response. The audience has recognized it. You deserve your exhilaration! Cheers!

7. When you're receiving compliments, you're not in the best possible shape to remember them (unless they're in the unforgettable category we just talked about). The reason: your mind is having a party. Your presentation is over! You're probably a bit giddy. The compliments may be floating right through your consciousness.

Whoa! Settle down. Compliments can be rich in insights *and* opportunities. Soon as you can, jot down a few things from the post-presentation period. They can be valuable later. A few examples: When someone says, "Really terrific, once you got into it," you are being given a suggestion as well as a compliment. When someone says, "Quite a presentation . . . where did you get your material?"— you've got honest skepticism being registered. Toughen up your documentation. Compliments can be extremely constructive. Well worth remembering.

Or, there can be opportunities buried in compliments.

Example: "That was fascinating. You know, our executive staff ought to hear that presentation." The comment is made, and—quite possibly—forgotten.

Or, "Great stuff. I'd like to hear more about it some time." Nice words, but they evaporate in the euphoria of the moment *unless you write them down.*

Your Presentation Diary

Here's the idea: Write down some key things right after you've heard your compliments (and may you have *more* compliments than you can possibly remember!). There's a simple, pictographic form at the end of this chapter.

How would *you* grade your presentation? Ten being perfect—one being a turkey. What was the *best* thing about it? What *didn't* work? Then, key words from the compliments. What did the compliments tell you, if anything? Finally, what needs following up? Who, what, when?

YOUR PRESENTATION DIARY

Date _____

(to be completed ASAP after your presentation)

Name of presentation _____ Occasion _____

How would you rate your presentation? (overall)	10	9	8	7	6	5	4	3	2	1
	Perfect									*Hopeless*

What pleased you about it?

What needs fixing?

What was said afterwards?

(compliments, comments, key words only, but try to identify who said what)

Follow-ups needed?

Requests to be filled? Invitations? New business leads? (Check the business cards you received)

Start a file of these sheets. They'll help you help yourself.

This is where you write your own private thoughts and recollections about your presentation.

Let's give this post-presentation review a name . . . *Your Presentation Diary.* The diary is here—ready for your recollections. All you have to do is make a presentation and fill in the blanks. Do this for your next three presentations. You'll discover things you never knew about yourself as a presenter *and as a person.* You'll also detect an improvement in your presentations.

What's more, you'll have the compliments to prove it!

63

"Here's looking at you, kid!"
—on viewing
your *first* videotape

*L*et's look at the tapes.

Looking at videotapes has become a part of the game in collegiate and professional athletics.

If a team in the National Basketball Association, for example, has been trounced in a big playoff game, the scrutinizing of the tapes may start immediately following the game and continue into the early morning hours—then resume again after breakfast with coaches and players viewing and reviewing crucial actions.

The New York Times quoted Chuck Daly, coach of the Detroit Pistons at that time, following his team's 1987 playoff loss to the Boston Celtics.

> "There is only one way to stay on top of it; when you watch it on films. Only then can the players and coaches see what went wrong. There are no make-believes with the films, and sometimes it takes a couple of viewings before it sinks in."

Aspiring presenters should listen closely to Coach Daly (who, like many coaches, tends to use tapes and "films" interchangeably when, in fact, tapes are magnetic tape, and film is film).

Videotapes of you, presenting, can be invaluable as you prepare for your next presentation.

What you'll see isn't you *live* (videotapes tend to flatten people out), but it's you as you *were* when the cameras were rolling, and it's probably the most realistic motion picture of yourself that you'll ever see. As Coach Daly says, "There are no make-believes with the films."

You may discover that you're ignoring half of your audience—or seeking inspiration in the ceiling. You may find that you're smiling self-consciously—or scowling heavily when you weren't even worried. You may want to speed up your voice, or slow it down, or *calm* it down.

Or, you may realize that all of those little tics and twitches that you thought were so bothersome *aren't even noticeable*!

You'll know what to fix and what to leave alone. You'll have a picture of yourself that you can modify as you see fit.

It's an exciting prospect, isn't it? If you've never seen yourself on tape before, you'll have—for the first time in your life—a perception *of you* that is based on your reality, not somebody else's.

So, you've done it. You've made a tape. You've videotaped a rehearsal or the actual presentation. (The equipment can be rented with a phone call, and rates for suitable cameras are modest—$75 or $85 for the day, plus tapes. You can even rent a cameraman, if you want, but the minimum goes up to around $225 for the day.)

You slip the tape (according to your unit's directions) into your videotape player (VCR) and snap on your receiver. The screen lights up and, in a few seconds, *there you are!*

You are presenting to yourself, seeing and hearing yourself as your audience sees and hears you. You are the audience for you, the presenter.

Your first videotape can be a landmark experience in your life, moving testimony that you *exist*, and—in all honesty—it can also be a trifle unsettling.

Here are some tips to ease the trauma and chart the course:

—*Be an audience of one at the first viewing.* Just you, alone. That way, you're less likely to be defensive. You, looking at you for the first time, can create considerable self-consciousness, especially if someone else is watching you watch yourself.

Just sit there (it's best to be sitting down for your first viewing) and observe yourself *out of sheer curiosity.* (You'll be tempted to say, "Is that really me?" It is.) So, relax—lean back—and get used to the sensation of seeing yourself from *outside* rather than *inside.*

—*For the second viewing, become your boss,* or whoever your most critical audience may be. Try a little role playing. Look and listen to that presenter on the screen as if he or she were working for you. Would you be impressed with your good judgment in hiring that person up there? If you were your boss, how would you characterize the speaker's greatest strength, and most troubling weakness? What would you tell that presenter if you were the boss and wanted to pass along a few words of compassionate criticism?

—*Look at your videotape with the sound turned all the way down.* This will show you, silently, how you are communicating *nonverbally.* With the sound off, you'll become aware of the "chemistry" you're projecting. Are you animated or staid? Do you smile or frown? How's your poise? Are you comfortable? This, of course, leads into all kinds of other questions you can try on yourself. "Do I trust that person? Do I like that person? Would I want to see that person again tomorrow?" Looking at the *nonverbal you* can provide a dramatic and revealing portrait of how you are perceived as a presenter.

—Now, push that sound back up and look away from the screen. What does your voice alone tell you *nonverbally?* Would you want that voice to be the captain on your next long-distance flight? Does that voice *know* anything? Does that voice *believe* what it is saying? It's absolutely amazing what your voice can tell you just by its tone, texture, and general attitude. Some presenters discover, with a little help from the tapes, that their *words* don't really match up with their nonverbal communicators. Example: the words can be urgent—the delivery can be off-hand, uncaring. Guess which message the audience takes away?

—For the fifth viewing, invite a colleague to watch your tape with you. Turn on the tape (you'll be an expert by this time), and position yourself in the darkened room so that you can watch your audience out of the corner of your eye. Watch your visitor's facial language, body language. You'll get a review of your performance by keeping an eye on your audience (which is true of all audiences—large or small, taped or "live"). How does that review match up with *your* analysis of yourself?

■

Videotapes offer the presenter one more reward, and it may be the most valuable one of all.

In the past, before videotape, presentations had very short lives.

They were given and they were gone. Presentations were ephemeral, evaporating into the atmosphere. *Poof!* There goes another presentation.

Now, with videotapes, presentations are *tangible*—preserved for as long as you please. The presenter has something to study, analyze, set aside, and consider again.

The tape *doesn't* evaporate.

Tapes are good, solid *tools* that you can use to upgrade your presentation skills—and maybe even your self-image.

Here's looking at you, kid!

64

"The next step is . . ."

Ten days before your next presentation, take this list full of nuggets on the next two pages and pin the whole glittering array to the wall of your office, den, kitchen, basement, or wherever you're going to be.

Add your own notes and nuggets as presentation day approaches. The night before your presentation, review each point (*visualize* it, if possible).

You'll discover that you feel remarkably comfortable about yourself as a presenter—and confident about your presentation.

So, flip this page and start thinking about your next presentation. You're going to be dazzling!

NUGGETS FOR YOUR NEXT PRESENTATION.

1. Make a "hot button" seating sketch. Works well in small meetings. Set up your meeting so that seating is prearranged. Then, make your sketch—identifying each seat by the main concern of the person who will be sitting there. *Visualize each concern.*

2. Most presentations are *two* things: (1) a solid base for your basic premise or point of view; (2) an idea that relates directly to an audience need. Make sure you've got both.

3. Fill your head with knowledge before you prepare your presentation. You should have at least *seven times* as much useful information as you will actually use.

4. Use a camcorder instead of a notebook. Pictures bring words to life.

5. Try this format next time: Say it. Show it. Sum it up.

6. Get inside the mind of your audience before you begin. Remember, you are building a relationship.

7. Present yourself to yourself. A full-length mirror would be perfect.

8. Rehearse everything exactly as it will be. Say every word. Make every move. Afterward, get a compassionate critique from your "Stanley Kubrick."

9. State your point of view early on. Most people are too busy (or too smart) to be held in suspense for very long.

10. Never give a "generic presentation." Localize it. Personalize it. Relate it to the news of the day.

11. Shift, as quickly as you can, from self-consciousness to audience-consciousness. Put yourself in their shoes. It's the best way to beat nervousness.

12. Let your convictions show.

13. Watch for "the barometer" in the audience. There's usually *one person* who reacts more quickly and demonstrably than the others. Let that person help you anticipate the overall reactions.

14. Make pictures out of numbers. Pictographs.

15. Keep coming back to your theme. It's the glue that holds everything together.

Pin this up on your wall. It will help you shine!

_____

_____

_____

_____

_____

_____

_____

_____

_____

_____

_____

_____

16. Substance is essential. Technique usually breaks down at the point where substance is thinnest, or ceases to exist. Great presentations are never made on technique alone. It's just not possible.

17. If you've got a sense of humor, it will blossom when you feel you really *know* your subject.

18. If you're using cards or charts, you don't have to cover one with another. One advantage of cards is that they can be placed around a room to help your audience remember where you've taken them.

19. Get out of the gray—demonstrate. Use audio/visual aids that give you freedom. Improvise within your knowledge. Don't break eye contact for more than ten seconds.

20. Be more of your strongest strength. Put your faith in what you like best about yourself—and your weaknesses will fade away.

21. Be sensitive to the sensitivities of your audience. Identify their "nerve endings"—like age, gender, locality, "colloquialisms."

22. Every question you get is an indication of interest. *Welcome it!*

23. Answer questions *graciously*. Presenters who pounce on questioners lose points.

24. Keep looking for ways to crystallize issues, so that varying views can reach areas of agreement. "Isn't *this* what everybody's saying?"

25. Most people would rather say: "That presenter told me what I have long suspected to be true," than, "That person told me a lot of things I never heard before."

26. Offer lists (like this one).

27. You're always *for* your audience. You're on *their* side—first, last, and always.

28. The enthusiasm of the presenter is often the point-of-difference in the product.

29. Remember there are thirty-three million business presentations every business day. You've got *lots* of competition.

30. Close your presentation *strongly*. Ask your audience to do something specific. Leave something behind (a proposal, article, summary checklist), something to remember you by.

319

Epilogue

Each time you make a presentation, you are accepting a moral responsibility.

Before this begins to sound like a locker-room pep talk, let me offer you one quick story to make the point.

■

A major convention was being held in Lakeland, Florida. It had been highly promoted throughout the state, and a lot of important people showed up.

One of the highlights was to be a restaging of a big-league competitive presentation by two of the outstanding marketing firms in the region.

What made the idea *interesting* was that neither one of the companies had *won* the competition (which had been recently completed), but both of the companies learned—from unimpeachable sources—that their presentations had been worthy of winning. I was to be the referee. After explaining the rules of the matchup to the audience, I was to jump out of the way and let the combatants roar into action with all of the spunk and fervor they had brought to the original meeting.

As we were discussing things at dinner the night before, I said, "This is a terrific thing you're doing. It will be of great interest to the audience, and—after seeing both presentations tomorrow—the people in your audience may be able to give you some observations that you can use to win your next time out."

You know when the coach gets the tub of Gatorade dumped on him in the last game—and tries to act like he really loved the whole sticky mess?

That's what happened to me. I got cooled off in a hurry.

Both competitors said they would brook no criticism of any kind. No way.

Then, I was told not to expect much from their presentations the next day. After all, they weren't *real* presentations. There was no business to be won. They weren't getting paid for this. They were there merely to acquaint the audience with a few of the nuances of new business. It all sounded very public service-y.

Next day, the competitive presentation took place—with no sparks. It was sort of a walk-through.

The audience was respectful, but eager to draw some conclusions. They turned to the referee. I gave them what I thought were some helpful comments (being careful not to trample on any toes), and the two competitors eventually joined in. But I never forgot their attitudes. "Don't expect much from us. Nothing in it for us."

■

Here's the point: *audiences are sacred.* There is no such thing as an unimportant audience. If for no other reason, your audiences are important because they came to see *you.* What an incredible compliment! These people, sitting out there, have taken time from their busy lives to hear what *you* have to say, and see what *you've* got to show.

They figure you've got a responsibility to them because *they're there.* And they're right! You owe them the best that's in you.

And that, dear friend, has been the objective of this book. To help you give your best to those good people who think you *are* the best.

I wish you compliments by the score and riches beyond wealth.

Ron Hoff

Suggested Reading

- Boettinger, Henry M. *Moving Mountains—or The Art of Letting Others See Things Your Way.* New York: Collier Books, 1969.
- Calamandrei, Piero. *Eulogy of Judges.* New Jersey: Princeton University Press, 1946.
- Detz, Joan. *How to Write and Give a Speech.* New York: St. Martin's Press, 1984.
- Goffman, Erving. *The Presentation of Self in Everyday Life.* New York: Doubleday & Company, Inc., 1959.
- Goldberg, Robert and Gerald Jay Goldberg. *Anchors Brokaw, Jennings, Rather and the Evening News.* New York: A Bird Lane Press Book, 1990.
- Hodgson, John and Ernest Richards. *Improvisation.* New York: Grove Press, Inc., 1966, 1974.
- Leech, Thomas. *How to Prepare, Stage, and Deliver Winning Presentations.* New York: Amacom—American Management Associations, 1982.
- Morris, Desmond. *Bodywatching.* New York: Crown Publishers, Inc., 1985.
- Nizer, Louis. *Reflections Without Mirrors.* New York: Doubleday & Company, Inc., 1978.
- Rusher, William A. *How to Win Arguments.* New York: Doubleday & Company, Inc., 1981.
- Samuels, Mike, M.D., and Nancy Samuels. *Seeing With the Mind's Eye.* New York: Random House, Inc., 1975.
- Schanker, Harry H. *The Spoken Word.* New York: McGraw-Hill, Inc., 1982.
- Thourlby, William. *You Are What You Wear.* Kansas City: Sheed Andrews and McMeel, 1978.
- von Oech, Roger. *A Kick in the Seat of the Pants.* New York: Harper & Row, 1986.
- Valenti, Jack. *Speak Up With Confidence.* New York: William Morrow & Company, Inc., 1982.
- Webber, Andrew Lloyd. *CATS: the Book of the Musical.* Photographs and drawings by John Napier. Orlando: Harcourt Brace Jovanovich, 1983.

Dear presenter,

Do you have any "presentation stories" (real life experiences) that you will never, ever forget? Seems like everybody has at least one.

I've found that you can often learn more from a funny disaster than a flawless triumph.

So, if you'd like to send me a "funny disaster"—or any "presentation story" that sticks in your mind—I'll make sure you get full credit when it appears in my next book. You can also FAX your stories to (312) 642-8487.

Ron Hoff
P.O. Box 10305
Chicago, IL 60610-0305

Index